The Career
Counselor's
Handbook

The Career Counselor's Handbook

by

Howard Figler

Author,
The Complete Job-Search Handbook

and

Richard N. Bolles

Author,
What Color Is Your Parachute?

TEN SPEED PRESS

Ten Speed Press
P.O. Box 7123
Berkeley, California 94707
www.tenspeed.com

Distributed in Australia by Simon and Schuster Australia, in Canada by Ten Speed Press Canada, in New Zealand by Southern Publishers Group, in South Africa by Real Books, and in the United Kingdom and Europe by Airlift Book Company.

Cover design by Thomjon Borges
Typesetting by Star Type, Berkeley

Library of Congress Cataloging-in-Publication Data on file with the publisher.

First printing, 1999
Printed in Canada

ISBN 1-58008-157-6

4   5   6   7   8   9   10 — 03   02   01

Acknowledgments

Authors rarely toil alone. When they are at their best, they toil as part of a community. We, the nominal authors of this book, are deeply aware of the community out of which this book has risen. For it will be evident to all who know us that we could not have come up with all these ideas simply on our own. We acknowledge the help we received from many career counselors, in person, on the phone, or by correspondence, wherein they shared with us their insights, their problems, and their inventive solutions. They made this book possible, and by their gentle prodding, they brought this book to fruition -- after we had merely talked about writing it for many years.

We offer especially warm thanks to Dick Knowdell, in whose *Career Planning and Adult Development Network Newsletter* many of these chapters and ideas first appeared, albeit in a more primitive form, more often than not. These include "A History of Ideas and Events in the Job-Hunting Field during the Twentieth Century," "How to Do 1-2-3 Career Counseling," "How to Use Just One Hour," "A Return to the Real America," "Schooling and Entrepreneuring," "Five Business Cards Instead of One," "Helping Clients Define Success," "Doing Well and Doing Good," and "Adding Value."

Howard would like to express his thanks also to Betsy Collard, H. B. Gelatt, Janice Klar, John Krumboltz, Constance Stevens, Helen Scully, and Patrick Ferris.

And Dick would like to express his thanks to Daniel Porot, the late John Crystal, Sidney Fine, Dick Lathrop, Harvey Belitsky, Arthur Miller, Tom and Ellie Jackson, Ellen Wallach, Rita Morin, Dave Swanson, and Carol Christen.

Needless to say, however, none of them are responsible for any errors that may have crept into this book, despite our most vigilant effort to keep those errors out.

-- *Howard Figler*
Dick Bolles

Contents

The Present: Special Problems

The Present: For Clients Who Want to Be 'On Their Own'

The Present: Values

The Present: Spirituality

The Future

The Authors

Howard Figler, Ph.D., is a nationally known speaker, author, and seminar leader, and has been for the past twenty-five years. He is the author of five books besides this one, the best known of which is *The Complete Job-Search Handbook,* a bestseller which has sold over 100,000 copies, and has been featured by the Quality Paperback Book Club. As a training-seminar conductor, he presents seminars for career counselors who work in educational, industrial, military and governmental settings, as well as private practice. His clients have included AT&T, Chase Manhattan Bank, Chemical Bank, Mercy Healthcare, Procter & Gamble, Sun Microsystems, Stanford University, Washington University, the University of California, Private Industry Councils and the United Way.

Howard earned the Diplomate in Counseling Psychology from the American Board of Professional Psychology. His Ph.D. is from Florida State University. He has a Master's of Business Administration from New York University, and a Bachelor of Arts degree from Emory University. He is the former Director of the Career Center at the University of Texas at Austin (1982–1990), and currently resides near Sacramento, California.

Richard N. Bolles is acknowledged as "the most widely read and influential leader in the whole career planning field" (*U.S. Law Placement Assn.*) and as "the one responsible for the renaissance of the career counseling profession in the U.S. over the past decade" (*Money Magazine*). He has been in this field for thirty years. He is the author of the most popular job-hunting book in the world, *What Color Is Your Parachute? A Practical Manual for Job-Hunters and Career-Changers,* which currently has over 6,000,000 copies in print. The book has been on the *New York Times* best-seller list 288 weeks thus far, in its lifetime, was listed in 1995–1996 by the Center for the

Book at the Library of Congress as one of "25 Books That Have Shaped Readers' Lives," and has been popular in such diverse countries as the U.S., Canada, New Zealand, Australia, and others. It has been translated into twelve languages: English, French, Spanish, German, Dutch, Italian, Polish, Portuguese, Russian, Slovenian, Chinese and Japanese. Dick is the author of several other books in the career field, as well.

He is an alumnus of the Massachusetts Institute of Technology in chemical engineering, a graduate of Harvard University in physics (*cum laude*), and the General Theological (Episcopal) Seminary in New York City, from which he holds a Master's degree in New Testament studies. He has been the recipient of two honorary doctorates, and is a member of Mensa. He served as a National Staff member of United Ministries in Higher Education (1968–1987) and was director of their National Career Development Project (1974–1987). He is listed in *Who's Who In America,* and *Who's Who In the World.* He lives in the San Francisco Bay Area.

Preface

Howard Figler and I have been friends for over twenty years. We live near each other, see each other often, and have worked together (we both appear every November at the California Career Conference/International Career Development Conference, and in addition, Howard has been on staff at my two-week workshop, held each August in Bend, Oregon).

One day we were discussing a lamentable lack in this field. Namely, the need for a comprehensive handbook that could be given both to seasoned career counselors who were seeking to reinvigorate their passion for what they do, as well as to those just seeking entry into the field.

After discussing who we should recruit to write such a handbook, we decided to do it ourselves. We chose topics, assigned or volunteered for this chapter or that, and set to work. Howard did all the prodding (let's get this done!), the setting of timelines, and so forth.

We made no effort to enforce consistency on the way this work is written. Not only are our writing styles quite different, but there is no consistency even within our own bodies of work. So, we let the material shape the style of each chapter, rather than search for the Holy Grail of uniformity. Thus, these chapters vary widely in organization, arrangement, and style.

Fortunately, in thought and viewpoint Howard and I are virtually one. I have commented for years, that I search his writings in vain to find something I really substantially take issue with. And so says he. And so say we all.

As you approach this book, think of it as mining for gold (in the old Gold Rush days). Back then you found a promising spot, and got shovelfuls of dirt, which you ran through a sluice pan in some stream, looking for nuggets of gold. Since Howard and I both live in California, we like this metaphor. It states our wish for you, dear reader: may you find some nuggets, as you go!

-- Dick Bolles

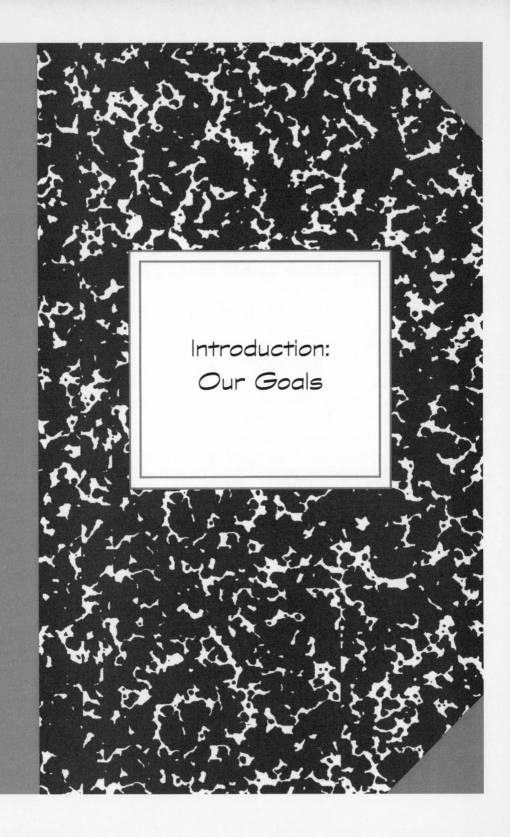

Introduction:
Our Goals

CHAPTER 1

"So You're a Career Counselor! Just Exactly What Do You Do?"

by Dick Bolles

It would be nice if all of us who try to help people with their job choice and their job-hunt could say we basically do the same thing.

But happily (or unhappily) Career Counseling is a *very* broad field. To understand how broad, consider just *some* of the job-titles that belong to this field: vocational psychologist, employment counselor, life/work planner, guidance counselor, vocational-rehabilitation (or voc-rehab) counselor, job-developer, executive search personnel, outplacement specialist, placement director, career counselor, counseling director, vocational counselor, counseling psychologist, test administrator, manpower expert, and career coach -- and they keep going, on and on. Yikes!

One way to simplify it, a bit, is to disregard job-titles, and simply consider what it is a person *does* in this field. Turns out there are basically seven subjects that we may occupy ourselves with, in Career Counseling:

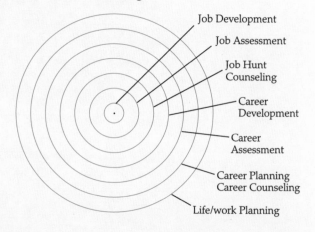

- Job Development
- Job Assessment
- Job Hunt Counseling
- Career Development
- Career Assessment
- Career Planning
- Career Counseling
- Life/work Planning

If we want to simplify it still further, we can ask whether in our work we are:
• Primarily (not exclusively, but primarily) occupied with the job-market, and what's *out there;* or,
• Primarily (not exclusively, but primarily) occupied with the individual, and what's *in there;* or,
• Equally occupied with both job-market information and the individual's needs.

Alternatively, we can describe what we do in this field by identifying what we see as our primary goal:
1. Is our goal primarily to dispense **information**? or
2. Is our goal primarily to impart **knowledge**? or
3. Is is our goal primarily to share **wisdom**?

Since these last three questions are rarely discussed, I think it is tremendously helpful to discuss them here, and see how we become expert in any one of these, regardless of which goal we pick.

As we shall see, they form in some sense a journey that we all take *in our own lives,* as we grow older. Our progression is not merely from "young adult" to "middle-aged" to "senior citizen." It is, sooner or later, from "Information" to "Knowledge" to "Wisdom."

And so we all begin with:

Information

When we first start out helping people, we tend to think that what they most need is information. Information first of all about the labor market (what is available?), and then information about themselves (what do they want to do?).

This need for information seems, at first sight, to be the easiest task in the world; after all, do we not live in 'the Information Age'? There are bunches of paper-and-pencil exercises that people can use for self-inventory. And the amount of information available about 'what's out there', either in books or 'online' is staggering particularly if it's fields, careers or larger companies that we or they are researching.

We come only slowly to understand that one may use information (and information sources) for years without ever understanding the true essence of information. It is easy to think information is just a bunch of facts.

No one is expert with information until they have learned that information has two basic departments, in essence: and they are **Symbols,** and **Silence.** Let us look at each of these in turn.

Symbols. Information is conveyed to others primarily through symbols: the alphabet, or pictures (graphs, charts, diagrams, etc.). Symbols have two characteristics: they are not 'the thing' but only a representation of 'the thing.' And even at that, they only represent *part* of the thing, and not the whole. To illustrate, a Myers-Briggs afficionado is wont to come up to me from time to time and say, 'I would guess that you are an ISFJ.' Well, the code is accurate; but in the larger sense of course I'm not 'an ISFJ' and neither are you. We are both "persons who. . . ." *Persons who* have certain characteristics, talents, gifts, and characteristic ways of acting, only *some* of which can be described by Myers-Briggs.

'Holland code' users also use symbols. The Holland code is essentially a new alphabet, comprised not of twenty-six letters, but of six letters only. And those six letters are used to spell out a number of words, such as RIASEC (if one uses all six), or, let's say, 'SIA' (if one uses only three). But, again, nobody is 'an SIA.' We are *"persons who . . ."* have certain characteristics, talents, gifts, and characteristic ways of acting, only *some* of which can be described by SIA.

The moral of all this is that Information becomes dangerous whenever we forget that all information is conveyed only in symbols, and all symbols are partial.

Silence. It is clear to all of us that when we deal with music, half of the music is comprised of silence between the notes. Consider Glenn Miller's "In the Mood," or Dave Brubeck's "Take Five," or Beethoven's Fifth Symphony.

Likewise, when we deal with information, half of the information is in the silences, and we have never begun to understand information correctly until, after listening to the facts/symbols, we ask ourselves "Where are the silences?" Consider the following bit of information: "It was revealed today people with a certain disease who don't drink wine have twice the mortality of those with that disease who do drink wine." Twice, eh? How awful, how calamitous, how doomed are those who don't drink wine.

But my question is, "Where is the silence in that information?" Well, of course, it is obvious, once we ask the question. We don't know what the original mortality rate is. Not drinking wine causes twice the mortality of those who do, but how many people are we talking about. Let us suppose the mortality rate of that disease among those who do drink wine is 150 out of 100,000. That means 99,850 survive, out of that 100,000. From this we deduce that the mortality rate of that disease if you don't drink wine is 300, twice the preceding. But that still means that 99,700 out of 100,000 do survive. *Pretty good odds, even without the wine!*

In other words, information is filled with a lot of formulas like "twice x" and therefore means nothing until we know what "x" is. We are never skilled with information until we ask about the x's that are hidden in the silences. To put it more bluntly, half of the information we seek is never really given to us. And sometimes it is the crucial half.

In music, silence is essentially to its beauty. In information-giving, the silences can be deadly.

Knowledge

Well, in time we learn how to become truly expert in dealing with information, its partial symbols and its silences. And, what then, for the career counselor?

Then, we begin to realize the people we are trying to help need something more than information. They need knowledge.

Knowledge is the next level up from information, and is distinguished from 'mere information' by two characteristics: knowledge is information that has been **Organized**, and it is information that has been **Applied**. Let us see what these two descriptors mean.

Organized. To illustrate this, suppose I tell you that the key to the job-hunt lies in finding the answers, and remembering the answers, to 275 issues. You will most likely throw up your hands in dismay. "275 things to memorize? You must be kidding!"

But if I tell you that everything about the job-hunt can be organized under just three headings: WHAT (do you most want to do?), WHERE (do you want to do it?), and HOW (do you find the person who has the power to hire you and show him or her how your skills can help them with their problems/challenges?) -- then you will probably feel great relief. "Oh, just *three* parts to the job-hunt, eh? Great!"

You feel relief because an immense number of issues that were lying across the landscape in great disarray have now been organized under just three manageable headings.

Thus we see the difference between information, and knowledge. Knowledge is information that has been organized, under headings, and into categories.

Knowledge, as we just saw, brings 'relief.' And from that relief comes 'healing.' Many of the people we are trying to help need relief, and healing. Hence, they need more than just "information." They need it organized, and applied.

Applied. "The sun is a bright bright object up in the sky." That's information. It doesn't demand any immediate practical application.

But: "If you send a thank-you note to an interviewer, after the interview, your chances of being offered a job greatly increase." That's knowledge. It's information that does have a practical application. Rightly understood, it leads to certain actions. Important actions, sometimes. That's why we say, "This is important to *know*" not "this is important to *inform*."

Information serves 'the mind.'

Knowledge serves 'the will.'

Information is concerned with intellectual puzzles, for which it tries to find answers.

Knowledge is concerned with practical problems, for which it tries to find solutions.

In our increasing mastery of our field over the years, we generally move from thinking that what our clients most need from us is information, to the realization that actually they need information that is organized, and applied. Ergo, they need from us knowledge.

Wisdom

But as we grow older, we realize that as career counselors there is an even greater gift that they need us to teach them, and that is: Wisdom. Wisdom is the next level up from knowledge, and is distinguished from knowledge by two characteristics: **Context** and **Weight,** as in "this is a very weighty matter."

Context. I have a friend in a distant city who was operated on for cancer of the prostate. During the first year, his recovery was miserable. It seemed to preoccupy much of his thoughts and conversation on a day to day basis, as I discovered whenever I would phone.

But after a year, when I called to ask how he was doing, he no longer talked about his misery. Instead, he started to tell me all the projects he was involved with. "Well," I said, "it sounds as though all your physical distress has cleared up." "Oh no," he said, "it's still the same. It's just that I decided I can't spend all my time thinking about it. I had to get on with my life." Then I knew that my friend had found wisdom.

Wisdom involves setting our present problem or situation in some larger context, in this case 'his life.' Often this is how we find the ability to cope with whatever problem is bedeviling us.

Weight. 'A larger context' gives us perspective, strength, and hope -- largely because once we have put our problem in a larger context, we are then able to give that problem its proper and appropriate *weight.* Things we thought were terribly important turn out not to be so important, when looked at in the larger scheme of things. When my friend placed his handicap in a larger context, he saw it didn't deserve so much weight as he had been giving it. That is the very essence of wisdom: learning what weight to give things.

All successful career counseling depends on our learning for ourselves, and then sharing with others, how to put things in context, how to give things their proper weight, no more, no less. For that is the essence of Wisdom. And wisdom is what our clients most need in their lives. And what they most need from us.

Information + Knowledge + Wisdom = Spirituality

What is "career counseling"? It is our attempt to share with our clients certain tools; and those tools are: wisdom, knowledge, and information.

And what is "Life/work planning"? It is that discipline which tries to give people these tools, *with special emphasis upon their application to the arena of work.*

Our work has six parts:

1. To teach the importance of always looking for the largest **context** for everything; and

2. To teach the importance of learning what **weight** to give various problems and solutions; and

3. To teach the importance of **organizing** the information we have in our life; and

4. To teach the importance of **applying** the information we have in our life; and

5. To teach the importance of **silence**; and

6. To teach the importance of understanding that words and pictures are only **symbols** of a much greater reality -- in us, in others, and in the world.

The most fundamental issue, in every field, is whether the basic nature of the field is material, or whether the basic nature of the field is spiritual.

In the case of career counseling, the basic nature of the field is clearly spiritual. Information + knowledge + wisdom is the very essence of career counseling and life/work planning. And information + knowledge + wisdom is the very essence of spirituality.

This is never more clear than when we examine the six parts of career counseling and then see that traditional God-centered spirituality has the very same six parts:

1. **Context.** In traditional spirituality, God is the context within which everything is set. "For in Him we live and move and have our being."

2. **Weight.** The Ten Commandments of Judaism, the Sermon on the Mount and The Two Greatest Commandments of Christ, are designed precisely to define what things in the world should have the most weight in our lives.

3. **Organizing.** Theology, literally "the words about God," reflect the attempt to organize all the key information that we have learned about God over the past six thousand years, into meaningful categories.

4. **Applying.** Ethics and moral values are the attempt of spirituality to apply what we have organized, to the guidance of our daily life.

5. **Silence.** Traditional God-centered spirituality sets forth prayer and meditation as essential to our life, because they underline the silences in our daily life, and fill them with meaning.

6. **Symbols.** Worship is both the proclamation of the importance of symbols, and the judgment upon the partiality of all such symbols, in comparison with the great living God.

Thus, spirituality and career counseling turn out to be twin sisters.

Conclusion

Information + Knowledge + Wisdom. What this means is that these are the basic hungers of our clients. Therefore the basic work of career counseling is to give them these tools.

Information + Knowledge + Wisdom = Spirituality.   What this means is that while the issues our clients are wrestling with may find their *immediate* answer in their work and career, the *ultimate* answer to our clients' concerns may lie in the clients learning how to deepen their own spiritual life.

In our clients' lives what begins as a quest for bread often ends up being also a quest for The Bread of Life.

CHAPTER 2

What Does "Career" Mean?

by Dick Bolles

Sometimes two career counselors use a word and *think* they are talking about the same thing, when in fact they are not. Each is using the word in a different sense. Therefore, any handbook for career counselors must begin with **definitions** of some of the common terms used in the career counseling field, so that we have agreement on what we mean when we use them.

JOB. This refers to a particular place where a person is employed, as at General Motors.

OCCUPATION. The word **occupation** refers to a **job-title**, such as engineer. Thus an engineer may, over a number of years, hold down four different jobs, at four different engineering firms. Of course, people change jobs, but it is common also to change occupations. This is most commonly described, however, not as *an occupation change* but as **a career-change** -- particularly if the change is dramatic (e.g., from high school teacher to shoemaker). The average person may expect to have three different careers before they retire.

CAREER. The word **career** is used in the world *out there* in several senses -- all related to the general subject of occupations or jobs in the world of work:

1. It is used, first of all, in contrast to **learning** or **leisure**. Thus when clothing ads speak of "a career outfit," they are referring to clothes which are worn primarily at work, rather than during learning-activities or leisure-activities.

2. It is used, secondly, to sum up a person's **whole life in the world of work**. Thus when people say of someone at the end

of their life, "He [or she] had a brilliant career," they are not referring to a particular occupation, but to all the occupations this person ever held.

3. Thirdly, in its most common sense, it is used as a synonym for the word **occupation** or **job** -- particularly where that occupation or job offers opportunity for promotion and advancement, toward the top.

I have more to say, and at length, about the origins of this word, further along here in this chapter.

CAREER CHOICE. Occupation or career choice is typically first made when a person finishes high school or college. One can choose today from among at least 12,741 different occupations/careers/job-titles, which have some 8,000 alternative job-titles, for a total of over 20,000.

DESCRIPTIONS OF CAREERS. In the U.S., a description of all these 20,000 occupations is/was to be found in the *Dictionary of Occupational Titles*, familiarly known as the *D.O.T.*, found in almost every public library in the U.S. It was published by the Department of Labor's Bureau of Labor Statistics, with its core material from 1977, supplemented in 1982, 1986, 1987, and 1991. (Fourth Edition, Revised).

O*NET. There are a number of ways in which all this information can be reduced to a more manageable quantity. The first is to forget about all 20,000, and discuss only those occupations into which most people (95% of all U.S. workers) go. This is the U.S. Department of Labor's strategy with what they call O*NET (The Occupational Information Network): they are replacing the *D.O.T.*'s 12,741 job-titles with just 1,222 of their own -- the ones that 95% of the workforce goes into. Unfortunately, of course, anyone who comes to you for career counseling probably wants one of the missing 11,519. *The O*Net Dictionary of Occupational Titles (1998 Edition)* print edition is available, now, from a variety of places, including: JIST Works, Inc., 720 North Park Ave., Indianapolis, IN 46202.

CLASSIFICATION SYSTEMS. The second way to save us from having to deal with 20,000 job-titles is to gather those 20,000 job-titles into a smaller and more manageable number of "families" or "clusters." The federal government, through the Bureau of Labor Statistics in the U.S. Department of Labor, has done such classification for many years, which it publishes in the *Occupational Outlook Handbook*. The number *and titles* of such families have varied from time to time, but at this writing all 20,000 job-titles, occupations, or careers, have been gathered up into just **19** families. They are:

CAREER OR OCCUPATIONAL FAMILIES

1. Managerial and Management-Related Occupations
2. Engineers, Surveyors, and Architects
3. Natural, Computer, and Mathematical Scientists
4. Lawyers, Social Scientists, Social Workers, and Religious Workers
5. Teachers, Librarians, and Counselors
6. Health Diagnosing and Treating Practitioners
7. Registered Nurses, Pharmacists, Dieticians, Therapists, and Physician Assistants
8. Health Technologists and Technicians
9. Writers, Artists, and Entertainers
10. Technologists and Technicians, Except Health
11. Marketing and Sales Occupations
12. Administrative Support Occupations, Including Clerical
13. Service Occupations
14. Agriculture, Forestry, Fishing, and Related Occupations
15. Mechanics, Installers, and Repairers
16. Construction Trades and Extractive Occupations
17. Production Occupations
18. Transportation and Material Moving Occupations
19. Handlers, Equipment Cleaners, Helpers, and Laborers

CAREER QUESTIONS. There are six questions (or groups of questions) that the skilled career counselor can use, to sort out what career direction a person wants to take:

1. Careers are either in **Agriculture** or **Manufacturing** or **Information/Service**. So, are you interested in a career which is primarily agricultural, working with growing things; or are you interested in a career that is primarily manufacturing, working at producing things; or are you interested in a career that is primarily service or information oriented, aimed at helping people? As background here, it is worth noting that careers and career patterns have changed dramatically over the years. There was a time, around the turn of the century, when the majority of the workforce -- that is, over 50% of all workers -- were employed in agriculture. Then, by mid-century, that had changed, and the majority of workers were employed in manufacturing. Today, that has changed again, and the majority of workers are employed in careers which deal with information, and/or render services to people. Consequently, though many individuals still choose a career in manufacturing or even in agriculture, it is the services/information sector that is growing the most rapidly today, and therefore creating the most job opportunities. Opportunities should never be the determining factor in choosing a career, but obviously it is *one* of the factors that should be considered.

2. Careers deal with either **Things, or Data, or People.** In any career field there is wide latitude about what kind of work you do, and what skills you use, within that field. Within agriculture, for example, you could be driving tractors and other farm machinery -- and thus working primarily with Things; or you could be gathering statistics about crop growth for some state agency -- and thus working primarily with Information; or you could be teaching agriculture in a college classroom, and thus working primarily with People. All careers can thus be typed. So, are you interested in a career which has you working primarily with things; or primarily with data/information; or primarily with people?

3. Careers deal with different **Fields Of Knowledge.** That is to say, every career requires you to know quite a bit about *something.* Fields of knowledge include such areas as: health, construction, law, computers, buildings, art, Japanese, oceanography, physics, psychology, the human body, religion, building materials, cars, gardening, sports, drama, and so forth. Even if you choose a career where you enjoy using the skills it calls for, if you have to use them all day long with knowledges you hate, then that career is not for you; e.g., a secretary who hates legal subjects, such as laws, torts, depositions, and so forth, finding herself working at a law school. So, what kinds of knowledge do you, or would you, like to be using all day long?

4. Careers have **Different Preparation Times**. So, you need to examine carefully how long it will take to train or otherwise prepare for each career that matches your skills and preferred fields of knowledge. If schooling or training is required, how long will it take? How long do you want it to take? Some careers require college, all four years of it, and often even more time than that. Fortunately, there are many careers with splendid opportunities available, that require only two years of preparation and training at most -- and sometimes as little as a year. Community and junior colleges offer such training, as do technical institutes, vocational schools, and even the armed forces. Proprietary schools, such as schools for travel agents, models, etc., also offer training, but as these range greatly in quality, thorough investigation needs to be made before signing up. For those who do not like or have access to a classroom, there is learning by mail through correspondence schools. Moreover, some careers offer apprenticeships or on-the-job training.

5. Careers have **Different Kinds of Workplaces.** So, as you look over each of the 19 families, ask yourself if a particular career requires you to work indoors or outdoors. And if indoors, in what kind of place? Do people in this career spend most of their day in a store, shop, office, garage, laboratory, hospital, car, building, loading dock, factory, library, agency, or

where? Which of these workplaces, or others, are the kind of place where you would *like* to spend all day?

6. Careers are either **Prescribed** or **Discretionary.** Within career fields, some jobs are very prescribed: you have to follow instructions carefully, and do the job in exactly the way you are told. Other jobs are very discretionary: it is entirely up to you as to how you go about doing it, so long as you get the job done. So, which of these two do you prefer? This will help determine at what level you want eventually, to be working, in the career you choose.

THE DEEPER MEANING OF THE WORD 'CAREER.' The origin of the word which shapes our field, is very interesting. It came, way back, from the Latin word **carrus**, cart; S. **carrera**, road; Fr. **carrière**, race-course.

Its descendant, **Career**, has been both noun and verb, and has had the following various meanings, over time:

A cart. "Carrus" meant from the beginning a two-wheeled vehicle for transporting burdens, such as a wagon or chariot. From "carrus" have come the English words "car," "cargo," "cart," and "carry."

A horse. "Career" has meant the short gallop of a racehorse at full speed, implying swift motion. It has also implied a rapid and continuous course of action, an uninterrupted procedure. Further, the horse's turning this way or that as it runs, has been reflected in such metaphors as Coleridge's "the mad careering of the storm."

A road. "Career" has meant also the ground on which the race is run, the race-course.

The road, the horse, and the cart -- these have endured down through time, as the three different attitudes people have toward their career. Let me show you what I mean:

1. **The Road or Race-course.** For those who hold this view of "Career," their job is seen above all else as *Action*. For them, it is the exhilaration and excitement involved in action that is the point of it all. They love the risk, the wheeling and dealing,

the thrill of the roller-coaster ride. The driving force that guides them is self-described as *Ambition*. They like it best when -- on a race-course -- they feel their career is an irresistible force, propelling everything else out of its path. For them, the emphasis is all on *Winning*. Excelling others is their motif. Power over others is often their goal, whether that power be overt (as in politics) or subtle (as in fame).

2. **The Horse.** For those who hold this view of "Career," their job is seen above all else as something that pleases the self. They aim for the elation of the horse as it races for the pure pleasure of running, with nostrils flaring. They take pleasure just in the doing of their work. If there is personal movement or advancement during the course of their career, what pleases them about it is not the degree to which they are excelling others, but the degree to which they are excelling themselves. Growth, rather than power, is their driving motif. They measure their career by how much they personally grow, in enjoying their work, in responsibility, in mastering their field, in transferring their skills to another field or more complex work.

3. **The Cart.** For those who hold this view of "Career," their job is measured above all else by what their work carries to others. For them, the horse may race down the race-course, nostrils flaring, beating all others, but the main question is: what's in the cart? What is being carried, by one's work? They define it as "their values" or "their Character." They look at every person not in terms of "what do you do?" but "who are you?" And they ask the same question of themselves. Character is their main concern, and they know well that the business world is not normally conducive to the development of character, as John Steinbeck pointed out, eloquently, in *Cannery Row:*

> "It has always seemed strange to me," said Doc. "The things we admire in men, kindness and generosity, openness, honesty, understanding and feeling are the

concomitants of failure in our system. And those traits we detest, sharpness, greed, acquisitiveness, meanness, egotism and self-interest are the traits of success. And while men admire the quality of the first they love the produce of the second."

But for those who value the "cart" view of "Career," if there is a conflict between Character and their work, they will quit their job rather than do work that runs counter to their beliefs and values. They believe that no career is worth anything unless a man's or woman's character becomes stronger for the doing of it, rather than weaker. If a job carries with it opportunities for them to be more honest, or more courageous, or more trustworthy, or more faithful, compassionate, and kind, then that for them is a worthy career. In their view, **carrus** (career) should lead to **carus** (caring).

Conclusion

Well, there you have it. Our definitions. And our attitudes. The Road, the Horse, and the Cart: three different and distinct views of what is at the heart of "Career." Every working man or woman holds one of these views. And so does every Age.

In this Age -- speaking personally -- I have no patience with The Road concept of "career." Career counseling books that deal with "power" and "looking out for #1" and "how to win" at your job, have always dismayed me. They seem to turn career counseling into simply the institutionalization of self-centeredness, self-absorption, and selfishness. This is not a noble path for career counseling to set its feet upon.

That leaves the other two: the Horse, and the Cart. Between them, we see two very winsome views of "Career." The one, emphasizing how much we must enjoy the work we choose, the other, emphasizing how much we must ensure that our work carries with it values and character that we can be proud of.

Which to choose, between these two? Well, they're both terribly important. But, on balance, I think the world is filled with a great deal of enjoyment, but demonstrates again and again, in the daily newspapers and in life, a tremendous hunger for character.

So, in this case, if we are forced to choose one over the other, then I think it's time that we in career counseling put the Cart before the Horse.

CHAPTER 3

What Does It Mean "to Counsel" People?

by Howard Figler

The word "counselor" creates confusion from the very start. It sounds as though we "counsel" people, or tell them what to do. But we don't -- or at least we shouldn't. If a career counselor tells someone else what job or career is good for them, they're doing a disservice, because no counselor can divine what kind of work a person will like, nor where they will succeed.

Thus, good career counseling is the reverse of giving counsel. It enables the clients to counsel themselves. The career counselor creates a process which allows the client to assemble what she knows about herself and act on that self-understanding. Far easier said than done. Suppose a client says, as many do, "I have no clue about what I want."?

The art of career counseling starts right there. It begins with encouraging the client to talk about her wishes, aspirations, thoughts, feelings, meanderings, and idle conjectures about what she *might* like to do. From such ramblings come the seeds of her exploration, a search that can begin immediately.

Career counseling seeks not so much to reach decisions as to get a client moving -- toward experiences that help her "reality-test" her daydreams. While the client is exploring, she can have one or more "interim jobs" or whatever is necessary to earn a living as she is testing out her long-range aspirations.

Counselors understand that clients proceed at their own pace. But they also recognize that clients can immobilize themselves by saying such things as: "I'm so depressed . . . I should make up my mind by now . . . I need a job but I don't know who would want me."

Counselors believe that you're less likely to be depressed if you find your core enthusiasms and translate that energy into putting one foot in front of the other. Depression, in one sense, is lack of action. Any kind of constructive movement has a good chance of shaking a person loose from the tentacles of self-pity. Even random behavior is better than no behavior at all. So, we get people out of their rooms and onto the streets, sometimes with no purpose other than to see who's doing what.

Right there is the single molecule that often makes career counseling effective -- the one element that can be found in every organic compound known as positive career development. That molecule is called "talking to people about their work and observing them."

Career counselors help people put their experiences in motion. We want people to act on their hunches about themselves, because we trust that if the client keeps following his nose, trying experiences that fit his drives and values, he will eventually land in something good or perhaps create it along the way.

That makes our job sound simple. As if anyone could do it. What's so hard about getting people moving? People who say that haven't talked with any confused career seekers lately. There are a lot of people out there who are totally flummoxed about what they want to do and what to do about it.

Career counselors sit on that bridge between the inner motivations of the confused client and the vast grocery store of options known as the world of work. Clients have enough trouble seeing inside themselves. When they try to imagine what's on the other side waiting for them, it feels as though they're peering across a large body of water on a very foggy day.

However, bewildered and resistant clients do not discourage an experienced career counselor, because counselors know two truths that serve as their well of optimism when clients flap around in search of direction:

1. **Every client has motivations.** Every human being is motivated towards something, even if it looks like nothing more than watching ships go by, talking aimlessly, or whittling wood. Anything more than catatonic is a sign of hope. A counselor begins by finding where the client's energy is, what she does with herself, what she pays attention to. In these subtle clues lie the hints of what may happen next in her career treasure hunt.

2. **Every possible career idea can be investigated and pursued.** Hey, this is America here. You know, freedom of choice. There's no legislation or code of conduct that says you cannot consider entering any job or career at all. The possibilities do not hide under rocks. They're out there whenever you're willing to start looking.

These are obvious messages perhaps, but they're the groundwork for every person's career change. Anyone has the possibility of moving to a wide variety of careers, if he's willing to do what's necessary to qualify. Sure, and I can play piano at Carnegie Hall next year. Have we officially entered fantasyland? No, I said the "possibility" of changing. How far you go depends upon how motivated you are and how much you focus your energy. Talent helps too, but we can cite many examples of people who have succeeded without great heaps of talent.

Motivation and pursuit

Motivation and Pursuit -- the two great engines that every career counselor tries to mobilize within his clients. Without them, little happens in one's career. With them, lots of things happen, and many great moments are possible. Rudyard Kipling wrote (in his poem called "IF"):

> *If you can fill the unforgiving minute*
> *with 60 seconds worth of distance run*
> *Yours is the Earth and everything that's in it . . .*

By that I presume Kipling means that active, energetic pursuit of a desired goal always gives you a fighting chance of getting it, and furthermore, the pursuit itself is equally as important as the objective. Whether you reach your goal or a different goal is almost beside the point. By trying to reach it, you gain every step of the way.

The art of career counseling is the art of helping people to rediscover and gather the energy for working that they've had all along. Sometimes good people lose faith in their ability to act, or they don't give themselves permission to pursue. They come to a career counselor to find the sparks they know are within them. We help them rediscover that pushing, kicking, laughing, falling down and getting up are better than feeling sorry for themselves or despairing or whining.

They've been trying to have these conversations with themselves, but somehow it took the presence of another person, a listener to hear their inner voice, to get the experience train rolling toward something good.

The career counselor's talent lies in her ability to nudge clients toward hearing themselves, sensing the gifts that are within them, gathering steam from their own imagination, and moving themselves to action. It's a tale that may start in the counselor's office, but it's a story the client writes herself.

CHAPTER 4

The Six Objectives
of Career Counseling

by Howard Figler

What's a career anyway? People who work have an opportunity to touch the lives of others. Ten thousand days in which to --

- give warm service or treat 'em like cardboard
- find things to laugh about or things to whine about
- build a new mousetrap or tear something down
- help people or hurt them
- build relationships or neglect them
- enhance your community or ignore it

Some would prefer to work only for money. To them I say -- you get what you work for. Career counseling here is oriented toward those who regard work as an opportunity, not simply a necessity.

Purpose and meaning are at the center of most satisfying careers. We want career counseling to enable clients to focus their purposes and develop strategies for pursuing them. However, purpose does not come to you in a blinding flash. It develops over time:

> Meaning is not something you stumble across, like the prize in a treasure hunt. Meaning is something you build into your life. You build it out of your own past, out of your affections and loyalties, out of your experience of humankind as it is passed on to you, . . . out of the things you believe in . . . out of the values for which you are willing to sacrifice something. The ingredients are there. You are the only one who can put them together

into that unique pattern that will be your life. Let it be a life that has dignity and meaning for you. If it does, then the particular balance of success or failure is of less account.   -- John Gardner

Objectives of career counseling

Foremost, the counselor seeks to accomplish what the client wants to accomplish. It is tempting to be seduced by our own ideas of what is "good career development"; however the client has ideas of her own. A client may decide that rushing off to Pakistan to ride camels for several years is her idea of a good career. Or perhaps a good career is living a very marginal existence by selling her paintings on street corners.

Lest we have ideas of "careers" that we believe are more suitable than others, our first responsibility is to the client. It's easy for career counselors to prefer certain careers that reflect their educational, cultural, or family backgrounds. The alert counselor must guard against these biases.

Here are six objectives that apply to all clients, regardless of the kinds of work they want, their levels of actual or aspired education, their age, or other characteristics. Counseling relationships of both short- and long-term duration are implied here. A counselor often likes to see a client numerous times over a period of months, but many clients only come once or twice. While a larger number of sessions has certain advantages, briefer counseling may serve to "get the client moving" more quickly, because he has to take more responsibility when the counselor is not an ongoing presence. Purpose and meaning are more likely to be reflected in clients' careers if the counselor helps the client to accomplish the objectives described below:

1. **Assume responsibility.** Counselors want clients to take charge of their career development, make their own decisions, and act on these decisions. While the client welcomes input from others, as Howard Kirschenbaum says, she is always "the

chairperson of her board of directors." This means that clients trust their own judgments of themselves and are willing to endure the risks that are always present in making choices.

Assuming responsibility is the key that makes all the other objectives possible. Clients often don't want this responsibility and will dance a fancy jig to get the counselor to relieve them of the burden. They may look to others for direction when they first seek counseling, so the counselor's initial objective is to encourage self-empowerment.

Many clients say: "Tell me what I ought to do." Some counselors are happy to oblige. It is tempting for the counselor to provide career advice under the guise of: "your test results suggest . . ." or "here are a few ideas that may fit you." You feel as though you're being helpful, but in fact you're doing the opposite. By providing such advice, the counselor makes it difficult for clients to take charge of their own career development.

2. **Imagine career ideas.** Most people unconsciously imagine themselves in careers every day ("How would I be as an actor?" "What if I had my own consulting business?"), but they often dismiss these ideas and don't allow them into the daylight. Novelist-adventurer-wine steward-executive. Why not? When career counselors tell clients to "be realistic," the client's initial career sparks may be snuffed out. With careers, there is no such thing as "unrealistic." When a career drive is strong, many people make their own reality. You think not? Talk to those who have built business empires, artistic careers, political organizations, or community service organizations -- from nothing.

Every client has had a rich variety of life experiences whether they know it or not. Ice fishing, science fairs, intense athletic competition, family crises, the local flood or other natural disaster, friends' illnesses, etc. -- from these experiences, they have formed hundreds of impressions about what they might like to do.

Clients thus have a ton of material in their imaginations. They don't need tests or other artificial devices to produce career ideas. Unfortunately, their career imagination often lies fallow.

It's the counselor's job to tap into these impressions and urge clients to use their experiences as a base for generating career ideas. Experiences which have strong feelings attached -- either positive or negative -- sometimes can lead to strong career motivations. Thus, some of the best help that career counselors offer is to urge their clients to be "unrealistic."

Career counselors should ask questions such as: *"Given that experience you just described, what kinds of jobs or careers does it suggest to you?"*

A friend named Algonquin (yes, that's his name) took his love of 18th and 19th century American history and created a museum on the Industrial Revolution, specializing in railroads. Everyone had told him "A museum? Get real."

Izmelda wanted to bring books to poor people. Her friends and family told her it was "do-gooder daydreaming" and she should dispense with it. But Izmelda knew that libraries were throwing away books! (to clear away room for new books) and she wanted to save them. Izmelda founded The Book Recovery Project, secured funding from seven different United Way agencies, and put this nonprofit endeavor on solid footing, delivering books to people who could not afford them, to raise the literacy level of the county.

The next Maya Angelou, Carl Sagan, or Aaron Copland is probably sitting right in front of you, but you don't recognize them. There are clients who dream of curing diseases, inventing newer, safer vehicles, performing magical dances, or helping impoverished countries (not all the same client, you understand). Many such ideas wither away, because of shaky support. Career counselors can be the catalysts for their clients' deepest career longings.

Some of the best career paths emerge from wild dreaming and ideas that seem ridiculous at the time. The counselor must separate the idea-generation process from the evaluation process ("will this career work out?," "can I do it?"). The evaluation must be kept at bay, saved for later, because clients are much too quick to judge and stifle their career possibilities.

Clients have abundant career imaginations. The counseling room is the place to let ideas fly around and be talked about, after which the client can decide those she wants to explore the most.

3. **Use one's favorite functional and adaptive skills.** Why give anything less than your best? One of the most fundamental dimensions of career counseling is helping people to discover and build the skills they most like using. While clients have vague ideas of what they're good at, their typical self-reports are incomplete, because they're not often asked about their "accomplishments" and they may not have the vocabulary to assign to the skills they used in these experiences. It is vital to ask:

"Tell me about some things you've done in your life that you've felt good about."

Though it may take a while before the client can trust the counselor enough to talk in detail about these experiences, this kind of self-disclosure is pivotal, because the client affirms what is unique about herself. Knowledge of one's strengths provides a foundation of confidence for moving into the work world. The client can believe:

"I have something valuable to offer."

We want career counselors to tap into the wealth of information people have about themselves. By doing so, clients discover not only their key assets, but also many clues about their most important values.

You would think that people automatically know these things. Au contraire. They often take themselves for granted or overlook key skills by saying: "Awww, that was nothing."

4. **Deal with negative emotions or thoughts which inhibit career progress.** Wham! Bam! Ooof! The body blows of rejection and the self-inflicted wounds of self-doubt can flatten many careers before they even get rolling. Clients will often have anxieties, fears, or self-defeating thoughts that lead

to outright avoidance of career action. The counselor helps clients work with and overcome these negative forces.

Too much complaining and inhibition can devour the client's resolve. Negative emotions -- anger, fear, excessive anxiety -- can undo one's career progress. The counselor listens to the client's complaints and then helps her to (a) develop strategies for overcoming the stated problems, and (b) find ways to manage the negative emotions.

5. **Know how to determine "steps to a career goal."** Counseling should make it possible for a client to find out how she can get from Point A (here I am now) to Point B (that is the career I may want to be in). It's usually best for a counselor to direct the client to outside resources (books, the Internet, etc.), rather than trying to describe these "steps to a goal" from her memory.

You would think that clients could discover that careers have entry requirements and that these requirements make them accessible to almost anyone, but many believe either that:

• "I can't do that kind of work. I'm not cut out for it." Or
• "Career paths are mysteries, known only to the anointed, such as career counselors."

Career counselors must counter these two mistaken ideas by:

(a) Encouraging clients to believe that one's motivation and skill development are the strongest determinants of career progress. Career development is about cultivating the skills you need to do the work you want. We are not "cut out" to do things. We grow into them. And

(b) Showing clients that the information about "steps" to a particular goal is readily available.

Talk must lead to action. Some clients talk a good game but don't do anything. Some action is usually better than none, even if it leads to mistakes and false trails, which it often does.

If clients translate their career ideas into "steps to a goal" and then follow their action plans, that indicates they are motivated. Which leads us back to the foundation that undergirds the most satisfying career choices -- meaning and purpose.

6. Choose work that has a sense of meaning and purpose.
A counselor helps the client to state her career purposes and express the feelings associated with them. A strong purpose has many benefits -- it leads the person to acquire new skills, helps her to weather the hard times, allows her to maintain direction even in an uncertain labor market, and gives her the deepest sense of satisfaction from her work. (Mission and the spirituality of careers are discussed later in this book in Chapter 32.)

When discussing purpose and meaning with clients, the counselor should include unpaid work as well as paid work. The labor market will not always pay people to do the things they value most, but they still need to keep those purposes alive. Musicians and artists are obvious examples. But let's suppose a person's strongest drive is to help the environment. Even if she can't get an immediate job in that field, she can stay involved and keep looking for opportunities, while earning income in other ways.

Clients need purposes that include economic survival but also transcend it. The counselor helps them to integrate their larger purposes with their need for earning income.

One of the challenges of career counseling is paying attention to all six of these objectives without shaping them into a strict agenda which would stifle the client. Don't try to push any particular objective on a client by implying: "We need to talk about this objective now, because Mommy (or Daddy) knows what's best for you." A counselor with an agenda is not an effective listener. The client must establish the topics of conversation based on her priorities.

You will learn how to integrate these six objectives with clients' statements of their key concerns. Sometimes you will give less attention to certain objectives, because that's not what the client wants at the moment. But eventually all six will become part of the conversation.

CHAPTER 5

The 12 Most Important Skills
a Career Counselor Uses

By Howard Figler

When the door closes behind you and the client gives you that look which says: "Well, go ahead -- do it!," what do you do?

This chapter will focus on the categories of responses you have available when you're counseling a client. Each of these forms of response is a skill. Below are the 12 kinds of responses (skills) that are most important to your effectiveness as a career counselor, regardless of the number or length of sessions that you see a client.

The objectives of career counseling, discussed in the previous chapter, give you a framework for using these skills, but the art of how to use each skill will unfold as you work with clients. Don't be rigid or formulaic about when and how to use your skills. Adapt these skills to a counseling style that works best for you. Be willing to experiment and consistently ask for feedback from your clients and from other counselors.

Your client's needs provide the best cues about which skill you're going to use next; she sets the agenda. You apply your skills as she reveals her aspirations, problems, and desired actions. How you integrate your counseling skills will be different for every client, because each one organizes her world in a different way.

Many clients are impatient to get "advice"

Giving clients advice about what careers they should choose is the quickest way to negate the value of all the 12 key career counseling skills.

The approach to career counseling in this book reflects the "client-centered" theory of Carl Rogers. It derives from the belief that the individual can generate his own decisions based on processing his internal "data," and that such decisions are more valid than advice offered by others.

Many clients would much prefer to receive "expert advice" about what careers are best for them. However, an advice-centered approach is counterproductive and harmful because: (1) it encourages the client to be dependent upon the counselor's so-called "insights"; and (2) the counselor cannot know "what is best for the client," no matter how much data she has. The client's choices come from her intuitive and unconscious mix of drives and priorities that only she knows how to decipher. One of the counselor's biggest jobs is to help clients access their inner voices and honor what they hear.

Advice giving can be a powerful lure to career counselors. The counselor may be under time pressure, and the client has a desire to be given "the wisdom of the professional." Be aware that a slight suggestion ("Well, your skills and values do seem to point toward working in this area _____") may be taken as gospel truth by clients who are eager to be directed.

The temptation to be "authoritative" can be hard to resist, especially behind a closed door, with a client aching for direction. So resist anyway. "Offering an idea or two" can feel as though you're being helpful. The client gets such "ideas" from everyone. Why not from you? Because the career counselor is presumed to have special knowledge. Just as some people believe that psychologists "can read my mind," others think the career counselor "knows what I'm best suited for." Don't take on that role; there are many skills you can use to help clients make their own choices.

Many clients who seek advice are looking to the professional as they would toward a doctor. They want "answers" and they believe the career counselor has them. However, career counselors are not "experts" like doctors, who know more than we do about the mechanics of our bodies, or like carpenters who know more about putting nails and wood together.

The client (not the counselor) is the expert on the materials that the counselor is working with -- the client's skills, needs, values, etc. The career counselor's expertise consists of helping clients to organize and act upon what they know about themselves.

Doctors might consider being more client-centered, because their patients would take more responsibility for their health. Many physicians already practice in client-centered ways and their patients benefit from it.

The 12 Key Skills of the Career Counselor*

1. **Clarifying content.** *Restating what you believe to be the essence of the client's statement.*

This is one of the two primary listening skills. By restating, you help both of you to understand the client's meaning. It is essential for a client to "hear himself talk." You're distilling the essence of what he said. This keeps the counselor "on the same wavelength" with the client. People need to be understood, especially because they are often misunderstood by family and friends. People close to you love you, but they sometimes don't listen well.

2. **Reflecting feeling.** *Restating the emotional quality of the client's response, identifying the feelings and the content to which they were attached.*

Most of what the client feels is not stated directly by him; thus the counselor must "read between the lines." Feelings are usually observed from the client's nonverbal behaviors. When a counselor sees joy, sadness, anxiety, anger, or other feelings,

*This classification of the twelve key career counseling skills was developed by Howard Figler and Kathy Strawser Worgul at the University of Texas at Austin Career Center.

she should let the client know she's observing those feel-ings. Once again, this helps greatly in the client's sensing he is understood. Often, the feelings are even stronger and more meaningful than the content.

"I'm angry that I have to earn more money because my hus-band's family is borrowing from us."

When clients feel alone with their emotions, they may over-magnify them and get into behavioral ruts. Counselors can use feeling identification as springboards to action:

"What do you think you might do differently to change that feeling?"

3. **Open-ended questioning.** *Asking questions that encourage the fullest range of possible responses.*

Such questions usually begin with What, How, or In What Ways. The open question is the single most useful tool for ex-tracting deeper layers of meaning from the client. A counselor can use open questions that "get underneath" a client's initial statements to uncover new layers of meaning, unexpected di-rections, and feelings that are closer to the core of the client's experience.

Many statements from clients are superficial. If he says: "I really love research," what does that mean for him? By asking, "What do you like about research?," you help him to deepen the meaning.

If a client says: "I am good at getting things done," you can ask: "How do you go about getting things accomplished?"

Bandler and Grinder's book, *The Structure Of Magic, Vol-ume I* (Science and Behavior Books, Palo Alto, CA, 1975) helps you to learn how to use questions to help clients deepen the meaning of what they say.

When you are stuck in career counseling, think of an open-ended question that is related to what the client just said. You will get unstuck by asking the client to explore his self-understanding more fully. For example, *"What bothers you most about your pres-ent job?"*

4. **Skill identifying.** *Naming the specific areas of talent or strength revealed in the client's description of her past experiences.*

Clients seldom know much skills language. By listening to clients talk about their successful experiences, the counselor can expand their skills vocabulary, using an inventory of skills such as the one given in Bolles's *What Color Is Your Parachute?*

Counselors want their clients to eventually learn how to select or name their own skills words. They can ask: "What skills do you think were most present in that accomplishment?"

5. **Value clarifying.** *Identifying the sources of enjoyment and satisfaction in a person's description of past activities and experiences.*

When clients talk about their good experiences, the counselor can spot values that are prized by the client and report them back to her. Skill identification and value clarification go hand in hand. Every positive experience has both imbedded within it.

When clients identify the skills they like best and the values they seek most, they have a language for talking to themselves and others about what they are looking for in the world of work.

6. **Creative imagining.** *Methods which encourage the client to envision job and career possibilities through open-ended brainstorming, imaging, visualizing, fantasizing, etc.*

The counselor should stimulate this by asking questions such as:

- *What kinds of careers have you thought you might like to do?*
- *What pictures do you have of yourself in the world of work?*
- *You've said you like organizing numerical data and writing technical reports. What kinds of careers might enable you to do these together?*

Imagination and visualization tap into the right side of the client's brain, where intuition, play, dreams, and pictures float freely. Many of the best, eventually most functional careers start with fantasies. Some insist that all the best careers start that way. Thus, dreams often become highly "practical."

7. Information giving. *Giving key pieces of job or career information that enable the client to understand better a particular job or career or a particular process (such as job hunting).*

As explained in a later chapter, information giving must be very limited and selective, so that the session does not mistakenly become a one-way process of teacher-to-student. This would discourage the counseling dialogue and the client would lose the opportunity to talk about her career skills, needs, and values.

8. Role-playing.

Role-playing is an opportunity to bring into the counseling room situations that the client will face later. It can be a practice job interview, a conversation between spouses, or a meeting between a person and her boss. The counselor can help the client practice what she will say, how to say it best, and how to deal with the expected responses.

In role-playing, the counselor can play the respondent (interviewer, spouse) so the client can practice her skills, or she can be the client herself in order to model behaviors she would like the client to learn. Often a counselor will see opportunities for role-playing that occur impromptu during counseling.

9. Spot-checking.

Ask the client if the conversation, so far, has met her expectations, or has covered the concerns she had when she first came in. *"Are we on track regarding what you most wanted to talk about?"*

Counselors often forget to do this. It is absolutely necessary to spot-check once or more during every counseling session. You may be "off track" and he is afraid to say anything, because you're the authority so "you must know what you're doing."

On the contrary, the client is the "authority" regarding the conversation, because his feelings and thoughts are primary. *When you spot-check, often a client will redirect the conversation.* This is good. Don't worry that the client will disrespect you for "missing" his priorities. Instead, he will appreciate that you asked. Spot-checking allows you to stay close to the center of the client's problems.

10. **Summarizing.** *Collecting what the client has said thus far, and reviewing it for purposes of moving forward.*

Career counseling needs breathing spaces and these are provided by summarizing. The counselor can pause at various junctures and say: "Now let's see if I can summarize the key things you've said so far."

Summarizing also can help the client to regroup and decide where he wants to go next.

"You've said you'd like to get free of your government job and start a tax accounting business, but you're afraid of the risks. You'd like to try it on an experimental basis. How do you want to test the waters?"

Summarizing helps you be a more effective counselor because you can't easily remember everything the client has said. You may also consider asking the client to do his own summarizing.

11. **Task setting.** *Asking the client to gather information or engage in experiences that are directly relevant to her job or career objectives.*

Tasks can include reality testing (information interviewing, brief work experiences), collecting data about career options, talking to family members, or anything that fits within the client's career action plan.

Task setting usually takes place toward the end of the session, after the client has talked about what she needs to begin moving toward her objectives. The best tasks usually are ones which can be done most immediately, because any time lag between counseling and action usually lowers the chances that the client will do it. Immediate tasks need to be readily available and doable.

12. **Establishing the Yes, Buts.** *Identifying the client's chief concerns, main obstacles or roadblocks she believes may stand in the way of her job or career goals.*

These are also called "Yes, Buts." This skill involves eliciting a certain amount of negative talk ("I don't know if I have the talent to do it"; "My wife would throw a fit"), but clients need to talk about their problems in a nonthreatening, nonjudgmental atmosphere.

Clients may do a full-court press on you for answers to their seemingly intractable Yes, Buts. Avoid quick-fix answers; they inevitably will be off the mark. This skill involves listening, drawing out the depths of the problem, synthesizing what you hear, and encouraging the client to develop her own ways of dealing with the problems.

Other Skills

Open invitation to talk. Often used early in the session. "Tell me about your situation as you see it" . . . "What happened then?" . . . "Tell me more about that." This is a key skill in developing trust, because it communicates to the client that you're genuinely interested.

Focusing. Directing the conversation toward topics the client has identified as high priority, to make the best use of the limited time available. "You said you wanted to identify jobs that you could get immediately. What kinds of skills do you have that you think might be marketable?"

Leading. Making a direct statement that asks the client to continue speaking about a given topic. "You were talking about your parents' expectations of you."

Encouraging. Providing emotional support for a course of action that the individual is considering, one which you believe to be positive --"I believe you're right that practice job interviews would be helpful."

CHAPTER 6

The Mystery
of Career Choice

by Howard Figler

The heart has its reasons, which reason cannot know.
                                            - - Blaise Pascal

The best careers are those that emerge from the depths of a person's being, revealing her strongest drives and aspirations. A career counselor's job is to let people sing their songs.

Career choice is a mystery, because human beings are mysteries. Why do people climb up the sides of buildings? Why does Renfru go off to raise goats in Wyoming when he just completed his electrical engineering degree?

No two people make their decisions the same way, and that is as it should be. Counselors often force career decisions into artificial structures ("consider these factors when you're making your decision"), but they should not. Instead, the essential uniqueness of a person's decision process must be acknowledged and encouraged.

Choosing a career is giving yourself permission to be who you are. This is easier said than done. There are always competing forces. Some people surrender to motives that are not their own. They may have "successful" careers, but eventually regret that they followed someone else's ideas, not their own. Others recognize their priorities and act on them with conviction.

Jack grew up in a poor family of Jewish immigrants amidst the industrial soot of Elizabeth, New Jersey. He had the talent and inclination to be a doctor, his parents' fondest dream, but so did his sister Rachel. This was a Great Depression family, when the son was supposed to have the serious career and the daughter support a man's ambitions, but Jack was insistent:

"The family can't afford to send even one of us to med school, much less two. It's too much debt. So, I'll make money and help Rachel be the doctor. I have my music. I can make enough money to get Rachel through. One doctor in the family is enough."

His being a musician did not warm the hearts of Jack's parents. This meant vaudeville -- low status, long nights, creepy atmospheres, and drinking -- a litany of his parents' worst fears.

It didn't look good on paper. One would think that Jack had made a poor career decision that he would rue forever. Instead, what he did was exactly right for him. He had given himself permission to follow his two most important values -- (1) to provide for a family member when they need it most, (2) to play music.

Jack performed in every band that would take him, handed the money to Rachel, and never looked back. He became one of the most renowned of "big band" musicians and won the Gold Drum Award given to the best drummer in the nation.

Why do people need to give themselves permission to be who they are? You'd think it would come naturally. For some it does. For others, "practical" considerations get in the way. People argue you should go to the professions or where the jobs are, or where you'll save money, or where there are good living conditions. Such practical considerations have merit, but they don't speak to the heart.

A career may provide food and shelter for your family but how does it feed your soul on a drippy, rainy night when you have a nightmare about your job . . . and you wake at 3 AM in a sweat and say thank you, thank you, there's still time to get out.

Getting and Giving are intertwined in every career choice. The more you have of one, the more you have of the other, but it all begins with Giving:

- If you're a business, give the customers what they want and need the most.
- If you're a dental hygienist, give the patients' teeth the best prophylaxis they've ever had.
- If you're a teacher, give your students all that's inside you.

A career counselor's job is to help clients release their internal drives, and then get out of the way.

A "career" must bore deep within to find energy that the client may have hidden from herself:

It doesn't interest me what you do for a living.
    I want to known what you ache for . . .
I want to know if you will risk looking like a fool
    for love, for your dream, for the adventure of being alive.
. . . I want to know what sustains you from the inside
    when all else falls away. . . .

-- Oriah Mountain Dreamer, May 1994

Clients should not pretend to fully understand why they want what they want. Much of it is unfathomable, and that is fine. "I just know that it feels right to me" is good enough.

Remember that many of the most dramatic career stories were lived by people -- Winston Churchill, Barbara Walters, Ted Turner, etc. -- who had not-very-promising beginnings. Yet they plowed ahead, because they gave permission to their inner selves to take them where they wanted to go.

My ego was so damaged by high school, which was big and judgmental, that I graduated in the bottom tenth of my class. . . American University was just about the only college that would take me . . . but there I found soulmates . . . my advice to aspiring writers is never be defensive . . .

And don't waste time trying to answer to people who don't understand the mystery that goes into writing. Most people don't.   -- Ann Beattie

Beattie's message is not only about writers. Everyone can be the "author" of her own career if she acts on her inner wisdom. By doing what you were meant to do, you're writing your own story.

Hockington, who was raised by wealthy parents, wanted to create a circus without animals. "Well, there goes the inheritance," he said, as his family looked on disapprovingly. In the first two weeks, he broke his back trying the flying trapeze, but Hocky got the business going and put together a team of performers for a successful circus road show.

You cannot predict the whole from the parts

Assessment traditionally precedes career choice. It has been assumed that if one knows the individual's parts (skills, interests, etc.), these can be "added up" to suggest career options. However, this approach to career choice is wrong. If you assume that any given skill or interest may suggest certain career areas, you undermine the individual's desire to define a career path that reflects her unique motivations and values.

A career choice emerges from hundreds of factors, many of which are unconscious and/or unmeasurable. Trying to capture the "truth" about any given person is like trying to catch raindrops in the dark. Assessment produces some data, but it misses what is most important about the person.

For example, you may have a client named Mary who has exceptional ability with numbers and also likes working with statistical data. Does this mean she should be a mathematician, accountant, or statistician? Many counselors would think they were doing "good counseling" if they steered her this way. However, other factors are at work in her choice process.

Even though Mary likes numbers, she has a stronger drive to do human service and does not especially want statistics in her career. She also wants to be in a learning environment with people contact, not confined to working with mathematical models in a room by herself.

People often get free advice about their career ideas whether they like it or not.

"Oh, you wouldn't want to be a sportswriter. They don't make a good living and they travel all the time."

A lot of this advice is evaluative or downright negative -- warning against the problems of a given career. Most input is biased by the experience of the observer. The career counselor's job is to provide a bias-free environment.

When a client proposes a career, she should expect some people to disagree with her, because no one knows her "reasons" as well as she does. Resistance from others is a sign that the client is doing her own thinking.

You don't look at a client's attributes -- skills, values, interests -- and attach them to careers that seem to "fit." You ask a client to generate her own career hypotheses, regardless of whether they line up with her attributes or not.

What if a client's career ideas are "not realistic"?

Not realistic? According to whom? No one knows what an individual is capable of doing until she tries it herself. Decisions about the suitability of careers are made in real life, not the counseling room. The client will learn only dependence and frustration if she's told: "That's not a good career idea for you." Counselors should recognize the difference between information giving and advice giving. Timely information can be helpful. Subtle manipulation is not. Even the most "unrealistic" looking career ideas can and must be reality-tested. Better to fail six times and learn from your experiences than be told not to do something and regret not having tried it:

> *For all sad words of tongue or pen, the saddest*
> *are these: 'it might have been'*
> -- John Greenleaf Whittier, "Maud Muller"

People often succeed when you would least expect them to. The counselor's job is to believe in them and encourage the pursuit of their goals. Thus, 'tis better to have tried and lost than to never have tried at all.

How does the counselor elicit career ideas from clients?

1. **Ask directly.** "What kinds of work do you think you'd most like to do?" People often know the career ideas they're thinking about and they need to talk about them. When you ask this question early in counseling, some clients will say "I don't know." If you persist gently in asking the question later on, after the client trusts you better, she may offer some ideas she had kept buried earlier.

2. **Mental imagery.** Various methods can be used to stimulate imagination. Guided visualizations are effective, because they are supported by relaxation techniques and they don't ask for any explanation. Working on paper can also be useful:

"Make a picture of yourself where you'd like to be in the world of work, and what that world would look like."

These methods encourage free-form imagination and de-emphasize the judgment that you are choosing the "best" career.

3. **Focus on the client's accomplishments.** Ask the client to describe things they've done which they felt good about. Help the client to identify key skills they were using and which of these skills they'd like to use again. This process is described in great detail in Richard Bolles's *1999 What Color Is Your Parachute?*

Following clients' statements

You will find many opportunities to ask clients to propose career ideas for themselves:

"What careers come to mind when you consider using some of your favorite skills?" "What kinds of careers might give you the freedom that you're talking about?" "What kinds of things would you like to build?" "What kinds of careers would have your kind of independence?"

This brings us to Career Choice Junction

The client has various ideas and asks herself: "What is my front-runner? What career will I look into first?"

Consult the client's intuition.

I'm saying that we should trust our intuition. I believe that the principles of human evolution are revealed to us through intuition.
                                                    -- Jonas Salk

"Reason" is a small circle of what you know about yourself that you can explain. "Intuition" is a much larger circle of all the things you know about yourself that you cannot identify or explain, but that are true nonetheless.

Experts on the mind have verified that unconscious intuition is responsible for a great proportion of human behavior:

Most of the information that passes through a person is not picked up by human consciousness, even when this information has a demonstrable effect on behavior. . . . we do not possess awareness of very much of what goes on inside us.
                          -- Tor Norretranders, *The User Illusion*, 1998
                                                    (page 161)

Can we trust the career ideas that clients dream up?

Why not trust them? Who are we to say that any particular idea is good, bad, or in-between? An idea has merit for the client because she has energy attached to it.

Some counselors will object to letting clients follow their intuition. They'll say such things as:

"They can't be wasting time making wild choices without any direction."

"Clients don't know anything about careers. They'll choose things for silly reasons and then regret them later."

Sounds parental, doesn't it? Counselors are on very shaky ground when they hint that a certain career might be the right one. A counselor is not a prediction machine. It's important to avoid that role, because many clients think that's exactly what a counselor should do -- "tell me what I oughta be." The wise counselors and parents recognize that no one can tell an individual what they oughta do.

Imagine if you had been parents of the Marx Brothers. They probably thought a professional life for their sons would have been nice. But they backed off and let the boys be themselves. Would anyone have wanted to stop Groucho, Chico, Harpo, Gummo, and Zippo from doing what came naturally?

If there is a formula for career choice, I don't want to know it. I like mysteries. The forces which enable a bridge to stand are numerous enough, but they are grossly simple compared to the complex unconscious forces that drive a human being. Let the client stay in charge of this mystery. Our job is to keep her career imagination cooking. Don't mess with the process inside. It's bigger than both of us.

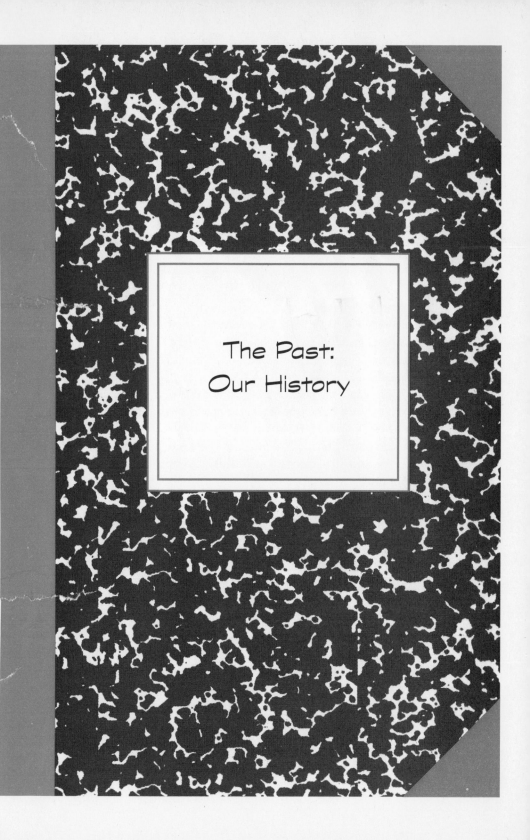

The Past:
Our History

CHAPTER 7

A History of Ideas
and Events in the Job-Hunting Field
During the Twentieth Century

by Dick Bolles

Most fields have a history of ideas, which history is well known in that field, with names. Gravity, Sir Isaac Newton; pasteurization, Pasteur; the airplane, the Wright Brothers; psychoanalysis, Sigmund Freud; the telephone, Alexander Graham Bell; etc.

But alas! This field of job-hunting has no written history. If you asked a bunch of career counselors where their favorite idea came from, or to whom we are indebted for that idea, you would draw a blank. No one knows; no one remembers. It just seems as if the major ideas in this field have . . . *always* been around.

We need a better sense of our own history than that. Hence I have here set forth an outline of some, though not all, of the major job-hunting ideas in the twentieth century, and how and when they came to be, as best we can tell. For this history, I supplemented my own *voluminous* files (and memory) by interviewing many of my old friends: Sidney Fine, Harold Sheppard, Harvey Belitsky, Arthur Miller, John Holland, Bernard Haldane, Tom Jackson, Bill Batt, H.B. Gelatt, Sandra Hirsh, Dick Lathrop, Howard Figler, Dick Knowdell, Walt Hopkins and the late Bart Lloyd. I am very indebted to every one of them for their help, though I alone am responsible, of course, for any misstatements of their ideas, or other glitches which may appear.

R.N.B

1909

Idea first published in 1909: **We must learn to match people to jobs**: the trait and factor approach.

We take for granted today the idea that jobs and workers should match each other. We forget there was a time when it wasn't obvious. Frank Parsons was the man who set forth this idea, in his seminal work, Choosing a Vocation, *Houghton Mifflin.*

1918

Idea first discovered in 1918: **a career was defined as "the expression of one's own personality,** *working through some medium.***"** For an artist, the mediums are paint, drama, etc., etc. For nonartists, the mediums are four:

1. Ideas
2. People
3. Things or
4. $ symbols (= economic symbols).

John Mills, of Western Electric, came up with this idea. In interviews, he would have these four categories on separate cards and ask the job-applicant to arrange the cards in order of decreasing interest to them personally. Written up in 1921, in time this idea got lost, as so many job-hunting ideas have; and had to be rediscovered some time after World War II. This idea of John Mills's is of interest, because it was apparently the first time that anyone came up with an idea akin to that of Data, People, and Things -- now the cornerstone in our understanding of transferable skills (see **1942** *&* **1950***).*

1929

Idea first developed in 1929: **Groups wherein job-hunters could meet**, be taught job-hunting techniques, and share their stories and problems with other job-hunters as well as with a trained counselor.

"The Depression has caught us unprepared," wrote one writer of that time. However, a number of private attempts were soon made to help job-hunters, both individually and in groups. 'The group idea' eventually prevailed.

The longest-running group was founded in 1933, and was called the Thursday Night Club. Its founder was a man named Carl Boll. It was dedicated to helping graduates of the Harvard Business School find work. The Thursday Night Club met for at least forty years, under his tutelage.

The largest group was founded in October of 1935, and was called the 'Man Marketing Clinic.' Its services were free, and in spite of its name it was open to women as well as to men. Its founder was a man named Sidney Edlund. In the first twenty years of its operation it was used by over 500,000 persons. Sidney wrote up his approach in a book that was first published in **1938** *-- which see.*

Other job-hunting groups which subsequently formed were often called 'Job Forums' and were run by university alumni groups, Chambers of Commerce, service organizations, sales executives clubs and advertising clubs. The Man Marketing Clinic, for example, was eventually taken over by the Sales Executives Club of New York. This group idea is still alive to this day -- see **1973**, *Job Clubs are born.*

1933

Idea first developed in 1933: **You have to sell yourself to an employer, convincing him of your uniqueness: that you are 'one man in a hundred.'**

This idea, now commonplace in the job-hunting field, was a very new idea at this time, spoken in the language of that time (today, of course, we would say "you are 'one person in a hundred.'") This was Carl Boll's brainchild (sounds like *Bolles's* -- but isn't), *for his Thursday Night group described above. Carl did not write up his ideas for nationwide publication until* **1965** *-- which see.*

1936

The event in 1936: **The publication of the first true job-hunting book in America.** It was entitled, *Your Work Abilities: How to Express and Apply Them Through Man Power Specifications,* by A. W. Rahn. Harper and Brothers Publishers 1936.

While many career counselors today think that the 'creative job-hunting process' was invented by either Dick Bolles **(1970)**, or John Crystal **(1968)**, or Bernard Haldane **(1947)**, in fact most of the elements of that approach were discovered years earlier by A.W. Rahn.

In this book back in 1936 we find most of the elements of what we know today as 'the creative approach to job-hunting.' Ideas first published in this book:

1. **The idea of the self-directed job-search;**
2. **the raising of WHAT, WHERE and HOW questions that the job-hunter must answer -- What can you do? Where can you do it? Who needs this? Why have you come to me?;**
3. **the writing of a work biography;**
4. **the analyzing of that biography for functional skills;**
5. **the avoiding of a resume** 'that sums up only your past';
6. **the avoiding of job-titles** ("talk only of tasks you can perform");
7. **the writing of a one-page paper summarizing what you can do in the present** (Rahn called it "Your Man Power Specifications Sheet" -- the title at the top of the sheet was *Functions I Can Perform*) -- essentially your five best functions, with a lengthy paragraph describing each ("Five will describe satisfactorily what a man can do.");
8. **the showing of that paper to everyone, asking for their advice** ("Will you take three minutes to read these specifications of what I can do, in case my services might be helpful to you or your associates, either now or later?");
9. **the choosing of places where you would like to work rather than places known to have a vacancy;**
10. **the researching of those places ahead of time through directories;**
11. **the strong use of contacts;**
12. **the going face to face with employers;**
13. **the presentation of yourself to employers as a resource rather than as one begging for a job;**
14. **the showing to each employer a one-page summary of what you can do for him or her;**
15. **the use of functional skill language as a kind of 'lingua franca' between job-hunter and employer;** and
16. **a reported success rate of over 80%.**
    It's all here.

*Alphonso William Rahn was, like Mills (**1918**), an engineer who worked for Western Electric. He was very concerned with helping men who were out of work. He developed the approach I have just outlined (which he called* The Rahn Plan*), in order to help unemployed job-hunters, for whom he felt great compassion.*

But while his book was detailed beyond belief, and enjoyed a second printing within two years of the first, it does not seem to have been widely known even ten years later.

In a sense those who came after Rahn had to reinvent and rediscover all over again the things that he knew well, as manifested in his book.

In the first two-thirds of this century, the records of the previous generation tended to get lost (as above), or be little noticed (see 1938). In the last third of this century that changed: one book (*What Color Is Your Parachute?*) has remained popular and available for thirty years, thus keeping alive the same ideas. Until it was born (1970) however, each new age had to rediscover for themselves how to do the job-hunt well. Always they eventually came up with the same ideas as previous generations had -- this, because **a successful job-hunt is based on understanding human nature, and human nature alters not.**

Job-hunting ideas work across cultural lines. *What Color Is Your Parachute?*, for example, exists in many languages -- again because these ideas are based on human nature, and human nature alters little, from one culture to another.

1937

Idea first published in 1937: **You can find a job even in the most difficult of times, and regardless of what handicap you think you have, if you can show the employer how you will benefit them.**

It was two women who set out to prove this idea. They toured the country and were offered hundreds of jobs. The fact that they were female, and both over forty, was never an obstacle. They simply tried to show each employer how their assets and skills could help that employer get

more customers, more profits. They reported, "With that approach, no
one asked about age."

Their names were Clara Belle Thompson and Margaret Lukes Wise.
They wrote up their experience in the second job-hunting book to appear
in that decade: We Are Forty And We Did Get Jobs, *(J.B. Lippincott Co.,*
publisher, 1937). The book was summarized in the May 1938 issue of the
popular magazine of that day, the Saturday Evening Post.

Since the history of ideas in this field tended to be dominated by men, it
is worth emphasizing that both authors here were women -- and that in
the following item one of the two authors was also a woman.

1938

The event in 1938: **The publication of the oldest job-**
hunting book still in existence in the '90s. It is entitled, *Pick*
Your Job — And Land It! by Sidney and Mary Edlund, originally
published by Prentice Hall (1938), and thereafter by Sandollar
Press (Seventh Printing, 1973). Like Rahn's book (see **1936**), it
had all the ideas now regarded as "modern job search" down
cold, shortly after the Great Depression and before the Second World War. Ideas which first appeared in their book, or
were 'twists' on previous ideas:

1. The idea of having a goal of a particular field and job
before starting your job-hunt;

2. the inventorying of your assets only after you have in-
terviewed people in each field that interests you, to ask
what assets or personal qualities are required for success
in that field;

3. then looking to see if you have those assets or qualities
-- and proving it with personal stories;

4. the keeping of 'career work sheets,' to record your find-
ings for each field that interests you;

5. the idea that men and women are blind to their own ac-
complishments, that each of us has deeply hidden assets,
skills, talents, or aptitudes;

6. the discovering of your hidden assets by systematically
examining how you worked;

7. the searching for what unusual methods you used, when you worked;

8. the choosing which employers to approach, and of researching employers thoroughly, once you have made a list of your best prospects. "Research each name on [your list] very carefully. Squeeze out every fact you can find on the firm and its products."

(The Edlunds were the first to suggest such thorough detailed research.)

9. the use of the job interview to "analyze your prospect's problems and show them how you can help solve them"; *This, of course, was akin to the idea we saw under 1937, above: offering a benefit or a service to the employer.*

10. backing up every statement of what you have to offer, with stories that display your talents in action;

11. demonstrating a keen interest in that firm, and their products, during the interview;

12. closing strongly in the interview; "Be specific about your offer. Be specific about what you want. Be specific about what you have."

13. showing them by the close of the interview what makes you different from the other applicants;

This idea of course was first laid out in 1933, as we saw; here, however, it was much more strongly developed. They said you can find this out by having previously asked yourself such questions as:

- *In what ways have you handled your job better than it was handled before?*
- *How have you saved money for your employer?*
- *How have you helped your employer do more business?*
- *Were you ever given a special problem to solve? How did you meet it?*
- *Did you originate any new systems?*
- *Have you ever won favorable comment from your chief or fellow workers? For what?*

14. once in the job, keeping a record of your accomplishments, so you can later show your boss you merit the promotion or salary increase you're requesting; "Keep copies of the things you write, of the reports you make, of the sales you register, of the amount of money you save for your firm. Each birthday, set all your achievements of the past year on paper. Marshal all the evidence you can, so you can show your boss you merit the promotion or salary increase you're 'angling for.' "

*Sidney W. Edlund was the president of Pine Bros. cough drop company, and then of Life Savers, Inc. As mentioned under **1929**, he was also the developer of the hugely successful Man Marketing Clinics. His wife Mary Edlund was a department head for Chase National Bank in N.Y., and an industrial relations consultant. In this 1938 book, Sidney and his wife described his 'Man Marketing' methods to the general public.*

Though the book has not been widely circulated, it has had a long history. The seventh edition of it was printed in 1973, and it was still in print in 1996 -- fifty-eight years after its first publication -- making it the hands-down winner of the longevity award for job-hunting books in this century. It set forth the new ideas outlined above, that feature some nice 'twists' on previously-published ideas, plus some old themes -- "Only you can make a wise career choice for yourself," you must create a written sales presentation for yourself (they called it 'a portfolio') and the by-then-familiar dislike of the 'chronological resume'.

1939

The event in 1939: **The first edition of the *D.O.T.* -- the *Dictionary of Occupational Titles* -- was published, describing 17,500 jobs in the U.S., giving job-hunters, career-changers and counselors at last a menu of options to choose from.**

It was published by the Department of Labor's Bureau of Labor Statistics, and is found in almost every public library in the U.S. The second edition of the D.O.T. appeared in 1949, the third edition in 1965, and the current one appeared in 1977, with its core 1977 material supplemented in 1982, 1986, 1987, and 1991. (This last is called the Fourth Edition, Revised), There are now 12,741 jobs described in the D.O.T., with about 8,000 *additional, duplicate titles. Unhappily, 80% of the job descriptions in the 1991 book have not in fact been updated since 1977 (revealed by the Definition Trailer at the end of each listing, wherein "DLU 77" -- Date [of] Last Update 1977 -- is common). A lot of changes have occurred in the job-market since 1977. The U.S. Department of Labor as of 1998 is updating and in fact replacing the D.O.T. with O*NET: a classification system that describes just 1,222 occupations -- as 95% of all U.S. workers are to be found in those 1,222. Of course, most career-changers have no interest in those 1,222. They want the jobs found by "the uncommon herd" -- i.e., the other 11,519.*

1942

Idea first developed in 1942: **The transferability of skills**, defined by Sidney Fine as "the continuous use of acquired knowledge and abilities when moving from one job to another." Transferability is made possible by the fact that **"the methods, procedures and plans of attack** remain much the same in circumstances and for problems which at first sight appear very different from one another." *(Frederic Bartlett)*

Up until this time, the job-hunting field had pretty much operated without any checklists or standard nomenclature. Earlier job-hunting books left this pretty much up to the intuition of the individual involved. It was more of an art than a science.

But at last, a checklist was developed. During the Second World War, The United States Employment Service (USES) had a Job Family Program, which was handed the same problem as confronted the nation during the First World War, namely, finding equivalent military jobs for those coming into the Armed Services from civilian life, and then, after the war, equivalent civilian jobs for those leaving military life. The issue was the transferability of experience and abilities, wherein someone who could do one job was able to transfer to another field or career, without additional training or schooling. They looked for "factors."

The factors were called 'worker traits' and there were 48 of them. Under the direction of a man named Sidney Fine, jobs were analyzed and evaluated for their transferability according to these 48 estimated worker traits. 'Job families' were thus identified (hence the name of the Project), and these findings were published in the Job Family Series, Nos. 1–89, covering 77 occupations in all (1942–1944).

*The U.S. research on transferability, encompassing not only the Job Family Program but also the work done later for the D.O.T. (see **1950**) was ultimately written up by Sidney Fine, and published in* The Monthly Labor Review, *July issue, and August issue, 1957, under the title: "A Re-examination of Transferability of Skills, Parts I and II."*

1946

The event in 1946: **Executive job-counseling firms as we know them today, were born**.

Bernard Haldane became Associate Editor for the Journal of Commerce *with an office in N.Y.C. beginning in August of 1941. But in 1946, he also founded* the Executive Job Counseling Service *of the New York Chapter of the Society for the Advancement of Management, created in order to help returning veterans.*

In 1947, Bernard founded his own private firm -- thereby launching a whole new genre that was to become known over time as 'executive counseling firms', because (of course) they concentrated on offering "counselling services to middle-management personnel and professional men concerned with changing their positions or careers." Bernard's agency went under three titles -- 'Executive Job Counselors, Inc.', 'BHA,' and 'Bernard Haldane Associates.' BHA remains the oldest nationwide executive job-counseling firm still in existence to this day and it still bears Bernard's name, although he actually sold his interest in it around 1973.

*Since 1947, many other executive counseling firms have, of course, sprung up -- and the whole industry has become not only very wide-spread, but also very controversial (see **1965**) -- helping many, but also leaving many job-hunters high and dry.*

Bernard is the oldest figure still alive and active in the job-hunting field today (1999), is a creative thinker much venerated, as he has had a tremendous impact on this job-hunting field for over fifty years now, not only by his own lucid writings and teachings, but also through his disciples, former employees or associates -- including Saul Gruner, Eli Djeddah, Richard Germann, John Crystal, Richard K. Irish, Tom Hubbard and Tom Washington.

1947

Ideas first published in 1947–48, by Bernard Haldane:

1. **The irrepressibility of talents:** "The energies or talents that dominate your personality, that make you what you are, must have positive expression. If you fail to use them they will force themselves out in some form of erratic behavior, nervousness or neurosis."

2. **The importance of achievements:** "Don't try to learn from your mistakes; try to learn from your successes. Focus on your strengths, not your weaknesses, your accomplishments or achievements, not your mistakes or failures."

3. **The definition of 'Achievement,'** has dominated the job-hunting field ever since: "Something you feel you have done well, enjoyed doing, and are proud of. The way you felt about it, deep inside you, is what counts." *Today, he calls this a* **Good Experience.** *He coined the latter phrase in the '80s, when he found the concept of "achievements" was not well-accepted in other cultures (he was working with Vietnamese at the time).*

4. **The identification of talents through stories:**
Bernard advised you to choose two or three Achievements from each period of your life -- it could be every three years, or 'every few years'; try to list twenty, then arrange the ten most important to you in decreasing priority, proceeding to write about each of the ten in order.

5. **The use of a check-list of skills and interests:**
Bernard then gave people a chart to use in analyzing their ten achievements, a chart which had a check-list. This check-list had 52 items on it. Bernard called the 52 items 'success factors' which he defined as "factors that appear most frequently in people concerned with professional and management activities."

6. **The phrase, 'The Qualifications Outline':**
This concept is akin to Rahn's earlier idea of the Manpower Specifications Outline, was first coined by Bernard; cf. Richard Lathrop's later phrase, "The Qualifications Brief." (see **1959***)*

7. **The idea of staying away from the personnel department**: Instead, 'find out the names of men who would be heads of the departments in which you would like to work.'

8. **The idea of using contacts to get an interview:** Send an 'Appointment-getting Letter,' together with a commendation of you (get an executive friend to write and sign the latter, on his company letterhead).

9. **The idea of interviews as focused on 'Remembrance and Referral':**
Bernard invented the concept of 'Remembrance and Referral interviews'. With regard to "Remembrance," he advised people to use memory-fixing techniques so that the employer would remember you. As for "Referral," he advised: "Always ask for introductions to other executives who might hire you."

10. **The idea of writing a thank-you note, after an interview**, was for this very reason: "Always send a courtesy note afterward, a 'thanks-for-the-time-given me' letter, because it serves to keep you in the minds of those you met."

11. **The idea of bringing the spiritual into the job-hunt:** Bernard was early on with the idea of combining the spiritual with your job-hunt:"A little praying before you get to work on a job like this cannot do harm, and might secure for you the most beneficial kind of cooperation."

Bernard set forth most of these ideas in two ground-breaking articles, one in the Harvard Business Review, *Autumn 1947, and the other, a 1948 job-hunting booklet, entitled,* How To Get An Executive Job.

In these articles, the ideas which were new to this field are listed above. But there were also some themes we have seen in earlier writings, to wit:

*1. The idea that the two major rules of effective career-hunting are, **first**, know what you want; and second, know what your prospective employer wants.*

2. The idea that finding employment is a business, and should be handled like a business, with a job campaign carefully planned.

*3. He laid out the familiar questions (to the historian, by now): **What job would you really desire if you had a free choice? What functions must*** *you perform, and what qualities of personality must you express, in order to do that job well? What have you done, at any time, that proves you can perform each of those functions, and possess those personality traits?*

4. The importance of self-examination.

5. The idea that if you have done it before, that is proof you can do it again.

6. The way in which we take our best qualities for granted and are blind to our own abilities.

7. The idea (akin to Rahn's) that one should show a piece of paper summarizing your skills, to everyone including employers, though Bernard's accompanying words were somewhat different from Rahn's: "I don't expect you to have a job or to know of one, but will you look at this report on my skills and tell me if you think it will help me get a job?"

8. The importance of offering a profit-making service to an employer.

9. In the interview, high interest is the most important factor.

10. Create a written sales presentation for yourself.

Like those of creative souls in this field, Bernard's ideas have continually evolved as he has worked with more and more job-hunters of various backgrounds and cultures. This is evidenced by the ways in which his nomenclature has changed over the years, for example, Bernard has given various names in print to his program: Achievement Analysis (1948), Success Factor Analysis (1960), System for Identifying Motivated Abilities (1964), System for Identifying Motivated Skills (1974), and Dependable Strengths Articulation Process (1984).

Bernard's chart (mentioned above) has also gone by many published names between 1947 and 1994: A Factor Chart (1947), A Success Factors Chart (1960), A Motivated Skills Chart (1974), and a Dependable Strengths Exploration Chart (1984). Currently, he defines a Dependable Strength as a skill, talent or strength that occurs at least three times in one's seven top Good Experiences.

It is worth noticing that in the beginning, in 1947, this chart was not, strictly speaking, a transferable skills list as we know it today. Rather, it was (and is) an amalgam of skills/talents and products worked with, plus various kinds of data (budgets, controls, figures, ideas, programs, systems/procedures, words).

Over time, Bernard did move more toward a skills list; by 1960 he was in print with a list of 12 additional 'classifications' in addition to the 'success factors chart'; by 1968 he had replaced the 12 with 16 and now called them 'work areas'. These 16 were much more akin to what we know today as a list of functional/transferable skills, and indeed by 1974 Bernard was calling the 16 'skills or functions' clusters, and -- more recently -- 'Job Activity Clusters.' But the significance of the chart, when it was first invented, is that this was the first time anyone had published a list of any kind, that you could use to help analyze your achievements.

1950

Idea first published in 1950: **In all the jobs in the world there are only a limited number of** *functions* **('skills') being used -- 26 to be exact**[1] **-- and they could be divided into three groups: according to whether or not they were used primarily with Things, Data, or People.**[2] (This was akin, of course, to John Mills's idea of "mediums," which we saw under **1918.**)

Here, it was Sidney Fine who came up with this idea, but he described them not as "mediums" but as "orientations." He proposed that **people had primary orientations to one or another of these three; consequently, if they found themselves in jobs with primary orientations different from their inclinations, they would be in trouble.**

He further came up with the idea that **within each of these three groups, the skills could be arranged in hierarchies -- with the simpler skills at the bottom, and the more complex skills at the top;** later, in 1960, he would add the idea that **the simpler skills were highly prescribed, with little discretion left to the worker, while the more**

---

1. The number was later increased by Sidney Fine to 32.

2. Incidentally, until decades later the American researchers had no knowledge that the British had independently come up with the same concept.

complex skills were very little prescribed, with lots of discretion left to the worker.

Sidney's hierarchies of Things, Data, and People became the basis for both the Canadian and the U.S. Occupational Classification Systems, appearing in the 1965 edition of the *D.O.T.*, and continuing through the 1991 edition also (pp. 1005–1007, and throughout). The first time this concept of Things, Data, and People appeared in a general job-hunting book was in *What Color Is Your Parachute? --* beginning with its first Ten Speed Press edition, in 1972.

To update ourselves on Sidney's history, here (see 1942) Sidney continued the work he had begun with 'Job Families' in 1942, and then from 1950 to 1959 was the head of the Functional Occupational Classification Project. The Project's mission: to study 4,000 jobs, in order to learn their 'Worker Characteristics,' with a view to revising Part IV (related to counselors) of the D.O.T.

*In 1952 Sidney invented the phrase **"Functional Job Analysis,"** to describe the application of the above ideas to particular jobs. He further elaborated on this technique in 1967, 1969, 1971. He wrote up his findings, and their application, in* Functional Job Analysis Scales, A Desk Aid, *1973, revised 1989, and in* Functional Job Analysis: A Foundation for Human Resource Management, *1999. The latter is published by Lawrence Erlbaum, Mahwah, NJ. The earlier works are available from Sidney A. Fine Associates, 1229 North Jackson, Milwaukee, WI 53202.*

1953

Ideas first published in 1953: **Vocational choice is not an event but a process; one's choice of vocation is a way of implementing a self-concept; vocational maturity, or career maturity, can be defined -- in terms of five life stages: growth, exploration, establishment, maintenance, and decline; career crises are developmental stages, ill-handled. Career transitions are developmental stages, well-handled.**

Donald E. Super invented these concepts -- one of the great pioneering names in the field of the psychology of careers. He held many important posts in his lifetime, including that of Director of the Longitudinal Career Pattern Study, as well as International Coordinator of the Work Impor-

tance Study, and consultant to the Italian National Council on the Economy and Work. It was in a 1953 article in the American Psychology journal, entitled, "A theory of vocational development" that the above ideas first appeared. His subsequent books, further explaining these ideas, were: The Psychology of Careers *(Harper & Row) 1957; and (with R. Stahishersky, N. Mattin and J. P. Jordaan),* Career Development: Self-Concept Theory. *(College Entrance Examination Board) 1963.*

1959

Ideas first published in 1959: **Use 'a qualifications brief' instead of a resume. Employers are at least as anxious as job-seekers are about the interview, and job-seekers can help lead the interview.**

These appeared in Who's Hiring Who . . . the journal of jobs *which began publication this year, with a jobs directory of listings from 10,000 employers. WHW was published by Richard Lathrop on behalf of his employer, the Army Times Publishing Company. It appeared twice a year, and represented a major attempt to help ex-military find jobs in civilian life. Now 40 years old, the book is still published today, currently by Ten Speed Press.*

'A qualifications brief,' incidentally, is a substitute for the resume -- rooted in the present rather than the past. In concept, it is akin to Rahn's idea of a Manpower Specifications Sheet.

Idea first discovered in 1959: **'RIASEC.'**

John L. Holland, an Army classification interviewer during the Second World War, noticed that during interviews his pen was checking off answers ahead of the interviewee, and when he wondered why, he was led to the concept of 'types.' Said John later: "I'm a psychologist who pays attention to the obvious." Subsequent interviewing, for the Student Counseling Center at the University of Minnesota 1946–1950, confirmed this discovery, and resulted in his identification of six types, of people environments/skills/values which today are called 'Realistic,' 'Investigative,' 'Artistic,' 'Social,' 'Enterprising,' and 'Conventional' -- hence, 'RIASEC.' The six types went through five different sets of labels before arriving at their present definitions. Articles by John began appearing in 1959, beginning with the 1959 Journal of Counseling Psychology. *The book propounding his theory of types first appeared in* **1966**. *His SDS -- Self-Directed Search -- instrument first appeared in* **1971**.

Event first occurring in 1959: **Criticism of vocational and psychological testing as a guide to a person's future job-choice began.**

Robert Thorndike and Elizabeth Hagen began the critique, in their 1959 book, 10,000 Jobs, *reporting on a study of several thousand men given batteries of tests by the armed forces and then followed up over a ten-year period. "The conclusion reported is that the predictions made with the aid of these accredited psychological tests were no more dependable than tea leaf readings."wrote Bernard Haldane later.*

Teachers College at Columbia University was next, with their publication, in 1962, of a book called Epitaph for Vocational Guidance. *It reported that the great majority of tests had a built-in 40% margin of error, and concluded that intelligence and aptitude tests were "little better than guess work"as guides to a man's future performance.*

In 1966, John Holland added his voice: "Despite several decades of research, the most efficient way to predict vocational choice is simply to ask the person what he wants to be; our best devices do not exceed the predictive value of that method." The Psychology of Vocational Choice, *1966, Ginn and Company, Waltham, MA.*

Over the years since 1966, tests have continued to be subjected to a barrage of criticism, from such leaders in the field as Bernard Haldane, John Crystal, John Holland, Dick Bolles and Howard Figler, among many others. Howard is currently the strong warning voice, cf. his "Testing and Psychological Witch Doctorism," published in the Career Planning and Adult Development Network Newsletter, *November, 1992. His key idea: self-assessment is far more powerful and empowering than the parent-child relationship set up by testing; in addition to which, vocational tests have very little predictive power.*

None of this criticism, even from respected leaders in the field, has made even a dent in the popularity of testing. To this day a large proportion of those in the career counseling field depend heavily on testing, in their work with clients.

1960

Ideas appearing for the first time in 1960: **The importance of knowing the success rates of various job-hunting methods:** less than 5% of jobs paying more than a living wage are filled through employment agencies; 15% are filled through responses to 'help-wanted' ads or through letters of application. More than 80% are filled through the recommendation of friends already employed by the concern, or through 'contacts' or 'tips.' (This laid the foundation for the famous concept of **'the hidden job market.'**)

These ideas appeared in Bernard Haldane's book, *How to Make A Habit of Success,* first published in 1960. Other ideas which first saw the light of day in 1960 (all taken from his book):

The idea that it is the combination of several factors that is the key to understanding a person's gifts: "a strength is usually the presence of many strong factors."

The idea of a pattern of success: *Originally he defined a success pattern as consisting of those factors with* four or more *checks out of your* ten *achievements. By 1984 Bernard was calling an achievement a* Dependable Strength, *and defining a success pattern as a factor with* three or more *checks out of your top* seven *achievements or good experiences.*

The idea of pursuing small companies. "Don't disregard small companies. More people find success in small companies than in large."

The idea of talking for only two minutes at a time, before asking the employer (or contact) what else he wants to hear about.

How to Make a Habit of Success *was published originally by Prentice-Hall (July, 1960), then by Unity Press, then by Warner Books (revised, 1975). An excerpt from it appeared in the July 1961 issue of the* Reader's Digest. *It incorporated Bernard's instrument for analyzing achievements called "Success Factor Analysis," which had appeared in his booklet, 'The Best That's In You,' January 1958. Since 1960, and up to the present day (1998) Bernard has published many books, the best-known of which is* Career Satisfaction and Success *(Amacom, 1974).*

1961–1969

The event between 1961 and 1969: **Job-hunting books began to become more common.** Twelve other job-hunting books (but only 12) appeared during the rest of the sixties.

Their authors were Charles Miner (1963), Carl Boll (1965), Ess Wein (1966), Malcolm Kent (1967), J.I. Biegeleisen (1967), Maxwell Harper & Arthur Pell (1967), Auren Uris (two books: 1967, 1968), Robert Snelling (1969), Performance Dynamics/Robert J.Gerberg (1969), E.A. Butler (1970), and Lou Albee (1970). **These books were largely preoccupied with resumes, interviews, and salary negotiation.** *The books which hung around the longest were/are Gerberg's, Snelling's, and Boll's (see* **1965***).*

1961

Idea first appearing in 1961: **Certain individuals are characterized by 'achievement motivation,' defined as "an individual's willingness and tendency to persist and to excel in situations involving success or failure."**

The degree to which a person has 'achievement motivation' may be 'measured' by asking the subject to make up his own story about some pictures of men and women, with the counselor watching to see how often such words as *striving, achieving, succeeding, etc.* **appear in that person's story (or stories).**

This idea was set forth in David McClelland's Achieving Society *(Van Nostrand), 1961. Sheppard and Belitsky made extensive use of it in measuring job-hunting behaviors,* **1966.**

Idea first appearing in 1961: **The term 'motivated abilities'** appears, thanks to a man named Bill McConnell. The idea was fleshed out by Arthur Miller: motivated abilities were described as "the phenomenon that everytime a person does something which he enjoys and believes he does well, he repeats some or all of the same behavioral elements. When these elements are tracked through a number of a person's enjoyable achievement experiences, an entire motivational pattern of some twenty elements emerges." Other ideas based on this concept:

The use of an autobiography to identify one's motivational pattern, by adding up recurring words, phrases and themes of identical or closely similar dictionary meaning. After the autobiography is written, eight achievements are selected for detailed description, and then **a Motivated Abilities Pattern is identified by analyzing and listing the recurring words. That pattern is characterized by a central Motivation Thrust, outcome or payoff, which is fixed, irresistible, controlling, and insatiable.**

Bill McConnell, a Presbyterian minister on Arthur Miller's staff, first coined the term "Motivated abilities" during a project with NASA in 1960. His boss, Arthur Miller, was former Personnel Director for Argonne Laboratories, and founder of People Management Incorporated -- which exists to this day. In 1958, Arthur met Bernard Haldane and was impressed with his concept of 'success patterns.' Using this concept, plus his own work, not to mention Bill McConnell's concept, Arthur produced by 1963 the 'System for Identifying Motivated Abilities' (SIMA), a program wherein time is spent interviewing each job-hunter after they have written a biography; and then summarizing his or her 'pattern.' Arthur was in print by 1963 with the definition of Motivated Abilities quoted above, and by the next year he had developed a checklist of typical motivated abilities. SIMA was registered with the U.S. Patent Office by Arthur as both his trademark and service mark. Bernard Haldane quickly adopted this idea of 'motivated' abilities (1964) or skills (1974), but gave his system a slightly different name: SIMS -- 'System for Identifying Motivated Skills.'

1965

Idea first published in 1965: **'The broadcast letter'** as a very special kind of cover letter to send with one's resume.

The idea of sending a cover letter with one's resume -- if one uses a resume -- is so commonplace these days, that we forget there was a time when it wasn't obvious. Carl Boll either invented the idea or, at the very least, carried it to its highest art, in a technique he taught for decades (see **1929***). But he finally put it in print in 1965, with the publication of his classic book,* Executive Jobs Unlimited *(MacMillan), subsequently revised and updated in 1979.*

Event occurring in 1965: **The Christian Church begins to deal with vocational crises among its clergy.**

1965 was the year that various denominations began to open a series of career counseling centers, to help its clergy who were having vocational

*difficulties. The Presbyterian Church and the American Baptist Conven-
tion took the lead in establishing places, though their centers swiftly became interdenominational. The first of these was the Presbyterians'
Northeast Career Center in Princeton, N.J., and others followed. Typically,
these church centers would do a battery of tests, plus interpretation, over a
three-day period; they used such tests as the Strong-Campbell, the Myers-
Briggs Type Indicator, and Will Schutz's "Firo-B." The primary intent of
these centers was to help the clergy remain within the church.*

*But despite this intent, men and women began to leave the church or
the cloister in increasing numbers. The problem eventually came to national attention (the* New York Times *March 8, 1969, and* Time *Magazine, Feb. 23, 1970). Subsequently, informal private groups, often for
profit, arose, such as "Bearings for Re-establishment, Inc," which worked
primarily with disaffected clergy and nuns in the Roman Catholic
Church, and "Next Step" and "Mainstream International," which worked
primarily with disaffected clergy within the Protestant Churches.*

*No other profession has ever had so many career resources designed
explicitly for that one profession.*

Event occurring in 1965: Executive counseling firms begin to come under fire.

*The genre of 'executive counseling firms' began with very well-intentioned
men aiming to offer a genuine service. But the field in time attracted
others, who saw a chance to make a fast buck off people who were in trouble and therefore vulnerable. The primary criticisms of the genre, from the
beginning, revolved around firms which promised too much verbally (but
never in writing), and charged a large fee up front for promises never ful-
filled. Disgruntled clients had huge difficulties in getting any refund of the
large up-front fee. The exposure of such practices began with an article by
the late Sylvia Porter in May 2, 1965, and continued with articles in the
October 11, 1968 and December 10, 1968 editions of the* Wall Street
Journal, *and* This Week Magazine *(Dec.1968)*

*The criticism has continued, unabated, down to the present time, with
further articles appearing in -- to name but a few --* Business Week
(1/4/69), Iron Age Magazine *(1/15/70),* Retired Officer Magazine *(Sept.
1970), the* San Francisco Chronicle *(10/3/70),* Washingtonian Magazine *(Nov. 1970),* Money Magazine *(Nov. 1973), the* Wall Street Journal *(1/27/81, 1/29/81),* Savvy Magazine *(1981), the* New York Law

Journal *(2/26/82), the* New York Times *(9/30/82), the* Arizona Republic *(10/8/89), etc. The most complete and most recent critique is a series of articles in the National Business Employment Weekly, available still from their Reprint Service, P.O. Box 300, Princeton NJ 08543-0300, "A Consumer Guide to Retail Job-Hunting Services," $8.*

1966

The event in 1966: **John Holland publishes his *The Psychology of Vocational Choice: A Theory of Personality Types and Model Environments.***

This was a landmark book, setting forth for the first time John's RIASEC theory and typology (see **1959**), *in a form available to the public. The book eventually went out of print, and was succeeded in 1973 by a more detailed description of his theory, in a book called* Making Vocational Choices: a theory of careers *(Prentice Hall).*

Alongside the books, John invented some instruments. His original instrument, the Vocational Preference Inventory, *was conceived in 1953 and published in 1958. Starting in 1971, he came out with his far more-popular instrument, the Self-Directed Search, based on the book. The SDS has, as of January 1, 1999, been used by more than 24,000,000 people.*

Event occurring in 1966: **Someone decided to study the job-hunt scientifically.** Using an **"Effectiveness Index"** (dividing the number of persons using a given technique into the number actually finding jobs through that technique) they discovered which job-hunting methods or techniques worked best. Among their landmark findings:

1. **Job-seeking success is proportional to the number of job-search techniques the job-seeker uses; the greater the number, the greater the success.**

2. **Some methods work better than others. The most effective job-hunting technique for learning where jobs are is that of using friends, relatives, or other workers. This method is "twice as effective as the use of direct company application and the Employment Service . . . and about 11 times as effective as the use of newspaper ads."**

3. Among those who applied directly to companies, job-seeking success was related to how much the job-seeker disregarded whether or not those companies were known to have vacancies (thus increasing the number of companies that can be contacted).

4. How many job-hunting methods a job-hunter uses and how many places he contacts is related to three factors:

a) high achievement motivation (see 1961),

b) high achievement 'values' (as defined by Bernard Rosen, a sociologist at Cornell University: belief in individualism, in being active rather than passive, and in taking the future into account and not just the present),

c) low job-interview anxiety.

5. The more training and counseling a job-seeker receives, the higher the job-seeking success, particularly if the training focuses on teaching achievement motivation and values, and on reducing job-interview anxiety.

6. Job-seekers with low achievement motivation and high job-interview anxiety are the primary candidates for training and counseling, as they "tend to require an institutional intermediary in their quest for jobs."

This was a landmark study of the job-hunt, using 455 blue-collar workers in Erie, Pennsylvania, as their sample, conducted by Harold L. Sheppard and A. Harvey Belitsky. Their findings were reported in their 1966 book, The Job Hunt: Job-Seeking Behavior of Unemployed Workers in a Local Economy, *published by The Johns Hopkins Press, and in a 1968 pamphlet summarizing this book, "Promoting Jobfinding Success for the Unemployed," published by The W.E. Upjohn Institute for Employment Research, 300 South Westnedge Avenue, Kalamazoo, MI 49007. Both are now out of print. However, a summary of this research was made available to job-hunters in* What Color Is Your Parachute?, *beginning with the 1972 edition, and continuing to today.*

1967

Ideas first published in 1967: **There are three different kinds of skills -- functional, specific content, and adaptive.**

• Functional skills are those competencies related to Things, Data, People.

• Specific Content skills are the specific job content to which the functional skills are applied.

• Adaptive skills are those involved in managing oneself -- particularly with respect to *conformity* and *change*.

If a worker's adaptive skills (expectations) are not being met, that worker will not operate up to the level of their functional ability, and will try to escape that situation (new job, or new career).

This was another landmark set of ideas, invented by Sidney Fine. The idea occurred to him while riding crosstown on a bus, in Washington, puzzling over some work he was doing with Leon Sullivan's project in Philadelphia. Sidney first published these ideas in "Nature of Skill: Implications for Education and Training," from the Proceedings, 75th Annual Convention, APA, 1967. These ideas did not come to the wide attention of job counselors until they were popularized by Dick Bolles in his 2-week workshop, beginning in 1974, and in his book What Color Is Your Parachute? *where -- with slightly different words (Specific Content = Special Knowledges, and Adaptive = Self-Management) -- it was used in his "Quick Job-Hunting Map," beginning with the 1978 edition.*

1968

Event in 1968: **John Crystal began to write regular job-hunting columns for the** *Army and Air Force Times.* These columns attracted Dick Bolles's attention in 1969, and subsequently had a heavy influence on the very first edition of *What Color Is Your Parachute?* John was a former Bernard Haldane employee, and founder in 1963 of his own Crystal Management Services in McLean, Virginia. His columns reflected John's 'system', essentially an amalgam of ideas from three sources: John's experience with Bernard Haldane, of course; plus his experience as a spy in the Second World War (John used this experience to figure out how you could track down information about anything -- careers, jobs, places); plus his training in economics (he held a degree in this discipline from Columbia University).

John invented the idea of **the practice field survey** (see **1973**), now key to helping shy job-hunters get started on meeting people.

In addition, John gave a much stronger emphasis to ideas which had been in the field since A.W. Rahn's book (see 1936). Chief among them were these six:

1. **All teaching of job-hunting breaks down into just three basic questions**: Who, What and How? -- "Who am I?" "What are the realities of the world of work?" "What do I really most want to accomplish with my life?" and "How do I go about it?" (This last question, said John, "is the easiest part.") *This was akin to Rahn's basic formulations in his book* (see **1936**).

2. **Write a complete biography of your life before starting skill identification.** *This was akin to Rahn's idea (1936) and Arthur Miller's (1963).*

3. **Avoiding the personnel office at all costs.** *Again, earlier writers had advised this, but John elevated it to the level of a religion.*

4. The idea of writing **'talking papers.'** *This was akin to Rahn's idea of a Manpower Specifications sheet* (**1936**) *and Bernard Haldane's 'function papers'* (**1947**).

5. The idea of **offering a prospective employer 'a proposal' instead of a resume**. *John had a dislike for resumes -- as did others earlier in this history -- but John's dislike of them was awesome: he could rarely bring himself to even use the word 'resume' but referred to it as 'expletive deleted,' or as 'an obituary (the latter phrase probably borrowed from Bernard Haldane who had thus described a job application form). John proposed that no document be sent on ahead, except a "proposal" -- a concept akin to Richard Lathrop's idea of 'a qualifications brief' (1959).*

6. The **"low stress interview"** *(akin to Bernard Haldane's idea of "the coffee test").*

John Crystal's job-hunting columns for the Army and Air Force Times were called "Job Guidance;" Nos. 1–40 were published between November 20, 1968 and August 5, 1970. John's program, and ideas, evolved constantly, just as we have seen the ideas of Bernard Haldane and others did; the primary source of his new ideas after 1968 was a laborious 60 hour+

analysis that John did of each of his client's experiences and goals, wherein he himself did the skill identification, etc., for that client. John died in 1988.

1969

Idea first developed in 1969: **Setting up a non-profit employment agency comprised of job-hunters, solely for the purpose of enabling those job-hunters, in groups of eight to ten, to call employers, and -- representing the 'agency,' -- help develop jobs** *for the other members of their group.* This was Tom Jackson's idea.

Another idea of Tom's: **Doing 'group outplacement.'** Tom was instrumental in introducing companies -- beginning with Firestone in 1978 -- to the practice of 'group outplacement.' Prior to this time, 'outplacement' was a service offered by employers to individuals only, usually executives.

Tom's other key ideas are: **the self-directed employee, the importance of vision and target, the idea of the transformation of barriers,** and **the job-hunt as a series of No's followed by a Yes.**

Tom Jackson is the author of The Hidden Job Market (1976) *and* Guerrilla Tactics in the Job Market (1978) *and -- his most popular book --* The Perfect Resume (1981, 1990). *But back in 1969, he came up with this 'employment agency' idea, while working with laid-off aerospace workers, for the State of California.*

His special agency was called Opportunities Unlimited. *Laid-off workers received two days training, then worked on the phones for (typically) 10 hours per week, doing job-development and placement with prospective employers, on behalf of the other members in their group -- based on the well-known fact that it is easier to praise others than it is to praise oneself. "Hello, I represent Opportunities Unlimited, an employment agency. I have someone here who . . ."*

1970

Idea first published in 1970: **Only one job offer is offered, and accepted, for every 1470 resumes sent out by job-hunters.**

The raw data was in an Iron Age Magazine, *January 15, 1970, article; the final calculations from that data were made by Dick Bolles, and published in* What Color Is Your Parachute?

Event occurring in 1970: **on December 1,** *What Color Is Your Parachute?* **first appeared -- self-published, 8½ x 11" in size, and 162 pages in length.**

The book was written for campus ministers who were leaving the church by Dick Bolles, an Episcopal priest, working at that time for United Ministries in Higher Education, an umbrella organization for ten different religious denominations. When the campus ministers he was troubleshooter for, in the nine western States, asked him what to do as their next step after leaving the Church, he determined to find the answer to their question, and so -- with a travel grant from UMHE's Verlyn Barker -- traveled 69,000 miles researching how to change careers. He asked two main questions of all the people he interviewed during this research period: "How do you change careers without necessarily going back to school?" and "How do you search for a job, when resumes, ads, and agencies don't work?" He then summarized his findings in a book written in his spare time between Sept. 15 and Nov. 27, 1970. It was self-published, at a local San Francisco copy place (called Pronto Print), and first saw the light of day on December 1, 1970. After its publication it was distributed by Dick to campus ministers, and 2000 copies of the self-published edition went out, during the next two years. During that time span, many other organizations asked for a copy, outside the Church -- such as G.E., the Pentagon, UCLA, and City College of New York. "I've decided to bail out" was the common phrase of the day among those who were quitting their job, hence the flippant rejoinder chosen as the book's title. What Color Is Your Parachute? *had few ideas that hadn't been seen in this century already; its popularity lay rather in the fact that old ideas were presented in new forms, and organized well.*

1972

The event in 1972: **In November,** *What Color Is Your Parachute?* **was commercially published by a Berkeley publisher, 6 x 9" in size, and 201 pages in length. Since 1975, it has been revised or completely rewritten annually.** Ideas or instruments first appearing in *Parachute* (over the years):

1. The idea that **'Having alternatives' is the key to a successful job-hunt, or career-change.**
2. **The summarizing of the job-hunt as WHAT, WHERE and HOW** -- *What do you most enjoy doing? Where do you want to do it? How do you get hired there? -- (based on John Crystal's divisions of WHO, WHAT and HOW -- and akin to A.W. Rahn's WHAT, WHERE, WHO and WHY).*
3. The idea called **Informational Interviewing.**
4. **The summary of the three kinds of interviews:** The Practice Field Survey, Information Interviewing, and Interviewing for Employment. *Later systematized by Daniel Porot, of Geneva, Switzerland, as "The PIE Method" (see* **1996***).*
5. **The Prioritizing Grid** *(adapted from a more complex one that was invented by the Syracuse Research Institute).*
6. **The Party Exercise**, based on John Holland's RIASEC theory.
7. **The Quick Job-Hunting Map.**
8. **'The Flower.'**

The only way people could get Parachute *prior to this date was by ordering it from the author, directly. The significance of the commercial publication of the book was that this got the book into bookstores. It languished in the stores for almost two years, being frequently misfiled under "Sports" (Parachuting) before it started to become popular, and by 1974* Parachute *had come to the top of the best-seller lists, first in the Northwest, and eventually throughout the country, thus becoming the first book in this field in this century to become a best-seller. In May of 1994,* USA Today *listed* What Color Is Your Parachute? *as one of the top 100 bestselling books in the U.S., during the previous six months.* Parachute *has sold an average of 20,000–25,000 copies per month for many years now, has been on the N.Y. Times best-seller list (paperback, non-fiction) for a total of 288 weeks, and has been translated into ten languages.*
Other firsts:
• *It was the first job-hunting book to be revised every year. It is still revised every year, sometimes dramatically, with the new edition appearing in late October.*
• *It was the first job-hunting book with poetry, graphics (and, eventually, cartoons), and the use of color throughout.*

- *It was the first job-hunting book to dissect in great detail 'the numbers game' -- the traditional method of job-hunting.*
- *It was the first job-hunting book to list other job-hunting books, and the first to acknowledge its debt to many other job-hunting authors: Bernard Haldane, John Crystal, Arthur Miller, Dick Lathrop, Tom Jackson (and those listed next).*
- *It was the first job-hunting book to describe 'the creative minority' among job-hunting experts (Rahn, Edlund, Haldane, Miller, Crystal, Lathrop, Jackson, et al.), and to familiarize the general public with the ideas of Sidney Fine, John Holland, Nathan Azrin, Robert Wegmann, and Daniel Porot; additionally, it was the first to synthesize all their ideas.*
- *It was the first job-hunting book to contain a pure functional skills chart, based on Sidney Fine's classification system, as an aid to analyzing one's achievements.*
- *It was the first job-hunting book to use Sidney Fine's distinction of functional, specific knowledge, and adaptive skills.*
- *It was the first job-hunting book to give detailed instructions on how to choose a career counselor, and to list the articles critiquing shady practices in the executive counseling industry (as a consequence, the FTC, the New York State Attorney General's Office, and the President's Advisor on Consumer Affairs consulted with the author).*
- *It was the first job-hunting book to contain detailed lists of counselors and other resources.*
- *It is the first job-hunting book to have its title become part of America's everyday lexicon, as in the headline: "What Color Is Smith's Parachute?" The phrase "golden parachute" also came from this book, when some unknown writer in the '70s combined the common phrase of "golden handshakes" with the title of this book, to produce the misbegotten phrase "Golden Parachutes" -- used in a sense* (a 'cushy' retirement provided by others) *that totally contradicts the advice of the book* ('take charge of your own life'). *But the phrase is now part of everyday speech in the U.S.*
- *It is the first book in the career counseling field to be designated by the Library of Congress's "Center for the Book" in 1995 as one of "25 Books That Have Shaped Readers' Lives'* (along with The Adventures of Huckleberry Finn, Atlas Shrugged, The Catcher in the Rye, Gone with the Wind, How to Win Friends and Influence People, I Know Why the Caged Bird Sings, The Little Prince, The Secret Garden, Walden *and others).*

1973

The event in 1973: **John Crystal's system comes in for detailed study by the U.S. government.**

Dick Bolles, while a guest at the W.E. Upjohn Institute for Employment Research in Washington, D.C., was commissioned and funded by IEEE and the Department of Health, Education, and Welfare to make a complete study of John Crystal's program, with an eye to adapting it to electrical and electronics engineers leaving their profession. The charge was to turn John's 'art' into something more like 'a science.' The result was published the following year, as a training manual entitled, Where Do I Go From Here With My Life?, *by Bolles and Crystal.*

New ideas in 1973: **The Practice Field Survey** as a means whereby shy people could practice talking to people, by choosing a non-job-related "enthusiasm" such as skiing (John's idea).

Trioing as a means of doing skill identification within stories (Dick's idea).

The event in 1973: **Job-clubs are born. (Also called job finding clubs, or self-directed search.)**

Nathan Azrin, at that time a psychologist with the Illinois Department of Mental Health, and a leader in the field of behavioral modification techniques (particularly with toilet training), invented this job-finding technique called The Job Club. Using behavioral modification techniques, he formed groups of two to eight clients, beginning every other week. He reported this approach in 1973 in "An Experimental Application of A Social Reinforcement Approach to the Problem of Job-Finding," by R.J. Jones and Nathan H. Azrin, in the Journal of Applied Behavior Analysis, *Fall, 1973. Nathan later wrote up his techniques in the* Job Club Counselor's Manual: A Behavioral Approach to Vocational Counseling, *first published in 1980.*

In 1975, the Work Incentive Program (WIN) of the Department of Labor decided to test his theories, and so, funded five pilot projects serving welfare recipients, in Harlem, New Brunswick, Tacoma, Wichita and Milwaukee -- forming both a Job Finding Club and 'a control group' in each city. These were trained by Robert A. Philip, a former associate of Nathan Azrin. Excluding those who dropped out, 80% of the job club participants vs. 46% of the control group found jobs. The average counseled job-seeker started work in 14 days, compared to 53 days for the control group. Salaries for job club participants were one-third higher than that of the control group.

A nationwide network of such Job Finding Clubs was subsequently established in 17 states, by the National Office of Program Development, in Carbondale, IL, run by Robert A. Philip.

Other programs similar to Azrin's Job Club were started also in 1973, underwritten with funds from CETA (the Comprehensive Employment and Training Act). They were called "Self-Directed Search" Programs.

Their most notable characteristic was that they required participants to 'punch in' at 8 a.m. and 'punch out' at 4:30, and participants were paid a 'salary' (stipend) while job-hunting. Dozens of such CETA programs sprang up around the country, but four of them became particularly famous:

The Self-Directed Placement Corporation, established in San Diego, California, in 1973 by Charles Hoffman; The Job Factory established in Cambridge, Massachusetts, in 1976 by Joe Fischer and Albert Cullen; the San Mateo County Job Finders in San Mateo, California, run by Dick Wright; and the Sonoma Program Services Corporation in Forestville, California, run by Dave Perschau. In the Spring of 1980, David wrote a very detailed manual on how to run a job club, called "Group Job Seeking Course Guide" using his own particular orientation and synthesis.

Job clubs -- now called 'support groups' -- still thrive, but no longer pay stipends, and rarely have full-day programs.

Famous ones include: The Job Search Task Force at the First Baptist Church in Richardson, TX; The Racine Job Network, at St. Andrew's Lutheran Church in Racine, WI; The Employment Information Network in Pittsburgh, PA; The Interfaith Job Search Council in Dallas, TX; The Job Transition Support Group at the Colonial Church in Edina, MN, founded in 1977; Job Seekers at Trinity Church in Princeton, NJ, founded in 1982; the Career Transition Ministry (CTM) at the Presbyterian Church in Menlo Park, CA., founded in 1989; The Jewish Employment Network in Chicago, IL, founded in 1991; Career Connection at Canyon Creek Presbyterian Church in Richardson, TX, founded in 1992.

There are also commercial enterprises, modelled after Job Clubs, such as Dean Curtis & Associates, which began in 1985 and is modelled after Dave Perschau's "Group Job Seeking Course Guide."

Ideas appearing for the first time in 1973 (taught by Nathan Azrin):

1. **Job-hunting is a learnable skill.**
2. **Use the yellow pages and phone book to call every company listed in your field.**
3. **Ask who is in charge of hiring for the position you want, get his name, hang up. Call back and ask for him by name: secure an appointment without getting interviewed over the phone.**
4. **Have a script to follow (read it!) over the telephone.**
5. **Have a buddy who is listening in on an extension line, and gives you feedback after the call is completed.**
6. **In your interviews, emphasize how you can help the company** *(an old idea, of course).*
7. **Send a thank-you note on colored paper.**

1975

Idea first appearing in 1975: **A liberal arts education makes one highly marketable in the world of work.**

Howard Figler wrote this in: Path: A Career Workbook for Liberal Arts Students *(Carroll Press, 1994, 1979, 1975), where he set forth the idea (amplified in his* Liberal Education and Careers Today; *Garrett Park Press, 1989) that a liberal arts education enables graduates to cultivate skills -- thinking, learning and communicating -- which are not only highly marketable in the world of work, but often enable liberal arts graduates to outshine their 'vocational' counterparts in the business world and elsewhere.*

1976

The invention first appearing in 1976: **Card sorts** as a method for prioritizing skills, knowledges, values, etc.

(Actually, card sorts have a long history, antedating 1976: in the 1950s there were key-sort cards, with holes punched around the perimeter corresponding to various factors. These were then sorted -- first by needle, and then, later in the '50s, by machine. But in 1976, card sorts began to be used with job-hunters, and Dick Knowdell, then at Lawrence Livermore

Laboratories, was the inventor. He first designed a Career Values card sort, 'in-house,' based largely on Howard Figler's work. In 1978, Dick designed a Motivated Skills card sort. And in 1979, a Retirement Activities/Occupational Interests card sort. (All available still from Career Research & Testing, Inc., 1-800-888-4945.)

Other people, independently and often with no knowledge of Dick's work, also designed card sorts subsequently. These were: a Transferable skills card sort, with detailed definitions, plus color-codes ("SkillScan® Professional Pack") developed by Lorraine Gazzano, M.A., and Lesah Beckhusen, M.S., P.O. Box 587, Orinda, CA 94563-0557 (1987); another Transferable skills card sort ("Deal Me In"), developed by Career Systems, Inc., 800-283-8839 (1991); a Thinking styles card sort ("Diversity") produced by the Ned Herrmann Group, Applied Creativity, Inc., P.O. Box 3641, Seminole, FL 34642-0641 (1992); and, certainly not finally, a Fields of interest card sort ("Occupational Work Settings") developed by Paul Stevens & The Worklife Network Team, at The Centre for Worklife Counseling, 5 Earl Street (PO Box 407, Spit Junction 2088), Mosman, Sydney, NSW 2088, Australia -- based on Dick Knowdell's work (1994).

1977

The invention first appearing in 1977: **Detailed skill identification lists for homemakers** to use when going into job-interviews. It enabled them to describe their home tasks in the language of the marketplace.

They were called the "I CAN" competency lists, and were published by various organizations. Unhappily they were allowed to go out of print in 1994.

1979

Event of 1979: **The job-hunting field found its researcher.**
The late Bob Wegmann came along just when it was apparent that this field badly needed someone to dig into all the literature and pull out every useful statistic there was. Among many articles he was to publish before his untimely death in 1991, the most significant one was called, "Job-Search Assistance: A Review," published in the *Journal of Employment Counseling,* December, 1979.

His basic findings were not new, but whereas up until now these conclusions had been based on intuition and anecdotal evidence, Bob found empirical evidence for these facts:

1. **Self-esteem is crucial to a successful job-hunt.**
2. **Job-hunting is inherently discouraging, and almost everyone needs some kind of social support.**
3. **There is factual information about how to find and approach potential employers that can be taught in a group setting.**
4. **There are telephone and interviewing skills that can be practiced before they are used.**
5. **The more time one spends attempting to get interviews, the more interviews obtained. The more interviews obtained, the greater the probability that at least one of them will result in a job offer.**

Idea first published in 1979: **Job-hunting itself requires certain skills; there are 20 separate, observable skills that job-hunters typically need, in order to do a successful job-hunt.**

This idea appeared in Howard Figler's The Complete Job-Search Handbook: All the Skills You Need to Get Any Job and Have a Good Time Doing It *(published in 1979, revised and expanded in 1988 and 1999). The idea was derived from a book by Allen Ivey, called* Micro-counseling, *in which he attempted to identify the separate, observable skills that counselors use when they counsel. Howard decided to adapt this approach to job-hunting, by identifying the separate, observable skills that job-hunters use when they job-hunt. He found 20. His object was to help job-hunters understand what skills they needed, and then go acquire or improve the ones they needed. But of course one of the implications of his work was that some occupations required these 20 skills in the doing of the work, and therefore those qualified to apply for such jobs not only could do the job well once hired, but had a head start in doing the job-hunt well also, since it demanded the same 20 skills. A very important work.*

1980–1996

The event during this period: **The job-hunting sections in bookstores became** *huge.* Due to the popularity of *What Color Is Your Parachute?* as a best-seller (it remained on the *New York Times* paperback best-seller list for 288 weeks), every major publisher as well as many smaller houses set out to publish job-hunting books. So many, that *Fortune Magazine* (1/15/96 issue) reported that 3,100 books about finding, managing, and changing careers had been published just since 1990.

Aside from Parachute, *the most enduring have proved to be Barbara Sher's* Wishcraft, *Tom Jackson's books, the Bob Adams's "Knock-em Dead" series, and books by Paul Tieger & Barbara Barron-Tieger, most notably* Do What You Are (based on the Myers-Briggs "Type" Indicator).

1996

Event in 1996: **Daniel Porot writes** *The PIE Method for Career Success* (published by JIST Works, Inc., 720 North Park Avenue, Indianapolis, IN 46202-3431) setting forth his ideas for systematizing John Crystal's and Dick Bolles's approach to job-hunting, combined with many other ideas that are Daniel's own.

Daniel Porot is a Frenchman who lives in Geneva, Switzerland, where he is the founder and head of Cabinet Porot. His PIE method was previously published in French, with over 100,000 copies sold there. He has co-taught the annual What Color Is Your Parachute two-week workshop, with Dick Bolles, for 20 years.

1997

Event in 1997: **The 'welfare to work' movement gains momentum, and the movement finds its workbook in** *No One Is Unemployable: Creative Solutions for Overcoming Barriers to Employment,* by Debra L. Angel and Elisabeth E. Harney. (Worknet Publications, P.O. Box 5582, Hacienda Heights, CA 91745-0082.) Among the many original ideas to be found in this book, written for people reentering the workforce, are three in particular:

1. **Business is a foreign culture and must be approached as though one were going into another country and another culture: with its own language, customs, values, and rituals.**

2. **When a job-hunter is puzzling over a decision, it is useful to ask him or her to think of three options facing them, in that decision-area, list the pros and cons of each, and then choose which one they wish to pursue.**

3. **It is the task of the career counselor to help the job-hunter implement whichever of the three options they choose, regardless of whether or not the counselor feels this was the wisest of the three.**

1998

Event in 1998: **The 'career coach' movement gains momentum.** During the '90s the official credentialing of career counselors tended to become more and more rigorous -- requiring 48 semester units in a Master's degree program in counseling, plus 3,000 hours of post-Master's internship. This has spawned, inevitably, attempts to find alternative routes to credentialing that are quicker, and less burdensome. Enter "career coaching," a new way of getting credentialed (often in a weekend) and a new way of doing career counseling or a substitute for career counseling.

In theory, coaches are para-career counselors, similar to paramedics -- able to take on simple problems, often with stunning success, but adjured to leave the more complex problems to fully-credentialed career counselors. Yet, in practice, people with coaching credentials often try to take on any problem that a fully-credentialed career counselor would take on -- so the line is beginning to blur.

It is all part of a trend (I am indebted to Dick Knowdell for pointing this out) toward a faster, more impersonal way of life that is fast approaching with the new millennium: and in our profession, this is leading toward telephone coaching instead of face-to-face counseling, Internet advising instead of telephone coaching, e-mail solutions instead of Internet advising. But alongside this movement and trend, continues to be the hunger in many job-hunters (and counselors) for face-to-face meeting. It remains to be seen how these clashing trends will sort themselves out.

But we are children of our history, the history outlined here, and we who are counselors or coaches need to become very familiar with the ideas developed by those who came before us, or we will have to invent the *career-counseling* wheel all over again.

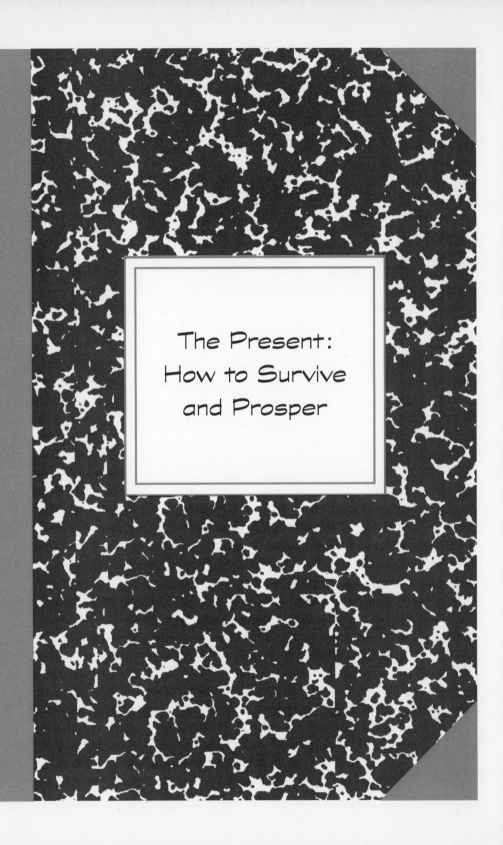

The Present:
How to Survive
and Prosper

CHAPTER 8

Finding Clients

by Howard Figler

Prospective clients are everywhere. If you don't believe it, just go to a party sometime and tell people you're a career counselor:

"Oh, do I need to talk to you! Do you have a minute?"

Go anywhere -- to your hairdresser, a restaurant, a Jiffy-Lube, your veterinarian's office, and ask: *"How do you like your work?"*

Of any 100 people, 30 are actively looking to change their work, and 20 more are contemplating it.

Even though there are thousands who could benefit from career help, most people do not become paying clients. That's because career counselors usually don't do an especially good job of marketing themselves. If you're like most counselors, you want the clients to come to you. It won't happen that way. Let's look at what you can do.

I. Finding clients for one-to-one counseling

People typically do not choose counselors who are completely unknown to them. They come on the recommendation of others. Therefore, consider:

(a) Relationships with other professionals. Many of your best referrals will come from others in professional roles -- career counselors, mental health professionals, health professionals, accountants, lawyers, financial analysts, etc.

Professionals want to be assured that they will deliver someone to good service. The best way they can judge you, other than hearing from your present or former clients, is to meet you. Thus, you must go out of your way to develop relationships with other professionals. This is where much of your business will come from.

Health and mental health practitioners in particular are in a good position to send you clients, because they often hear about job and career woes when they are performing their services. They're doing their own clients or patients a favor by sending them to you.

(b) Meeting people in general. In the world of personal services, face-to-face contact is everything. People are far more likely to trust people they have met. Friendships form that way. Future spouses are found that way. Similarly, referrals most often derive from in-person meetings.

Thus, you must commit yourself to being more outgoing than you're usually comfortable with. How much more? Fifty percent would be asking too much. Can you handle 20%?

This doesn't mean random, crazy socializing. It means purposely being in places where potential clients and those who refer are present. But it also means making yourself available for general socializing where you don't know who'll be there -- neighborhood block parties, hanging around your children's school for a few minutes, and getting to know people at the travel agency or the grocery store. You never know who you'll meet.

It doesn't happen automatically. Consider career counselor Gladstone Speezle. He hung out his shingle, put an ad in the yellow pages, rented his office and waited . . . and waited. It wasn't his name that worked against him. He didn't market himself. One day at a Little League game, sharing his woes with several parents, he tripped over a guy who had lost his job, fell to the ground, gave him some free help . . . one thing led to another and now he has a few clients. Gladstone learned his first lesson of marketing -- the clients don't drop into your lap when you're hiding in your office.

Treat your home area as a very small town

The first rule of getting prospective clients to know you is to "be as visible as possible." And a good strategy is to imagine that you live in a town of 1,000 or fewer, where you would introduce yourself to everyone, and build relationships because you're going to see people again . . . and again. In a small town, you cannot be anonymous with anyone.

In Texas they have a custom of beginning a business meeting by first talking on a personal basis. Texans call it "visiting." They will not discuss "bidness" until doing enough visiting to be comfortable with one another. Texans are suspicious of people (especially "furriners" such as New Yorkers) who want to talk business right away. And they are right. This practice enables them to develop a sense of trust for people before dealing with money.

"Visiting," Texas style, is what *you* must do first, before you ever consider asking anyone for their business.

In this era of hyper-technology, face-to-face contact is more important than ever. People want to look you over. It's much easier for prospective clients to trust you when they see you, rather than responding to you on the telephone or reading your advertisements or other less personal forms of communication.

What if you're a not at ease socially?

All this may sound as if you have to be a social butterfly -- be all over the place, flitting around making contacts every spare minute -- and many readers will recoil at the thought.

Not everyone socializes naturally or even willingly. Fortunately, socializing does not require shy or reserved individuals to change their personalities.

Socializing is a willingness to be present with others; but it does not necessarily mean dancing around as the center of attention. Social skills can be learned by anyone. Susan RoAne's book, *How to Work a Room,* is an excellent primer to help you be at ease in social settings. The title of the book sounds manipulative, but don't let that put you off. RoAne has dozens of sensible guidelines for communicating effectively in every kind of social situation.

> *If you want to manage the mingling at any event look around for people who are standing around with white knuckles. They are clutching (their glasses) so tightly their knuckles are white. They're scared to death and they are always alone. These people usually welcome your conversation because you save them from anonymity. . . . If you walk up and start a conversation, you're doing a good deed and also moving* yourself *away from the wall.*
>
> (Susan RoAne, *How to Work a Room,* 84–85)

(c) Participation in organizations. These include professional associations, social clubs, sports clubs, investment clubs, and others. Organizational memberships help increase your socializing. But you have to be active at the meetings and activities, not hide in a corner hoping that someone will find you.

Other methods

Free seminars. Call friends and professional contacts to invite them to your free seminars. What seminars? Programs you offer to any community organization, social organization, service clubs (Rotary, Kiwanis, etc.) or government agency which might want them.

Get yourself on or in the media. Propose possible radio-show topics, articles for the local newspaper, or even brief TV interviews. Career advice columns, call-in radio shows, and free resume clinics have great potential for career counselors but have not been fully explored.

Copresent seminars with another professional. Do programs with a financial counselor, a lawyer, a mental health professional, or others.

Less effective methods

Yellow pages advertisements in the telephone book aren't likely to attract as many clients as you may expect. Also, the people who find your name in the phone book are less likely to be "good clients." They frequently are "no-shows," they more often don't pay for services, and they require more explanation about what you do.

Don't spend much money for advertisements in publications such as newspapers or magazines. Your time, energy, and money are better spent in the activities described above.

II. Finding clients for group programs

"Group programs" refers to a combination of activities, including facilitation of workshops, training programs, seminars, and public speaking.

To get business for group programs, all the recommendations in the previous section apply -- socializing, educating the public, being in the media, etc. Because group leaders/facilitators, trainers or speakers are perceived as "experts" in their field, and because you want to be identified as an expert, use the following methods, too:

Publications. Writing is an effective tool for generating business. Since people are apt to believe what they see in print, they tend to give much credibility to any author and almost anything she writes. People who publish articles, newsletter columns, books, etc., are often invited to speak or lead workshops, because their publications imply that the authors are high-ranking in their fields.

Public speaking skills. If you intend to make income from groups, invest yourself in public speaking skills. Attend professional institutes, college courses, or other learning situations where you can practice your skills, observe others, and receive feedback. Toastmasters International organizations can be very helpful, and the National Speakers Association represents the highest level of professional speakers.

Speaking anxiety can be overcome through practice. Many accomplished speakers began as stutterers or those who once lived in terror of public presentations.

Publicity. If you're committed to having group work be a large part of your business, you may want to consider hiring a publicist, a person who will lay out a strategy for getting your name known in potential markets. She can do a lot of things described earlier in this chapter, if you don't have time for them.

Writing, speaking, and publicity can bring you quantum leaps in credibility

Notice that all three of the above categories start with the letters P-U-B. That doesn't mean to start drinking to ward off the stress of getting business. It means p-u-b as in public. If you make part or all of your living as a trainer, speaker or workshop leader, you are a public figure. Become comfortable with that role, and do writing and speaking to enhance it. Your reputation will grow and you will attract more clients.

III. Finding clients for organizational career development consulting

Networking is also essential in organizational career development consulting. Many consultants in this field spend 50% or more of their time meeting and socializing with human resource professionals, company executives, managers, and friends of friends in the corporate world.

What do they talk about? They do what any good salesperson does -- they listen to and interpret the needs of the client. You meet organizational people anywhere you can -- in professional associations, social settings, community work, and through referrals from people you already know. By the time you meet a prospect for the fifth time, you might be ready to say, for example:

"I think I can help you build a system of employee career development to fit the needs you've been telling me about."

IV. The portfolio approach

If you do a *combination* of professional work -- individual clients, group work (training, seminars), organizational consulting, outplacement, etc. -- you may expand the potential business that will come your way. As you apply your skills to a variety of clientele, there are more people who can consider hiring you for something else. Increasingly, career development professionals are building wide portfolios of skills and clients in order to have multiple sources of income.

We are still pioneering

Why are many people not paying for career services even though they need them?

• Many who need career services don't know what they are; some only have a vague idea that career counselors exist. Career counseling is not well understood or appreciated by a large proportion of the general public.

• Some prospective clients mistrust our services, because they have heard about people who paid a lot to "career counselors" who promised a lot and delivered little. While there are thousands of competent professionals who do not identify with unethical practitioners, their credibility is affected nonetheless by others who have delivered poor service and over-charged for it.

What can be done? We recommend the following:

1　Educating the public.

One of the best ways to create new clients is to enhance the general public's understanding of our profession. Counselors should accept frequent opportunities to speak to civic groups (Kiwanis, Rotary and other community service agencies), schools, Chambers of Commerce, etc., about what career counselors do, and how they help people. This "free work" takes time, but it's an excellent way to build public awareness and improve the market for all career counselors. Bring copies of the "Consumer Guidelines For Selecting A Career Counselor" (by the National Career Development Association).

Many of the involvements recommended in this chapter serve the purpose of familiarizing the public with career services. The public needs a lot of educating. When those people you meet at parties already know what you do and they start ringing your office phone off the hook, you will have done your job. Until then, it's educate, educate, educate.

2 Speaking out against abuses.

Because people's job needs are often desperate, there have been unscrupulous "counselors" willing to prey on these needs for many years. The virus has been hard to eliminate. Responsible counselors must tighten ethical practices within the profession, or else confusion and wariness will persist. Who can blame a person for hesitating to contact any career counselor when they hear that a neighbor paid $1000–$5000 up front for career help, and all they got was some general advice and months of futility in the job market?

3 Provide service for those who can't afford it.

Another way to improve public perception is to help those who need it most, when they cannot pay going rates. You can reach a lot of people by doing free or low-cost group work. You need not accept vows of poverty by doing all your work free; the people you help at low cost will tell others who may become paying clients.

While pioneering a profession is hard work, it's also exciting, in that you are part of "writing the book" about effective practices. When career counseling gains broad public acceptance, today's counselors will know that they had a role in shaping this successful transition.

CHAPTER 9

Learning Self-Promotion

by Howard Figler

Karen, a career counselor in private practice, decided to attend a Chamber of Commerce dinner which was honoring her friend Michelle, the guest speaker and author of a brand-new book. Karen saw this as an evening to relax, enjoy the conversation, meet a few people, with no pressure to do anything professional.

Yet only 10 minutes into the predinner conversation and she sat with hands shaking, stomach churning -- a bundle of anxiety. Karen wished she had never come. All thoughts of relaxation were impossible. The leader of the Chamber meeting had introduced an element of terror into the proceedings --
"I'd like to ask each of you to say something in 30 seconds or so, about the nature of your business."

"I look awful. I wore the wrong dress . . . I have no talent for talking about myself . . . it would be good if I could say something funny . . . yeah, I look like a clown, but I don't feel very funny . . ." *"How do I explain what I do in 30 seconds?" thought Karen. "I'll be stupefyingly boring . . . I'm supposed to say something that will attract business. Hah!! I'll drive them away . . . once they hear how dumb and ignorant I sound . . . can't I just pass out my business cards?"*

Self-promotion. It's such a misunderstood term. It has the flavor of standing around bragging about yourself. It seems vaguely low-class, certainly unprofessional. Yet, the business world is like this. You appear in public and people ask you what's your business. You can't say "I don't know," "I'd rather not answer that," or "Same to you, fella."

In the polite and orderly world of professional life, promoting yourself may feel out of place. Going out of your way to announce your services seems . . . well, like something a circus barker would do.

Career counselors have plenty of excuses for avoiding self-promotion

"I don't want to be pushy and obnoxious . . . I don't have time for self-promotion . . . I'm good, people will find me. I shouldn't have to do this stuff."

The relentless self-promoter is a pretty strange animal, probably not one you would like to emulate. Yet, counselors take the opposite end of the scale as though it were a badge of honor -- "The more understated and un-promotional I am, the more likely that potential clients will view me as . . . 'professional', classy, not needing the business, but deserving it."

There is something to be said for understatement, but you may be using it as a place to hide, hoping that you can make your services available without referring to yourself at all. Hiding will not get the job done. Self-promotion, on its most basic level, is simply letting people know you're available. Doctors do it. Architects do it. All market-oriented professionals do it.

Professional life without self-promotion is just not possible. Once you become comfortable with it, your practice will benefit. You need go nowhere near the crude, manipulative extremes of self-promotion, but you must learn to do the following:

1. Prepare yourself to comfortably, spontaneously tell about your work in 30 to 60 seconds -- anytime, anywhere. If you take longer than that, you're reaching beyond people's attention span;

2. Put yourself in many situations where you're going to meet new people who will repeatedly ask you to do #1 above. A steady flow of new faces is the lifeblood of an expanding practice. Being "out there" on a regular basis is good for your

complexion and it keeps people talking about you. This is how serendipities occur -- you just "happen to meet" someone who knows someone else and, wonder of wonders, there's a new client.

3. Take other measures to increase your name recognition, such as writing articles in local papers, doing considerable public speaking, and being visible and active in both community groups and professional associations.

But most of all, there are the endless occasions you'll have to deliver your "30-second commercial," which you must learn to love and embrace.

When Karen's turn came at the dinner, she said:

"I'm a career counselor . . . I counsel careers . . . I mean I counsel people . . . I mean I help people . . . that is, they help themselves . . . I mean I listen . . . oh, I don't know what I mean."

The first few times it's not easy. But learning to talk about yourself is a rite of passage in our trade. Karen did much better after some preparation and practice:

"I'm a career counselor . . . I help people assess their capabilities and investigate prospective markets for their talents.

I work with people who want to change their career directions, or those who have been laid off. I also help people who want a career 'checkup,' to see if they're getting the best possible rewards from their work."

Self-promotion is not evil, obnoxious, or low class. It is necessary. It can be done with taste and blended gracefully into your personal and professional life. Learn to do it well. Self-promotion is not about tooting your own horn. It means being open and accessible. We teach clients to promote themselves in order to advance their careers. We certainly can advocate this for ourselves.

CHAPTER 10

Prospering
As a Career Counselor

by Howard Figler

The trail to prosperity is not a lone-wolf expedition. Perhaps the best avenue to success is to find ways of expanding the market for all career counselors, not just yourself. A rising tide may well lift all boats. When you compare the thousands of people who need career services to the far smaller number who pay for them, the room for growth is large indeed.

Yes, other career counselors are your "competitors," but it's a mistake if you worry about their stealing your secrets or your clients. Career professionals create a larger pool of business if they work with each other rather than playing war games.

Career professionals need to cooperate to expand the potential clientele for everyone. Examples:

• career counselors can create a "hotline" phone service to answer questions for people who have lost jobs

• career counselors can team up to offer low-cost programs for public schools

• career counselors can create a radio call-in show to answer questions and familiarize people with career services

• career counselors can team to offer programs at Chambers of Commerce to help people who have been laid off

Career professionals have been much too inclined to work independently, thus keeping their services quiet and relatively unknown.

Prosperity comes from recognizing that there are thousands of potential clients out there and very few of them are getting the service they need. Many other industries -- telephone, computer, entertainment, etc. -- are finding ways to reach untapped customers, because they are convinced they have something people want. They imagine their broad audiences long before they reach them. Not too long ago a few people sat around and envisioned the fax, the modem, the PC, and the motion picture for millions of customers.

Think big and think boldly. Career counseling is in its infancy. A few generations ago, psychological services were virtually nonexistent. And now they have wide public acceptance. Computer services were someone's idea of lunacy maybe 50 years ago.

The vast potential market will not be realized until professionals ask each other -- "How can career counselors break through the resistance that people have? . . . What kinds of new services do people want? . . . What methods work best?"

Career counselors give precious little time to understanding their untapped market. They're too busy scrambling to find a few more clients. Prosperity will be more likely when counselors step back to look at the big picture. In the meantime, here are some individual guidelines that you can apply:

1. **Learn to sense market needs as they are developing.** That may sound as though you need a crystal ball, but an easier way to "read" the market is to stay in constant touch with people, asking them:

"What have you not yet seen available which would help you with your career?"

"What new forms of service do you think I should offer?"

"How can the emerging interest in spirituality be translated into a service that people will pay for?"

2. **Create a market niche wherever you can.** Look for services that no one else is making available. When you find a need not being met, follow a cardinal rule of the marketplace -- get there first. You might be the first on your block to offer any of these:

- a job fair where you and other career counselors answer job-related questions
- guidelines about applying for jobs in other countries
- a one-day group process for helping people improve their interviewing skills through video feedback
- a short course in selling skills for non-sales-people
- interactive resume preparation assistance via computer
- a workshop that teaches telephone and voice mail skills for job hunters

3. **Build for the long run.** You are building a long-term enterprise, and that enterprise will require you to "invest" some of your human capital. Go out of your way to provide high-quality customer service. Treat every customer as though he is the one upon whom the future of your business depends. "Personal attention" is the hallmark of any successful service business, whether it's a grocery store, a computer store, a plumber, or a career counselor. People want to be attended to, valued, and cared for. They will pay extra for it.

4. **YOU are the product.** Being your own business, especially a personal service business, is an ongoing clinic in human relations, public relations, congeniality, perseverance, resilience in the face of setbacks, and openness to others.

5. **Always imagine that you'll see former clients in the grocery store.** Small-town storekeepers know they're going to see their customers again . . . and again. If you think a client is just one of many whom you'll never see any more, you may get a little sloppy in delivering your service. Imagine that you will know the client and her career for a long time. By assuming accountability, you'll keep yourself in line.

6. **Cozy up to selling.** We've said it elsewhere in this book, but it bears repeating -- learn how to become comfortable with the art of selling yourself. Selling is a generic human activity. Anytime you ask someone for money in exchange for your services, you are selling. There's nothing illegal or

immoral about it. Furthermore, it's a WIN-WIN situation. You give something of value, so they're happy when they pay you -- and you're happy to be paid.

"But, it seems so crass and pushy to sell myself," you might protest. Only if you believe you're manipulating or taking advantage of the client. If you're doing that, don't be a counselor; find a service that is disreputable. Counseling is honorable stuff.

7. **Consider earning your income from several sources.** Many career counselors in private practice earn income from a combination of one or more of these activities -- individual counseling, group programs, consultation, teaching, testing, and program administration. Others may generate income from writing, public speaking, testifying as an expert witness, or research.

8. **Charge what you're worth.** When starting your work as a counselor -- whether you're doing individual work, consulting, coaching, group work, or something else -- charge what you believe your work is worth. Don't get involved in price wars. Often when you price your services lower than the competition, you will be perceived as less valuable.

This principle might be different when you're bidding for a contract. In such cases, one criterion by which you're evaluated may be the lowness of your bid.

9. **Don't promise what you can't deliver.** Clients may have expectations that don't correlate with what we can do for them:

"Get me a $100,000 job that I can keep forever, where I can have regular use of the company airplane."

"Get me a job where the boss won't bug me and I will be appreciated by everyone."

Notice how these expectations start with "get me a job," which is what many people expect from career counselors. Make your role clear. Tell the client what you can and cannot do for him. This is a sample opening statement you might make:

"I can help you develop several career alternatives that will reflect your skills and values, and then help you develop a strategy for exploring these career options. I can also help you with job search methods that fit your aspirations. On the other hand, I cannot tell you which careers to go into. I cannot get you a job, and I cannot guarantee that any of your career choices will work out exactly as you like."

Don't let your client's initial expectations scare you. Prospering as a career counselor comes from relationships, not one-time contacts. Teach your clients how to help themselves. They will trust you and value your services more highly.

10. **Don't keep your clients paying forever**. Although you want to have ongoing connections with your clients, you don't want to overextend them. Remember, the idea is not to hold onto your clients until they're gagging from helplessness because they can't make a move without you. Counselors must be conscious of the need to get people flying on their own. If you regret seeing a client leave because you're worried about how to replace him, remind yourself that a newly empowered client will probably refer new clients to you.

The importance of integrity, relationships, and resisting greed

Larry started his practice with a bang. He hustled day and night, attracting lots of clients. His calendar was filled for months. He was written up in the local newspapers and appeared on local and regional TV and radio programs. After his first six months, Larry had more name recognition than counselors who'd been in business for years. Larry had been a go-getter in grad school too: "He was always more entrepreneurial than the rest of us."

Monique, on the other hand, started slowly. Low-key by nature, Monique built her clientele gradually and made low net income her first two years. She wished she could have Larry's dynamic personality, but said: "I can't really be like him."

A year later, Larry was losing clients in large numbers and watching his net income take a nosedive. Meanwhile, Monique's profits had improved greatly over the year before, and she had a filled calendar of group and individual work.

Larry was likeable but not trustable. His country-boy manner was disarming, but he talked about his clients' problems to other professionals, boasted about money and complained about ways that he felt other professionals had slighted him. Other counselors saw him as preoccupied with himself and having questionable ethics -- "a fast-buck kind of guy." They stopped referring clients.

Monique didn't have the hustler's charm, but people trusted her. She focused on making sure each client was fully satisfied and continually sought feedback about how she might do an even better job. She preferred to build her practice slowly, rather than try to get more work than she had time to handle.

Monique is now more successful than Larry and that trend will continue. The factors noted earlier were operating here:

Integrity. Sooner or later, people will find out who you are, and they will decide how much they can trust you. In the long run, making a living will depend upon how much people believe that you'll do what you say you can do. Integrity builds slowly, but can be broken by a careless or selfish maneuver.

Relationships. A successful practice derives not so much from superficial "networking" as from building connections with people that last. In these days of companies that change ownership or reinvent themselves overnight, the ongoing relationships that you have will be all the more important. These include connections with other professionals, members of your local community, friends, and neighbors.

Resisting Greed. In any profession, there are always temptations that involve money. A counselor may see an opportunity to make a quick profit and want to slide past something

that is ethically gray or that would undermine a key relationship. Sometimes people don't recognize how they've been
compromised by money until it's already happened.

People move around the country a lot and therefore may
persuade themselves that integrity, relationships, and resisting greed are less important. Big mistake. Professionals' reputations follow them wherever they go.

CHAPTER 11

The Isolation
of a One-Person Practice

by Howard Figler

Increasing numbers of counselors are offering career services as a one-person business. The autonomy of a one-person practice appeals to many, because it offers greater control and ways of integrating work life with family life. All this sounds promising. But beware of one unanticipated downside -- isolation.

At first you look forward to working alone, being free of messy office relationships, commuting, and being tied to other people's schedules. No more doing it because the boss says so. And then one day you hear yourself saying:

"I hated all that stuff -- the endless, pointless meetings, the hubbub, the chatter, the pettiness, the gossip . . . why do I miss it so much?"

You miss THEM, the people you worked with, in all their squirrelliness, their outrageousness, their ability to distract you, their . . . and you also miss their lovability. You are lonesome and tired of talking to yourself.

You also miss the levelling influence of others' opinions. When you have only yourself to talk to, you get away with being pretty rigid. You need to hear how others react to your thinking.

Isolation can be both social and professional. You want human contact and you want ideas. This is a problem that may drive you back to a regular job if you're not careful, but there are ways to deal with it.

Lock the refrigerator, I'm working at home now

Another dimension of being isolated is that you become less civilized. The office socialized you. You couldn't stuff your face too freely with people around . . . could you?? So you waited until you got home. Now you're already home. That's trouble. When you're working at home, there's less fear of humiliating yourself. You're a carnivore again, hunting and gathering midday Yodel snacks, pizza, cheese doodles, and tilling the soil for harvests of corn chips.

A related problem -- since these food gathering labors are taxing you well beyond the tepid office routine you were once accustomed to, you're sometimes so completely spent that you must collapse into a heap of sleep at odd hours. The bed beckons. Napping was good for Albert Einstein, so it certainly will increase your productivity.

Help, I'm caught in the spin cycle

So, you put a chain around the refrigerator, but the isolation continues to haunt you.

The benefits of office companionship were so automatic. All you had to do was show up. How do you recapture some of this cozy interaction so you don't suffer that most dreaded affliction of the solo practitioner -- "the washing machine of your mind," which comes from having only yourself to commune with? Have you ever hatched an idea one morning in the shower and then, as the day went on, you thought about it, and thought about it, and by nighttime your big idea was . . . *exactly* where it had been that morning? Your glorious idea just spun in the same rut endlessly and never got any more coherent, because you were talking exclusively to yourself.

As a one-person business, you must compensate for the lack of regular unplanned, random office contact in your life.

The practice of career counseling is isolating enough. Closed door, confidentiality, and all that. You don't want to compound the problem by having an exclusive diet of clients all day, every day. You need connections with friends and professional colleagues.

Things you can do about isolation

1. **Involvement in your profession.** Any professional groups that relate to career development are vital places for you to stay connected. Especially if you think "I've heard it all before." That's when you need the contact most.

You may find that 70% of the time you're covering old ground, but it's the other 30% that you need, the chance remarks in a hallway, the new book you hadn't heard about, the one new idea that changes your whole perspective, the laughter that you absolutely cannot get by yourself.

2. **Makeshift social groups.** When you work large periods of time by yourself or only with clients, you need human contact simply for its own sake, not for any overriding "purpose." Socializing is absolutely necessary. Create any reasons you can think of to get people together -- individuals reading the same book, an investment club, people who've been to Alaska, people who want to share business ideas, people who want to share recipes. Whether the purpose for meeting is deep or shallow -- get together.

3. **Friends as mentors.** One result of a single-person practice is that you have appointed yourself as your own mentor. However, you and other solo practitioners can mentor for each other. If you don't have someone other than you who makes observations about your career, gives you a place to ventilate, and offers you gentle advice from time to time, you may be lost in a house of mirrors.

4. **Do some of your own marketing.** One of the best ways to break out of your isolation is to have direct (and/or telephone)

contact with prospective clients. You may be doing this by necessity, and perhaps hating every minute of it, but it keeps you involved with the real world.

Marketing includes introducing yourself, chatting, listening, getting people's attention, accommodating to others, being patient, and putting up with folderol. Every one of these skills reminds you that you're not the center of the universe.

If you delegate a lot of your marketing to someone else, watch and listen to what she does, go along on some of the sales calls, and ask her for feedback when you do the marketing contacts.

Your Uncle Howard will make you a promise. Do ten marketing calls in the next two weeks, and even if you get zero business from them, I promise something good will happen -- you'll hear about an exciting program, get some financial advice, track down an old friend, learn about a new business in town -- something will happen that will make you glad you called.

Isolation is not good for anyone. It will stunt your growth. It will also creep up on you when you're not looking. You're so busy "getting things done" that you have many days when your only conversations are strictly functional, no exchanges of ideas, no laughing, no altering your opinions about anything. Those are bad days.

Isolation can affect you negatively in two ways:

• **Social malnourishment.** No laughter, interchange of ideas, eating together, or meaningless conversations not only make you a dull boy or girl; this condition leaves you wanting to play when there's work to be done.

• **Professional decay.** Without the ideas of others, your own ideas will wither. Everyone sees things differently. You cannot float an idea and expect it to be clear if you haven't already bounced it off many other people. I'm talking about conversations with colleagues including not only serious discussions, but also casual reactions, serious joking, and "here's what I think of that."

Counselors who isolate themselves see life in narrow terms. When all you hear are career stories, everything looks like a transferable skill.

Face-to-face contact is fundamental

E-mail and all that may help to reduce isolation, especially when time, money, and energy limit your travels. Nonetheless, too much cyber-contact and telephone talk are weak substitutes for face-to-face interaction.

Electronic contact is fun, but no substitute for looking another counselor in the eye and saying:

"I don't agree with your ideas about how to handle a panel interview. Now here's what I think . . ."

Sure, this discussion can take place via computer, but face-to-face is more electric than electronic, and friendships are more likely to develop.

One day a scientific study will reveal that professional isolation makes you more opinionated, more grouchy, less responsive to rock and roll, and more likely to eat weird cereals. The longer you hide in your home, the more wax will grow in your ears, until you don't hear anyone at all.

The more your work keeps you at home, the more you need to get out of your home. Remember that prisoners are isolated as a most severe form of punishment.

Ever wonder why people pay $7 apiece (or $28 for a family of four) to see a movie they could rent a month later for a dollar? You want to experience the movie with other people. And you don't even see or know these people at all!

You are a social animal, and so is everyone else. Reap the many benefits of having a solo practice, but don't let your happiness or productivity be compromised by isolation.

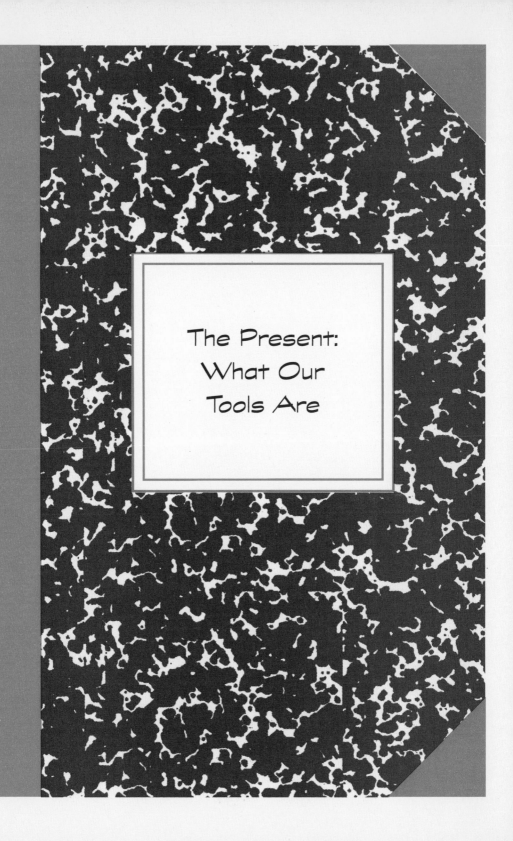

The Present:
What Our
Tools Are

CHAPTER 12

How to Do
1-2-3 Career Counseling

by Howard Figler

The themes that are present in all of career counseling are captured in three questions. An effective counselor weaves these themes together as though a fine string trio were playing in the background:

> 1. What do you want to do?
> 2. What is stopping you from doing it?
> 3. What are you doing about it?

Much of the counselor's art is her ability to stay close to these themes and not be sidetracked. By insisting patiently that the client answer these questions, the counselor is encouraging the client to take responsibility for her situation, and indicating that she has plans of action available to her. Any situation, no matter how muddy or difficult, can be forged into movement toward a goal.

Career counseling moves back and forth among these three questions. Progress in each one provides greater clarity for the other two. The counselor may pose each question again and again, because the client changes his answers as the counseling moves along. These three questions get to the heart of the matter.

Is career counseling "as easy as 1-2-3"? Not hardly. On the contrary, these questions confront clients with the complexity of their motivation, their struggle to keep themselves on track, the effort required to stay focused, the various motivations that confuse them, and the subtleties of understanding who they really are. 1-2-3 career counseling urges each client to acknowledge her strongest drives and put her actions where her heart is.

When clients follow this structure, they grow more comfortable with making their own decisions, because they are defining their problems and gathering data toward solving them. Clients may bounce among 1, 2, and 3 many times in order to explore their career possibilities. In doing so, they exercise their career development muscles. It is this very repetition that enables them to grow stronger and feel more confident in their choices of direction.

Let's take a look at how 1-2-3 career counseling works:

1 "What do you want to do?"

Endless numbers of clients will say "I don't know what I want. I don't have a clue." The counselor realizes that "I don't know" often means "I don't know for sure, forevermore." So she encourages the client to "talk about any fleeting career ideas you've had that you might consider, if you could."

The counselor might also say: "It's OK to talk about your thoughts, even though they're unclear or unformed."

The art of the question is that you can be there with the client even when you're not there. The counselor's questions linger while the client is mowing the lawn or driving in the mountains:

- What are some of the best things you've ever done and what do these suggest you need to do next?
- How has your work been different from what you've wanted it to be?
- What have you not yet done in your life that you really must do?
- Who are you as compared to who people think you are?
- What kinds of work feed your sense of purpose?

Talking about your vague career ideas is the first step toward getting stronger. The client recognizes that it's OK to experiment with career possibilities without knowing exactly what they are.

Clients are encouraged to investigate several career options at the same time. As they answer Questions 2 and 3 several times, they will discover which of these possibilities have staying power.

These days clients or their counselors may protest that "pursuing one's dream" is unrealistic. Tell that to Beethoven, Walt Disney, Emily Dickinson, Mary Kay Ash, and many other highly successful people who persisted with their dreams even though they were discouraged by many around them. Dreams don't unfold all at once. They may develop in fits and starts, including failures and periods of uncertainty. Clients must always be urged to continue the pursuit of what they're most enthusiastic about, because enthusiasm is what helps people overcome their obstacles.

2 "What's stopping you?"

For every stated career possibility, there is at least one rock or boulder in its path. Clients must be invited to talk about these obstacles. Often we call them "Yes, Buts." By describing these obstacles, clients give them shape, so they can deal with them. Clients may overstate the problems, but it's not the counselor's job to judge the accurate size of the boulders. That will happen later in Reality Testing.

Much of the discussion in career counseling will focus on "Why I believe it will be difficult for me to achieve this goal." The counselor's role here is to help the client unearth the problems and clarify them. The client should be encouraged patiently to reveal the very worst of his Yes, Buts, the problems that are most threatening and seemingly intractable.

"I'd like to own a flower shop, but I don't have any business skills, I don't have floral design talent, and my knowledge of flowers is sadly lacking." The counselor might be tempted to send such a person away, looking for a different career.

However, the key question is "How motivated is this client toward the flower business?" If he really wants to do it, he can acquire the business skills, and the knowledge of flowers and design. That's why we have step # 3.

Discussing Yes, Buts may seem like wallowing in the mud of one's indecision, but in fact it is quite often very helpful. The client may be clarifying her obstacles for the first time. Often she begins to develop possible solutions spontaneously as she identifies her Yes, Buts.

People come to career counselors because of their Yes, Buts. They fear the obstacles may be insurmountable. They need to talk about these fears and anxieties and have them understood. Half the battle in dealing with a Yes, But is defining it. This is letting the beast out of the hole so you can look at it. The other half is deciding what to do about it.

Sometimes a client uses a Yes, But as an excuse for not admitting that he's really not motivated enough to pursue a particular goal. That's why we have Reality Tests.

3 "What are you doing about it?"

Reality Testing allows clients to see how far their motivation will carry them. There are two ways that a person can respond to a "Yes, But" -- Reality Tests, Types A and B.

Reality Test Type A. How accurate is my perception of the problem? How can I get better data? For example, if you think you can't be a dental hygienist because you believe you don't have enough manual dexterity, take some courses where you can test your present skills against others.

Regarding Type A Reality Tests, people are usually very hard on themselves when they estimate how they stack up versus the competition, and they often base their self-judgments on small samples of information:

"I'd probably have to be a math whiz to be a real estate appraiser. How do I know? Uncle Harry told me."

As it happens, Uncle Harry is off-base, even though he likes to sound as though he knows everything. Math skills are important in real estate appraising, but not overwhelmingly so, and these skills are learnable.

More accurate information is available, but the client needs to be urged to get it.

Reality Test Type B. If Type A reality testing shows that I have less skill than I need, what can I do to improve my situation, to begin overcoming the obstacle? In the dental hygienist example above, the courses may improve my skill. In addition, I may find volunteer experiences in dental clinics or go to a dental school and ask their advice. Some dental school applicants practice by carving chalk.

One or more Reality Tests can be developed for any "Yes, But." Our aspiring flower shop owner can talk to such owners to see if prior experience is required. If so, she can work as a volunteer in their stores, take courses in flower design, and build the necessary skills.

Most everything in life has a learning curve attached to it, but does the client have the energy and drive to climb it? If a client says he's not sure he's good enough to do a certain job, then let him observe this job, read about it, and experience it firsthand before passing judgment on himself. It is usually possible to find temporary, part-time, or volunteer work, so that you can jump on the learning curve and discover how far you can and want to go.

Motivation and ability are both required to do a job. How much of each is necessary? Every case is different. A client should not be too quick to rule herself out on the basis of ability, because further experience may change her view.

Are there any situations when a counselor should tell a client: "You don't have enough ability to go into that field"? No, because: (1) The client can find out better through firsthand experience; (2) clients learn more about themselves by failing and then deciding how they're going to respond to these setbacks; and (3) often people seek one goal and then find another. By working toward one desirable goal, the client may find a related goal that is appealing to her.

In most cases, people don't know how much they are capable of doing until they allow themselves a fair trial. Often they achieve far more than they thought they would. As many times as we've impressed that lesson upon our children and ourselves, we must relearn it.

Reality Testing is always available if you look hard enough. Want to be a theatre set designer? They'll take some free help. Want to be a retail store buyer? You can learn from them if you're willing to be a nonpaid intern. Bob Weinstein details in his excellent book, *I'll Work for Free* (Henry Holt, 1994) reasons why nonpaid work is a first-rate career strategy.

Clients are not limited to Reality Tests that are unpaid. Often you can get part-time paid jobs or temporary work in fields that interest you, to gain experience and improve your skills.

Reality Testing allows clients to make judgments from their direct experiences. By deciding for themselves, they become stronger and learn that many things are possible, with focus and persistence.

Karen wants to be a book editor at a major publishing house. However, these jobs are very competitive and Karen is light on experience, skills, and contacts. Her reality tests include volunteer, part-time and eventually full-time work at smaller, less prestigious publishers, first as a proofreader, then as a copy editor, then finally as an editor. Karen does well in these positions and continues to like working with books. Eventually, she makes a contact at a major publisher in New York and gets her coveted job.

It could have gone a different way for Karen. She might have become disenchanted with book editing and taken her editorial skills to apply for a research job in the health industry, where she would edit research publications. Learning to change direction can also be part of the career development process.

Almost any Yes, But can be translated into one or more Reality Tests. Thus, there is a strategy for dealing with most any problem. The reality tests cannot assure success, but they give all clients ways to take constructive action toward their goals.

Little Joan Benoit said: "I want to be a runner, but I'm too small, I'm very unathletic, I'm from the far-out state of Maine, and I'm very shy." But she thought she'd try. So Joan ran and she ran some more. And some more. Until finally Joan was seen circling the track at the Los Angeles Coliseum in 1984, winner of the first Olympic Marathon for women. Her reality tests had overcome her Yes, But's.

The 1-2-3 sequence is a structure for taking charge of oneself. First, you give yourself permission to talk about those very tentative thoughts that you have inside you. Then you shape the problems that you feel stand in your way. Finally, you learn how big or small those problems really are, and how much energy you want to devote to overcoming them. This process allows anyone to take full responsibility for their career decisions. The client is active and involved and grows stronger with each cycle through the 1-2-3 process.

CHAPTER 13

How to Use
Career Assessment Tools

by Howard Figler

Once upon a time someone got the idea that you could ask people several questions about themselves and use the resulting information to direct them in their career choices. Whether interests, abilities, values, or other personal attributes are measured -- this has come to be known as "career assessment." Clients eagerly ask for it, counselors like to dispense it as morsels of revealed wisdom, and test publishers keep the pipeline filled.

There are, however, a few flies in this soup known as career assessment. First of all, tests don't mean as much as people think they do. Everybody wishes they meant a lot, and would love it if they really could forecast your "one right career." But there's less here than meets the eye.

We have enough anecdotal evidence to tell us that test results are often far off the mark and sometimes even laughable. Ever ask your friends what their test profiles were in school? "Yeah, mine said funeral director." "Mine said lawyer and I hate em!" "Mine said social worker and I have voted Republican ever since."

Do you want your career future decided by how you answer a small set of questions that have a dubious connection to career outcomes? Moreover, do you want your future career influenced by *any* method that has questionable validity?

What would have happened if Emily Dickinson, Lee Iacocca, and Carl Sagan received test profiles which did not fit their career aspirations?

"Carl, your profile points towards artistic careers, but stargazing is not high on your chart. I don't even know if it's on our list."

Test results imply that the high scores are where the person is more likely to be satisfied and successful. However, predictive validity studies seldom appear in test manuals, and there is hardly ever a study which shows significant prediction of career outcomes. All concerned -- client, counselor, and agency administrator -- assume that the tests are scientifically justified. Otherwise why would publishers make them available? Because people buy them.

Career counselors guide a process of self-examination, an exploration that has been underway in the client's life for years and will continue after counseling is done. Testing is an unnecessary and distracting sideshow in the counseling process, because test results compete with the client's understanding of herself.

We have fallen into a morass regarding career assessment, one that limits the career development of the individual. Assessment is largely defined by standardized testing, and it has many problems that work against the goals of career counseling. Practitioners have been unable to see farther than the horizon of testing and continue to ignore or minimize these problems.

What assessment needs most is an overhaul, a reconception of assessment that goes well beyond testing, so that it will promote the client's growth in more positive ways. This chapter will define (a) the ways that assessment must be reconceptualized, (b) the problems of testing that make it a negative force in career development, and (c) an approach to assessment that is more constructive.

A Broader View of Career Assessment

1. **The whole cannot be predicted from the sum of the parts.** No matter how much we ask questions, prod, poke, and gather data from an individual, the resulting scores will

not "add up" to the "right career choice" for that person. Career choice resists any such microscopic analysis. You cannot say that because an individual has specific skills, values, or interests that this suggests careers where he should look first. The right to decide a career direction must be reserved for the individual alone.

Tests are useful to help administrators select employees or place people in training programs, but they are not equal to the complex task of forecasting an individual's working future.

Do you want to find out what kind of careers people are really excited about? Ask them. They may not know *why* they want these careers, but they want them nonetheless.

2. **Initial career choice is overemphasized.** We have innocently assumed that, if a person makes a choice of career that seems to fit herself well, everything will go swimmingly after that. This assumption is off target, for two reasons: (a) Career choice is an ongoing process, not a one-time decision. The individual evolves, making subtle or dramatic changes in "career choice" every year. (b) Once the person decides a career direction, her career development has just begun. At this point, she must learn what the market will require of her, the skills she must acquire, how the market is changing, and what the market demands from successful people in that field.

Thus, when the client leaves with some career ideas that point her in particular directions, her "assessment" (which should be "self-assessment") is just beginning. Career success depends far more on later developments than upon the initial choice.

3. **Assessment must be future-oriented rather than stuck in the present.** This is perhaps the greatest disservice that testing often does to clients. Test results imply that "we have measured who you are; this is it, don't expect to change very much." Deliberately or unwittingly, test givers create the impression that test results are static. This is destructive from the client's point of view.

Often the client will not question test results, but will go home thinking: "Well, I guess that's it. I have to accept who I am." Once people accept test results as "genetic," they may lose hope of ever changing.

"I guess I'm just not a numbers person."

"I'd like to be a business owner, but I'm not a natural salesperson."

"I didn't score high on 'artistic.' I guess I'm not cut out for that."

This static view of test results tends to defeat the theme of optimism that is so vital for our clients. By contrast, the future-oriented counselor can foster hope, the belief that the client can acquire new skills, gain new knowledge, and grow into the kind of (career) person that she wants to become. It is this hope that helps a client's career development to thrive.

Ask yourself: *"How much better am I at certain skills today than I was when I was 18?"* This will give you a telescoped appreciation for any person's potential for growth.

For example, suppose that Anthony wants to be a newspaper journalist but tests have shown he's not good with words. However, he has enough drive that he's willing to mount a program to improve his writing skill. We cannot predict whether Anthony will progress enough to get a news reporter job, but what's important is that his counselor encourages him to strive for it, to assume that he can acquire new skills and that the goal is possible.

Assessment must ask the client: *"How do you want to be different tomorrow, so your career goals are more likely to come true?"*

The Problems with Testing

When the term "testing" is used here, it refers only to those standardized instruments designed to suggest or recommend that certain occupations or broad career areas are more likely to be successful and satisfying for the client. The tests most widely used for this purpose include the Strong Interest Inventory, the Campbell Interests and Skills Survey, the Self-Directed Search, and the Myers-Briggs Type Indicator.

There are many purposes for which standardized tests can be used, including personnel selection and placement in educational programs. The following discussion does not refer to those purposes. It is focused on the misuse of tests in an effort to assist one in making a career choice. In that regard, there are many problems with testing:

1. The Fortune-Teller syndrome.

People are only too willing to submit themselves to someone who will "tell me who I am and what I should do with my life." Many people cannot resist taking tests wherever they find them -- in magazines, school counselors' offices, private testing firms, etc. -- in the hope that someone will magically reveal their hidden potential. People want to discover their futures and they believe that anyone except themselves can tell them about it.

2. Testing encourages clients to be dependent.

Every principle of career counseling is designed to help clients become more self-reliant. Yet testing increases the very thing counselors are working so hard to eliminate -- dependence. The clients depend on the counselor to explain the meaning of test results so they will know what to do.

Counselors say that tests are "harmless." I say baloney. Despite counselors' valiant attempts to explain the limits of testing, too many clients look upon test results as though they were handed down from Mount Olympus -- a verification of who they are.

Worse yet, tests may discourage clients from pursuing fields of work where they have genuine interest. Once tests are given and scored, the cow is out of the barn. Counselors may not be able to help clients who decide to de-select themselves.

3. Testing gives the counselor a cloak of false authority.

"Come my child, let me introduce you to the mysteries of career testing." It is tempting to be authoritative. It feels good when clients think you know something. Tests, with all their squiggles, charts, and scores, may look to the client as though the career counselor really knows a lot.

The client wants to find out who she is. The counselor wants to tell her. Neither counselor nor client cares to examine too critically what the tests mean and don't mean, because the counselor wants to be knowledgeable and the client wants her authority.

Test givers may use the charts and data as a substitute for dealing with the complexities of the person. However, I encourage the counselor to give up the empty authority of tests so that clients can develop their own power by trusting their internal judgment.

When clients say: "Tell me who I am," the temptation to be "authoritative" can be very seductive. Some clients ask a counselor to narrow down the vast range of occupations to a manageable number. So, what could be wrong with helping point the client in a certain direction? It seems harmless enough, "just to get them started," "to give the client some options to talk about," "to give them something to react to."

I don't for one minute believe it. Clients who are offered shortcuts in the guise of professional expertise are being led away from themselves. A client's wisdom lies within, not from answering a bunch of questions that are far removed from their longings, passions, and complex inner musings. A key role of the counselor is to lead the client back home, to understandings of themselves that have always been there, but got buried or lost for one reason or another.

4. Clients believe that tests have high validity.

Clients often believe tests have the power to predict their futures. Career counselors can do all the hemming and hawing they want about the limitations of the tests; but clients may not hear them. Test profiles are designed to look as though they have much validity. How is a naive client to know otherwise?

5. Tests show little predictive validity, yet this is what they infer. A test profile looks scientific and science is seductive. When it shows that a person "ranks high" in certain occupational or career areas, the implication is clear -- that these areas are where she's more likely to be successful in the future. That's why the client took the test in the first place -- in the hope that she could get her fortune told. However, test manuals seldom ever show any predictive validity data.

6. Testing is a crutch for the counselor.

The counselor can lean on the independent presence of the test profile and use it to provide "direction," thus taking less time to help the client define herself in direct conversation. Tests are time-efficient. They can be given without the counselor being present. Tests offer a structure that looks "professional." The structure creates the impression of closure. The client believes she has "gotten the treatment" instead of recognizing that her career exploration has just begun.

7. Testing undermines the development of the career counseling profession.

Career counseling is dedicated to helping clients become more self-reliant and empowered. Testing, because of the dependence that it encourages in clients, flies in the face of this counseling mission. As long as counselors use tests, they will be relying on external means to "tell clients who they are." Such external assessments reduce the clients' ability to take responsibility for defining themselves.

I advocate not using tests at all in career counseling, because they are likely to have a negative effect on any client's career development, for the reasons described above.

It is difficult to use tests in moderation. The dramatic presence of a test profile tends to dwarf other methods, because such profiles look so "expert" to the client. Clients' belief in the analytical powers of computers adds to this mystique.

Career counselors, recognizing the limitations of inferences they can make from tests, usually claim that they use test results judiciously, so that clients are not misled. However, their defenses of testing are questionable. Here are some of the most frequent statements that counselors use to support testing:

- *"It's just one more piece of information."*

Clients don't look at test results this way. They view a test profile as unlike anything else that a counselor can produce. The all-at-once quality of a test profile grabs the client's attention immediately and often dominates his view of himself. By contrast, the client acquires self-understanding during counseling on a gradual basis.

- *"I explain all the limitations of the tests."*

Sure, and the clients' eyes glaze over while you're saying all this. Clients lack the sophistication to understand the inferences of complex statistical data. They're more likely to go for the simple interpretation: "The tests are telling me that I should go into human services or law, and that I'm not cut out for journalism or accounting."

- *"It's just a tool."*

No matter how the counselor uses the "tool," it's something that is happening *to* the client, rather than something the client is making happen herself. And as I pointed out earlier, there are too many counselors and clients who believe that tests have predictive powers far beyond what test manuals can support.

Test publishers have a **financial stake in** continuing to sell their products. Consider the thousands, perhaps even millions, of people who have taken career tests and you can estimate the amount of money that is represented by the testing industry.

Career counselors also have a financial incentive to continue using **tests in their practices**. Many clients ask for tests and regard the counselor as competent if she has a"battery of tests" available. Testing enhances the opportunities to sell one's services to clients. In the big picture, however, testing is undermining the marketing of career services because clients are discouraged from thinking for themselves. Dependent clients are ultimately dissatisfied clients.

Counselors, clients, and test publishers have joined arms to view assessment from a limited perspective. By force of habit, everyone continues with this narrow view, because there has been no larger picture of what assessment might be. The rest of this chapter will introduce an approach to assessment which better serves the career development needs of the client.

The client decides the direction

In this new approach, assessment is not done in the traditional manner, where tests or other data are used to predict, suggest, or otherwise predispose a client to certain fields of work.

Instead, the client is asked directly: "What do you think you'd like to do?" If the client says: "I don't know," the counselor engages the client in a discussion about her past daydreams and life experiences which eventually lead the client to propose career ideas for herself. The counselor asks such questions as:

- *What do you feel instinctively that you ought to look into?*
- *Which careers keep coming back to your mind?*
- *Which careers are you really curious to know more about?*
- *If you could have a magic wand and get to try any career you wanted for a year, which would it be?*

A fuller discussion of this method of career counseling is given in the chapter of this book entitled "How to Do 1-2-3 Career Counseling."

A new model of assessment

In the following structure, the client takes maximum responsibility for his career by: (1) exploring and reality testing the careers that interest him most; and (2) developing a strategy for learning the skills, attitudes, and knowledge required to succeed in a given career.

The client's assessment is ongoing. As her goals change or the market needs shift, the client assesses the skills, attitudes, and knowledge that she must acquire correspondingly. Once the client has identified a tentative career direction, here is the main question that career assessment is designed to answer:

"What does the client need to be successful in this kind of work?"

The client does research to identify what is required by the market for successful performance in her chosen field:

- skills required
- attitudes required
- knowledge required

The assessment profile

On the next page is an abbreviated example of a growth-oriented assessment profile. Based on her field research, the client can "assess" herself on a 1-to-10 scale for all the skills, attitudes, and knowledge required to be a journalist. The client rates herself by asking former teachers, employers, and others to give her feedback on how well she fits these attributes.

She then decides, once again based on her research, which of these she needs to improve in order to increase her chances in this career. The counselor helps her by looking at the "profile" of "strengths" (high self-ratings) and "gaps" (low self-ratings) and asking questions such as:

Which of these strengths or gaps do you believe are most important for Journalism?

Which of these do you want to work to improve?

Where do you believe you need further reality testing?

Career Assessment Profile[1]

Name _____

Date _____

10 = I have enough of this skill, knowledge, or attitude to be successful
     in this career
1 = I have none of the skill, knowledge or attitude needed in this career

Career Objective: Journalist

Key SKILLS needed in this career

Writing	1	2	3	4	5	6	7	8	9	10
Interviewing	1	2	3	4	5	6	7	8	9	10
_____	1	2	3	4	5	6	7	8	9	10

Key KNOWLEDGE needed in this career

_____	1	2	3	4	5	6	7	8	9	10
_____	1	2	3	4	5	6	7	8	9	10
_____	1	2	3	4	5	6	7	8	9	10

Key ATTITUDES needed in this career

Flexibility	1	2	3	4	5	6	7	8	9	10
_____	1	2	3	4	5	6	7	8	9	10
_____	1	2	3	4	5	6	7	8	9	10

1. The Career Assessment Profile was adapted from a presentation made by Betsy Collard and Howard Figler at the California Career Conference, Costa Mesa, CA, November, 1996.

The counselor helps the client's overall assessment by:

• Encouraging her to do field research to identify which skills, attitudes, and areas of knowledge are most important for her proposed career.

• Encouraging her to have a strategy for staying on top of what the market needs from successful performers.

• Teaching her how to gather feedback on her skills, attitudes, and knowledge from those who have observed her work.

The validity of this profile increases as the client collects more data about the skills, knowledge, and attitudes required in her intended career.

The counselor helps the client to gather data that will sharpen her understanding of the market and her ability to meet market needs. Thus, it's called the Career Assessment Profile. It is a continually updated map of the client's plan for pursuing a career.

CHAPTER 14

How to Use Occupational Forecasts

by Dick Bolles

When we look at the tools available to us as career counselors, one of our favorites is usually "Occupational Forecasts" -- predictions as to which occupations will need a lot of new workers, and which ones won't. These are often used by us to guide high school and college students, not to mention career-changers, when they ask us what occupations they should go into.

You will stumble across such forecasts in your local newspapers, or in magazines or in learned journals. They will look something like this (these are not current examples, so don't rush out):

Do you like selling? Good opportunities will exist for full-time, part-time and temporary employment in retail sales, due to growth of the field and high replacement needs. Openings are calculated at an average 190,000 annually.

Employment will increase faster than average in the metalworking industries, with 27,000 jobs opening each year in welding. Opportunities are rated excellent for skilled welders in nuclear power plants, pipeline and ship construction.

Prospects for engineering and science technicians are bright. The demand will come to 32,000 jobs a year in response to industrial expansion and the rising role of technicians in research and development.

While some private sources plus States and counties conduct their own occupational forecasts, most of the forecasts published in newspapers and magazines come ultimately from the following government sources:

• *Occupational Outlook Quarterly* (Superintendent of Documents, PO Box 371954, Pittsburgh, PA 15250-7954. Phone: 202-512-1800; fax: 202-512-2250, $8/yr domestic; $10/yr foreign)

• *Occupational Outlook Handbook* (BLS Publication Sales Center, PO Box 2145, Chicago, IL 69690. Phone: 312-353-1880, $42, paper; $28, CD-ROM)

• *Occupational Projections and Training Data* (BLS Publication Sales Center, PO Box 2145, Chicago, IL 69690. Phone: 312-353-1880, $6.50)

• *Employment Outlook* 1996–2006 (BLS Publication Sales Center, PO Box 2145, Chicago, IL 69690. Phone: 312-353-1880, $8.50)

The Virtue of Occupational Forecasts

The idea of starting out with what the market wants is of course a commendable one. The world of education and the world of work are often two distant kingdoms. Too frequently, the world of education seems to operate totally without awareness of the kinds of workers actually needed in the world of work. In a typical year, we may see colleges, universities and training facilities cheerfully turning out 150,000 graduates in a particular field, nationwide, when all the market has room for is 20,000 graduates in that field.

In a kind of perverse variation on the 1989 film, *Field of Dreams,* the colleges' motto often seems to be, "If we train you, employers will come." Ah, the heartbreak, when they don't, and a college grad can't find any jobs in the field for which he or she was trained.

Occupational forecasts are, therefore, an attempt we may applaud -- to bridge the gap between the world of education and the world of work, to get those two worlds talking to each other, and to introduce a healthy dose of realism into dream courses on college campuses.

But there are problems. There are problems with occupational forecasts that every career counselor should be painfully aware of, before we try to steer students or older career-changers into fields that the forecasts say are golden.

The Defects of Occupational Forecasts

1. **The source of the information is often biased.** Clearly, the Bureau of Labor Statistics is not in a position to know the future needs of every occupation, or every industry there is. Consequently, researchers from the BLS have to turn to coordinating councils of one type or another, and to leaders in that industry, in order to find out what the picture is for that industry down the road.

Now, suppose you are the leader that the BLS turns to, and you believe that 170,000 additional workers are going to be needed in your industry in the next ten years. Will you tell the BLS that figure? What if you are in error? What if there turns out to be a need for 70,000 more workers than you thought? You will have a bad shortage on your hands. Shortages are anathema. They drive wages up. The other leaders in your industry will roast you.

So, what do you do? Well, naturally, you "over-guess" a bit. Or a lot. And down the road a piece, if a few thousand extra job-hunters are attracted to your industry because of your over-forecast, and they then can't find jobs, well, no harm done. No harm, for you at least, in a surplus of workers. Surpluses are desirable. They drive wages down. The other leaders in your industry will salute you.

And thus we see that all forecasts depend upon people who are ultimately advocates for the employer, not advocates for the job-hunter.

And thus we see that occupational forecasts serve the needs of employers well; they do not necessarily serve the needs of job-hunters. Unless they are taken with a grain, nay a barrel, of salt.

2. There is a time lapse built into all forecasts. Let us depict the situation in a particular industry by a pendulum:

A SHORTAGE OF WORKERS   A SURPLUS OF WORKERS

The pendulum, for most occupations, is continually moving, swinging between shortage and surplus, between surplus and shortage. The only imponderable is how fast it is moving, or how slowly.

Now, let us suppose that for a particular occupation the pendulum is in the position shown above, at the time that the government is gathering the raw data for its forecasts. Naturally, when the forecast is published for that occupation, it will talk about this shortage. Aha! the job-hunter thinks, a field in which there is a golden opportunity!

But we must remember the pendulum keeps moving, in this case from left to right. It may have moved only slightly, because its movement is slow. Or it may have moved quite a bit, because the situation in that field is changing rapidly and people are already flocking to it. In any event, the government publishes its data based on the diagram above; but *by the time it has gotten into print*, the actual situation may be more like this:

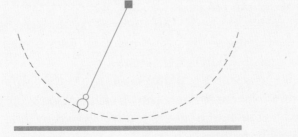

A SHORTAGE OF WORKERS   A SURPLUS OF WORKERS

High school or college students, not to mention career-changers, will of course think the picture is still as depicted in the first diagram, and choose that field. It will, however, take the high school senior or the college freshman some four or more years (in many cases) to finish getting trained for that occupation.

By the time their training is completed, and they are ready to seek a job in that field, the pendulum will have kept moving -- sometimes dramatically -- so the situation by the time they get there may actually be this:

A SHORTAGE OF WORKERS   **A SURPLUS OF WORKERS**

And they feel betrayed.

Compilers of occupational forecasts are, of course, acutely aware of this timelapse between data-gathering, data-publishing, and completed training. They try to deal with it by making three sets of assumptions -- low, moderate and high -- and by making their forecasts really long-range. But sad to say, like weather forecasts, the longer the occupational forecast, the more unreliable it is likely to be.

One career counselor I know likes to take old occupational forecasts from ten years previous and show them in an overhead to her students. The students laugh, because they can see for themselves that the forecasts often turned out to be widely (even wildly) off the mark.

3. **Forecasts don't actually know what the supply will be.** All forecasts are, of necessity, based not only on future demand, but on future supply -- a teensy-weeny little factor that is usually overlooked.

To illustrate, an occupation which was forecast to have the following pattern, would look like an excellent one for college students and career-changers to go into:

DEMAND

1st year	2nd year	3rd year	4th year	5th year
200,000	220,000	250,000	300,000	350,000

But suppose we toss in the missing ingredient, the supply of those who actually end up training for this occupation, then the prospects for this occupation are not so hotsy-totsy:

DEMAND

1st year	2nd year	3rd year	4th year	5th year
200,000	220,000	250,000	300,000	350,000

SUPPLY

190,000	215,000	270,000	330,000	390,000

As you can see, in the fourth and fifth year, at least, supply will far outstrip demand.

I came across an example of this, as far back as twenty-five years ago. I quote it without comment:

Money Magazine, January 1977: "Losers of the year (1976) in starting jobs: Architects, who are lucky to get a job, since there are nearly three new architects for every opening in architectural firms."

Occupational Outlook Handbook (same year): "Employment opportunities for architects are expected to be favorable through the mid-1980s. Several thousand openings will occur annually due to very rapid growth of the profession. . . ."

4. **Finally, forecasts make no allowance for different job-hunting behaviors.** *The Occupational Outlook Handbook* usually has the following kind of caveat (not often read by career counselors and coaches):

"The prospect of relatively few job openings should not prevent someone from pursuing a particular career . . . Even in occupations with relatively poor prospects, jobs are available because of the need to replace workers who leave the occupation. . . . "

Which is to say, there are openings for every kind of job in the world. All that forecasts actually do is *define the degree of competition.* Are there two people competing for every vacancy in a particular field? Three people? Ten? A hundred? That's all that forecasts really tell you: the degree of competition, according to the following table:

Demand much greater than supply	= Excellent job opportunity
Demand greater than supply	= Very good job opportunity
Rough balance between demand and supply	= Good job opportunity
Likelihood of more supply than demand	= May face competition
Supply greater than demand	= Keen competition

Career counseling has a rule, which no one should ignore: **the keener the competition, the more important is the manner in which the job-hunter looks for a job in that field or occupation.**

"Keen competition" does not mean job-hunters should avoid that occupation. It only means they need to place less emphasis on 'the traditional job-hunting method' -- resumes, ads, and agencies -- and more emphasis upon 'the creative method of the job-hunt' -- identifying their favorite skills, doing lots of informational interviewing, using their contacts to get in to see the-person-who-has-the-power-to-hire, showing that person how that job-hunter's skills can help the employer with their challenges and tasks.

Different job-hunting behaviors lead to very different results. People who follow the creative method are usually able to find jobs even in fields or occupations where the competition is fierce, and where their job-hunting compatriots who used only resumes, ads or agencies, are striking out.

Properly thought of, therefore, occupational forecasts are not directions about which field to go into. We should encourage students and career-changers to go into any field that interests them. All forecasts actually do is warn them about which job-hunting method they will need to use, if they choose that field.

CHAPTER 15

How to Use Information*
in Career Counseling

by Howard Figler

Working is reaching for a small piece of immortality. We all want to contribute something of value and work is one way to do it. Career counseling is a conversation about the meaning that clients would like to have in their jobs and careers.

But clients don't know how to talk about "meaning." Instead, they may ask for descriptive data about one career or another. Such information will not answer their need to understand themselves. The unique quality of career counseling is the opportunity it gives clients to examine their vocational longings and related conflicts. Therefore, information giving must be only a minor part of the counseling process.

Many clients will be reserved in the counselor's presence and will expect to receive information. Career counselors presumably "know all about the vast and unfathomable job market." Clients who believe that will sit back and listen, especially if the counselor holds forth about "where the jobs are." The client assumes: "Well, I guess she knows what she's talking about, so I'd better take in all that I can."

Because there is so much information in the world of work, and clients have so little of it, counselors often feel their information giving is justified.

There's a certain compulsive itch the counselor may feel he must scratch: "I can't let them leave without telling them this . . ." As though we have been derelict in our duty if we

---

* The term "information" here refers to data about the external world -- the labor market and job search processes. It does not refer to internal information which the client generates about herself.

don't deliver every piece of data we know that might somehow be helpful. This kind of compulsive worrying is nonproductive. A counselor's job is not to tell everything he knows.

Clients are often looking for the magic formula which will tell them what career to enter so they'll be happy forever after. This makes it tempting for counselors to offer their opinions regarding the labor market and how a client might match the opportunities available.

Information, in moderation, is useful. Too much information will undermine the counselor's primary role, helping the client to organize her thoughts and feelings toward constructive action. Counselors who give information for most of the counseling session may be taking a path of least resistance. The counseling dialogue is harder work.

The more a counselor views her role as an information giver, the less attention she pays to helping clients process their values, skills, interests, conflicts, and aspirations. In the extreme, information giving can degenerate into irresponsible advice giving:

"Since the counselor brought up those particular careers, maybe that's what she thinks I ought to go into."

Misuses of information in career counseling

• **"You have told me more about _____ than I wanted to know."** This is perhaps the most common problem. Where one piece of information is good, the counselor may think that five are that much better. And the client won't tell the counselor that he has gone too far.

• **"The information is OK, I guess, but it has nothing to do with my problem."** Tied for first as the top way that information is misused. Counselors sometimes believe that everyone wants or needs their information, and this overpowers their responsibility for listening to the client.

• **"I did not come here for a lecture."** Clients will often think this but not say it. "Being talked to" signals the client that maybe it's not OK to speak up. This happens more than you might think. The client doesn't like being spoon-fed, but he doesn't know how to resist it.

• **"The information you're giving me jars me. It makes me reconsider my career interests, and I'm not sure whether to do that."** Small items of information can have a strong impact upon a client, when given by an "expert," especially if they do not fit the client's previous image of a career field.

Each counselor acts as though his information is the best available, yet clients often get varying answers to the same information questions from different counselors. They can't all be right. As Howard Rosenberg, Associate Director of the University of Colorado Career Center and author of *How to Succeed Without a Career Path,* says: "Counselors should tell clients they're giving professional opinions, not facts."

Many of the information questions most frequently and eagerly asked are those having the most slippery, hard-to-agree-upon data -- salary ranges, "the hot jobs," and the supply-and-demand outlook for given occupations.

Other cautions regarding information giving

1. **The labor market changes every day.** Though career counselors need to be generally well-informed about the labor market, it's unreasonable to ask them to be up-to-date on every specific field a person may want to know about. If your client wanted to become an expert player on the flugelhorn, should she expect you to know where all the best teachers are?

2. **The labor market must be specific to the client's needs.** If a client wants to know the latest technology in photographic research and how she can qualify for jobs in this area, she should not expect her counselor to know all about it. The counselor can help the client refine her search by pointing her to the sources she needs.

Some typical resources would include the *Occupational Outlook Handbook,* the *Internet,* the *Encyclopedia of Associations,* the

Chambers of Commerce and the State Occupational Information Coordinating Committee (in the state capital).

Clients must sample occupations broadly, talking with at least three to five people in each field of work, to avoid being overly influenced by the bias of a single individual.

3. **Client expectations.** Clients will often want to believe that the career counselor knows exactly where all the "hot jobs" are, and will urge the counselor to tell everything she knows. Many clients will encourage their counselors to focus the session on information giving:

"Tell me, what are the technical skills most in demand today?"

"What are the best jobs for liberal arts graduates?"

"What kinds of jobs are electrical engineers getting?"

A counselor may feel uncomfortable if he doesn't have detailed responses to such questions, so he may attempt an answer in order to keep the conversation going. But the counselor should not inflate what he knows in order to appear "authoritative."

4. **Communicating entry requirements for careers.** Career information in a counseling session is often focused on the entry requirements for a particular field or cluster of jobs. Counselors should give such information with caution, because:

• entry requirements are in a continual state of change

• the counselor doesn't want clients to eliminate themselves from a career based on her best guess about the entry requirements

• what look like "requirements" are sometimes only "preferences"; people are often accepted without having any or all of the entry criteria. For example, many journalists don't have a college degree in journalism.

• the typical experience of entry-level people may be only a general norm. For example, some enter the computer field without any prior experience. They use their general intelligence and analytical skills to "catch up" to those with a history of computer work.

Ways to use information during the counseling process

Information is best used during counseling on a selective basis. Here are some ways to use information appropriately as a part of the counseling dialogue:

1. **Turn information questions into self-discovery questions.** Ask the client what the information she's requesting means to her.

"What is your image of what you'd like public relations to be?"
"Why is biological engineering of interest to you?"
"What do you think you'd like about X-ray technology?"
"What do you want to know about forest ranger work
that is important to you?"

2. **Don't jump up and grab occupational reference materials unless absolutely necessary.** Information grabbing will interrupt the flow of a counseling dialogue. By stopping to look in a book, the emphasis is directed toward the resource and away from self-discovery.

3. **When the client requests detailed information, promise that you can direct them to the resources they need, but only after you know more about their career priorities and goals.** Provide the resources *after* the counseling session.

4. **Give small amounts of career information as needed.** For example, a client may say:

"I think I'd like public relations, but I'm not sure what it is." The counselor could respond: "Public relations involves representing a company to its customers and the public. Writing, speaking, and interpersonal skills are required."

5. **The counselor should "contract" with the client.** Once having presented some information, the counselor should recommend that the client get additional information on her own. The two would develop a "contract" in which the client agrees to do certain information gathering tasks in the weeks ahead.

6. **Correct clients' misperceptions of careers when they occur.** Often clients have incorrect information that may affect their interest in a career. For example, a student may think a person must have a business degree to get a job in the business world. The counselor can advise her that many non-business graduates are successfully employed in the private sector and tell her how to conduct information interviews with them.

7. **Some clients are intimidated by the information gathering process.** Ask them: *"What will it take to get you to do this, to overcome your inhibitions?" "How can I help you feel more comfortable with asking people for information?"*

8. **Reveal the limitations of your knowledge.** Let the client know that you only have a fraction of the information that she can get from resource libraries and the Internet, and from in-person information interviews. Also tell them your information is only your best recollection and may not be accurate. Otherwise, clients will often believe that you are a "walking encyclopedia of careers."

As Marcie Kirk of the University of California at Davis Career Center has said: "Counselors should emphasize the need for lifelong career exploration, due to the vastness of the world of work."

9. **Explain why you are limiting your information giving.** "I am avoiding giving you lots of information, because I'm more concerned that we talk about what information you want and how it fits your career aspirations. It's a better way to make use of our time."

10. **Beware of making chance remarks.**

"I don't really know of any wild and crazy accountants."

I tossed in that snippet of 'information' when I was talking to a client named Sharon, who was considering becoming a CPA. She giggled, but said nothing and let my comment pass. I was just trying to lighten up the proceedings. Unknown to me, something entirely different happened, and it was a function of my innocent remark.

What I thought was lightheartedness was serious business to Sharon. My stereotypical remark about accountants stuck with her. Here is what Sharon thought but did not say to me:

"I guess all accountants have zero personalities. Why would I want to spend my time with that bunch? I like to have some fun at work too. I'm sure I can find other places to use my abilities where there are people who do more than breathe and work."

My passing comment had pushed Sharon's career away from accounting. She looked around for other fields where she would be sure not to encounter "dull" people. Sharon landed in the world of financial high rollers -- investment banking. She had enough talent to be competitive and got a job on Wall Street. Two years later she was back to accounting and told me:

"These investment banker people are not for me. What I liked originally about accounting was its stability, orderliness, and predictability. And I have since found to my surprise a lot of accountants who are fun, and even a little crazy."

I try not to make innocent throwaway remarks during counseling anymore. Sharon's story is an example of how "information" can be misused by a career counselor. Counseling is not information giving and it should not be focused on that. When a client hears "information" in the counseling session, she may overinterpret it, because "the counselor said it."

CHAPTER 16

How to Use
Just One Hour

by Howard Figler

How would you counsel a person if they gave you only one hour of their time? You know they're not going to return. One hour. That's it. The client isn't on your calendar until three days from now. You have some time to think about it. You'll never see this person again. What would do the most good?

The counselor should ask: "What can one-to-one counseling accomplish that is unique, that cannot be done by other methods or resources? What is individual counseling best suited for?"

Some counselors might use the hour to dispense the highlights of what they know about the labor market. This would not be a constructive use of the time. Clients are not well-served when counselors try to answer impossible requests such as:

"Tell me where all the good jobs are and how I can get them."

It is regrettable to see a career counselor acting as though he knows exactly what markets have "top jobs" and big payoffs when it is nearly impossible to have this knowledge. It's far better for a client to do her own research than to depend on secondhand inaccurate information.

Furthermore, you don't want their focus to be on the "hot jobs or industries," because what certain employers want may not be what the client wants to give. Instead, you want the client's focus to come from his strongest motivations.

Therefore, in the one hour available, I vote for a few "Why" and "How" questions that help the person get in touch with herself. People often don't know why they make career choices.

They may do what others are doing or act for no reason at all other than to get on with life. Your job is to help clients hear their own voices. These kinds of questions will help:

• "Why do you want to work in the first place?" (besides 'to earn a living')
• "How would you evaluate the work you've done so far in your life? What would you want to do differently?"
• "Why have you decided to make a change in your career?"
• "How does your work relate to your non-work priorities?"
• "How do you build meaning into your work?"
• "What things are most important in your life and how can your choices of work support these?"

These are questions that relate to a client's work values. Not every client will want to answer these questions. So what? Ask them anyway. Part of the counselor's job is to stretch clients beyond their comfort zones. If you don't have this conversation with them, who will? Perhaps they'll even thank you later.

Should you play the question-asking sage in the only hour you have available, when the client may want "practical" help, such as job search strategies, resume critique, or referral to information sources? Practical, schmactical. The client can get these answers elsewhere -- from books, career resource centers, videos, computer resources, or other counselors/advisors.

If they want a resume expert, let 'em find someone else. If they want a job search instructor, this is not the place, because you only have an hour. Let's get to the core of things. It's a checkup for their souls. When people don't know *why* they're pursuing something, they usually mess up *how to do it*.

Some insist they would avoid work entirely if that were possible. It's only a "necessary evil," they say. I don't believe it. Even if the person had enough money available to "not work," he or she would still want to be active, involved, and useful to others. That would mean "working," regardless of the pay involved.

In these days of scrambling to make a living, it may sound "unrealistic" to seek purpose and meaning in one's work. As many who survived the Depression have said: "You get work where you can and you do what you have to do." Well, yes, but that doesn't mean ignoring purpose. Meaning and purpose have economic as well as spiritual payoffs. If you're committed to the "Why" of your work, you're far more likely to succeed and make money doing it.

Asking the big questions is fun. You never know what you're going to hear:

"I like tools. They don't come to work late, they don't talk back, and they don't hurt me as long as I respect them." (carpenter)

"I work to trade abuse with the customers. I never miss a comeback. I'm a woman with wit and I love it." (waitress)

"I'm tired of sneaking away from my job to shoot pool. I'm going to start a pool room that is right for families. No smoke, no seediness, no gambling. My pool emporium will be a work of art."

Fine and dandy to ask the searching questions, but some clients are just not up for philosophizing. It either bores them or mystifies them, because they just don't think that way. Nonetheless, a career counselor can always focus on work values, even when the client is not conscious of it.

"Don't get all deep on me now. I just came here to get some help finding a job."

"Well OK, I can steer you toward books that will give that kind of help, but while we're talking, just tell me what you think about working in general."

"I think it's the pits."

"Then what would you like to do instead?"

"Find a job with flexible hours where the bosses don't lie to you all the time."

"What's important to you about flexible hours?"

"I don't want to be tied down to a strict schedule."

"How did lying become an issue for you in your recent work?"

"They never told me the same thing twice."

Having less time with the client may, paradoxically, allow you to do more good. Gurus on mountaintops are not available to see each individual for many sessions. They meet with you once, then you're on your own. So they pack a lot of meaning into each question. Similarly, career counselors can weigh a lot of meaning into the questions they ask. Less hands-on time with the counselor requires the client to take more responsibility and do more work on her own.

The counselor should probably consider using other skills during the one hour, such as task setting and identifying "Yes, Buts." However, the counselor should not waste precious time giving information since the client can get that elsewhere.

The best that a counselor can do for clients is to get them in touch with what drives them. Counselors don't motivate clients. They help them to work with what is already inside. A few well-placed questions and their responses fill an hour quite nicely. When clients answer questions about their root values, they stir the energy they will use throughout their career development.

CHAPTER 17

How to Use Group Work

by Dick Bolles

Good Career Counseling takes time. But sometimes we do not have the time. And, sometimes our clients don't have the time, either.

Therefore, since the early 1970s, Career Counseling has increasingly moved into group work -- via workshops or the classroom.

But often, even group work offers only limited time with clients, and we are perplexed as to what to try to cover.

It is, of course, difficult to give guidelines, because groups come in so many different sizes and shapes: their size may range from three couples, who meet in each other's homes on eight successive Sunday nights, to a full-semester course, taught for credit, on a college campus.

But despite the broadness of the category, some guidelines for group teaching do suggest themselves. Every mentor will of course offer different guidelines. We all have different prisms, through which we see the universe. My prism is affected by the perspective of *What Color Is Your Parachute?* (of course); and by my own experience of having led groups for well over 3,000 hours.

But if we understand that others may offer you very different guidelines, let me say that my experience is that there are four topics, basically, that need to be covered in a group setting. They are:

1. Introduction to the main problems in job-hunting or changing careers, and some outline of the main solutions to those problems -- followed, or preceded, by feedback designed to uncover what the concerns are, of each individual in the group.

2. What transferable skills, talents, or gifts, do you most enjoy using?

3. Where do you want to use them, in what field and place?

4. How do you identify places that interest you, and persuade the-person-who-has-the-power-to-hire-you that you are 'one in a million' for that job?

I have further learned that these four topics usually need to be given just about equal time (though the Introduction may be given less, if desired). It is useful to add up the total number of days or hours you will have with the group, divide that number by four, thus yielding some guidelines about the number of days or hours you should devote to each of the four topics.

Homework will have to be assigned, in most cases, because people are usually unwilling to meet in the group for the number of hours required to do this well. But, it is crucially important that exercises which are to be done a number of times, such as identifying skills out of stories you write, or doing informational interviews, you do at least one of each in the group, so that mistakes can be perceived early on, and triumphs rewarded, early on.

And what to do in the actual group meeting? Here are some *suggestions (only)* of what might be covered, for each of the four topics. *(In the following chart, "Student" refers to each member in your group, of any age, and not just to high school or college students.)*

1. Introduction

Objectives of This Unit for Job-Hunting:

To help each student understand:

• You will have to go about the job-hunt many times in your life.

• You therefore need more than mere services to help you with the job-hunt or career-change ahead; you need to master a process, so that you will be empowered to deal with all the times ahead, when you must job-hunt or change careers.

• There are two basic methods of job-hunting: the Neanderthal way (chapter 2 in *What Color Is Your Parachute?*) and
the creative method (chapters 3 and following).

• The virtues and defects of the Neanderthal job-hunt.

• The virtues and defects of the creative job-hunt; its virtues
are that it works for 86% of those who do it completely; its defects are that it requires work, self-discipline, and a lot of hard
thinking.

Implications for Life/work Planning:

To help each student understand:

• You are not a victim in life, you have the power to change
your life in whatever direction you choose.

• You cannot really *plan* your whole life, but you can *organize
your luck,* so that you are ready to take advantage of opportunities as they present themselves.

• A successful job-hunt and a successful life depend on always having alternatives -- a Plan A, and a Plan B -- in mind,
before you begin.

• You always have choices -- at least three options in every
case -- and the freedom to choose between them is the secret
of your power.

• You must choose your best option, as you see it, and give it
your best shot; but if you run into a dead end, switch to another plan, target, goal, method. Don't just keep doing more
of what didn't work in the past, for you.

Homework:

Students may be asked to:

• Read the pertinent material in the latest edition of *What
Color Is Your Parachute?* for each of these units, in turn (each
student should have their own copy, to help them in future
years as well as in this one).

• Go out and visit employment agencies, peruse newspaper
and Internet ads, to see the Neanderthal job-hunt in action.

Resources to Help You with This Unit:

What Color Is Your Parachute?

No One Is Unemployable by Debra L. Angel & Elisabeth E. Harney, 1997, available in bookstores, or from WorkNet Training Services, P.O. Box 5582, Hacienda Heights, CA 91745-0082, U.S.A. E-mail: worknetts@aol.com   Information about how to deal with "barriers" that people feel may keep them from ever getting employed. The book has an excellent "Encyclopedia of Barriers."

2. The Section on "What"

Objectives of This Unit for Job-Hunting:

To help each student understand:

• The key to finding a job, and finding one you love to do, lies in identifying your favorite transferable skills (verbs ending in *ing*).

• You probably don't know what your true and favorite skills are; a process for inventorying them is necessary. Trioing is the very best way to do this inventory (see the explanation of 'Trioing' at the end of this chapter).

• The key to enjoying your work lies not in the question "what skills do you have?" but in the question "out of all those which you have, which do you most enjoy?" Hence, once inventoried, your skills need to be reduced to your top ten *favorites*, in exact order of priority. A process for simplifying prioritizing is necessary.

Implications for Life/work Planning:

To help each student understand:

• In life, it is always useless to look back at the past before plotting one's future.

• In life, a list of anything is useless until it has been arranged in some order of priority. Since we have limited time and energy, we must apply it to the things which matter to us the most.

• It is important not only to set goals for your career, but also goals for your leisure time, and for your adult learning.

• Mastering the tools needed to make decisions about work (prioritizing, etc.) gives you tools for dealing with a lot of other decisions in life. That is, the tools -- like skills -- are transferable.

Homework:

In the group meeting, you will want to have each student write a story, then divide into trios to analyze each person's story for transferable skills.

If the group is meeting for many weeks, you should try to do more than one story and trio, in the group.

As homework, at home, each student should complete 5–7 such stories, meeting wherever possible with two other members of the group.

Resources to Help You with This Unit:

"The Flower" in the back of *What Color Is Your Parachute?* or: *The What Color Is Your Parachute Workbook.*

For additional help with the process of trioing, see the explanation at the end of this chapter -- which is based on page 69 in *Where Do I Go From Here With My Life?* by John C. Crystal and Richard N. Bolles, available from Ten Speed Press, Box 7123, Berkeley, CA 94707. Website: www.tenspeed.com/

3. The Section on "Where"

Objectives of This Unit for Job-Hunting:

To help each student understand:

• The transferable (functional) skills identified in the previous unit are transferable to any field you choose.

• The issue of 'where' is the issue of fields.

• It also requires you to deal with six different forms of that question:

where in terms of geographical preference;

where in terms of your preference for working with people, or things, or data/information;

where in terms of the kinds of people you would like to serve, help, or work with;

where in terms of the values you want your skills to serve;

where in terms of size of company or organization, their culture and working conditions;

where in terms of what level within that organization you want to work at: entry, boss, or somewhere in between (responsibilities and salary enter into this mix); the issue of self-employment gets treated here, as well.

• You must identify fields that interest you, from the foregoing, and then do Informational Interviewing, preceded by "A Practice Field Survey," to discover which priority those fields have for you.

• If you want/need/demand a shortcut, the best one is John Holland's RIASEC Theory of careers, using the SDS (Self-Directed Search) instrument or, when in a hurry, 'The Party Exercise' in *What Color Is Your Parachute?* -- as a way of focusing on possible careers that match the person -- employing the *Dictionary of Holland Occupational Codes,* after identifying one's 'Holland code.'

Implications for Life/work Planning:

To help each student understand:

• 'Where' highlights the issue of 'Place,' and 'Place' plays a very important part in determining the quality of your life, and your work.

• 'Conservation of your energy' will be necessary in your life, because you will never have enough time and energy to do all that you want to do; you have to be sure you expend it upon the most important things (to you). Hence the importance of prioritizing.

• Learning how to research *anything* through "The Practice Field Survey" can help you with many other tasks in life.

Homework:

Do the 'where' exercises in *The What Color Is Your Parachute Workbook* or "The Flower" in the back of *What Color Is Your Parachute?* You as leader should cover one or more of these exercises in the group, then leave the remainder for them to do as homework.

Have each student do a "Practice Field Survey," and then some "Informational Interviews" reporting back to the group about their experience.

Resources to Help You with This Unit:

The "Where" chapter in *What Color Is Your Parachute?* Also, *Where Do I Go From Here With My Life?* has additional exercises dealing with 'where.'

For more about "jobs as people environments," see *Making Vocational Choices: A Theory of Vocational Personalities and Work Environments, Third Edition,* by John L. Holland, 1997, available from Psychological Assessment Resources, Inc., P.O. Box 998, Odessa, FL 33556. Phone: 1-800-331-TEST. (They also have the SDS, and the *Dictionary of Holland Occupational Codes.*)

4. The Section on "How"

Objectives of This Unit for Job-Hunting:

To help each student understand:
• You do not wait for a vacancy to be advertised, but you go after any place that interests you.

• The question here is *how* do you get in to see the-person-who-has-the-power-to-hire-you, and persuade them you are 'one in a million'?

• There are different techniques for achieving this task, depending on whether it is a large organization or a small organization you are targeting. Contacts are the key in either case.

• The purpose of the first job interview at a particular place, is simply to be invited back for further interviews.

• Job interviews produce the most favorable reading of you, by the employer, when you talk half the time and the employer talks half the time.

• Thank-you notes, after each interview, are mandatory.

Implications for Life/work Planning:

To help each student understand:

• In accomplishing any work in life, your success depends upon finding allies -- people who share your enthusiasm, and can supply whatever you cannot: introductions, contacts, ideas, alternatives, etc.

• Talking to people successfully in life, is a matter of spending half the conversation on them, and half on you, 50–50.

Homework:

Have each student go out and try some of the techniques you are teaching them, while they are still meeting actively as a group.

Set up weekly meetings after the group has completed its studies with you, so they can exchange leads, information, contacts, etc., with each other.

Resources to Help You with This Unit:

The "How" chapter in *What Color Is Your Parachute?*

The Complete Job-Search Handbook (Revised & Expanded): All The Skills You Need to Get Any Job and Have a Good Time Doing It, by Howard Figler, Ph.D., 1999. Available from Henry Holt and Company, Inc., 115 West 18th St., New York, NY 10011. Fax: 1-212-633-0748. Website: www.henryholt.com/

Who's Hiring Who? by Richard Lathrop. 1989. Available from Ten Speed Press, P.O. Box 7123, Berkeley, CA 94707, U.S.A. Fax: 1-510-559-1629.

Well, those are my suggested guidelines for the four parts of a group career counseling experience -- seen from my perspective, as I said.

Of course, in the end, every career counselor will want to do their group work in their own unique way. If you like these proposed guidelines, my counsel is that you only begin with them.

Once you master these guidelines, I am confident you will inevitably see ways to improve upon them, and thus evolve your own distinctive style and curriculum, for career counseling with groups.

Addendum:
Skill Identification in Trios

Group Career Counseling At Its Best

Back in 1973, the U.S. Department of Health, Education and Welfare (as it was called at the time) commissioned me to study and write up John Crystal's life/work planning process. He was regarded by both that Department and IEEE (who co-sponsored the contract) as the leading practitioner in the field of life/work planning, and there was some fear that if a truck ran over him, he would take his secrets with him to the grave. I was asked to 'turn his art into a science.'

The W. E. Upjohn Institute for Employment Research offered me an office in Washington, D.C., so I took up residence there, as it was near John's office and residence in neighboring McLean, Virginia (at that time).

Each day, for two months in a row, I interviewed John in D.C., and discovered that most of his clients were ex-military, and that he did individual career counseling with most of them through the mail, running them through a complete 'course' that he had devised.

A great deal was demanded of John's clients, if they enrolled with him, including the writing not of seven stories, but of a complete (and hefty) autobiography, from "Day One" of their lives. They had to do that completely on their own.

But when it came time to analyze that autobiography to see what skills were used, John did all the work for them. Interestingly, he kept notations on the corner of their respective folders as to how much time he invested in each person, and after totaling up these "time notes" in dozens of cases, I discovered that typically he spent a minimum of 32 hours on each client. *(Inasmuch as he was paid by each client, at that time, only $600 for the entire 'course,' he was basically working for $6.25 an hour!)* I asked John how he did this 'skill identification' and he had a stock response, which he joshed me with, day after day: "Gee, Dick, nobody's ever asked me that, before." Well, I didn't argue. I simply handed him someone's autobiography and asked him to do skill identification right before my eyes. It was an awesome demonstration.

It was quite clear that there was a city inside his head. I saw I had my work cut out for me, if I were to truly turn 'his art into a science,' and teach others how to do what he did. In successive months, I had a chance to try out various techniques with various groups. These were the results:

I replaced the autobiography with just "several stories," because most people could not/would not take the time to write a complete autobiography. I learned, by trial and error, that the ideal number of stories needed to uncover the repetitive "patterns" of one's favorite skills, was seven stories. Not five. Not three. Seven.

When we turned to skill identification of those stories, I learned, very quickly, that a normal individual could not do this skill identification on their own. It was apparent that we see other people's skills clearly, but are blind to our own. To do skill identification anywhere nearly as well as John did it, we needed more than one person involved.

I then tried putting two people together to help each other on their skill identification. It sounded great, on paper, but it often didn't work, in reality. Reason? When two people were trying to help each other with skill identification, one of the two tended to be better at it than the other, and they settled quickly into permanent roles of 'teacher' and 'student.' Ever thereafter, when the 'teacher' pointed out to the 'student' a skill they did not realize they had, the 'student' tended to dismiss that skill identification, as merely an extravagant and misguided compliment. Twosomes didn't work well.

So I moved up to Trios, of course. Perhaps three people could duplicate what John could do. We tried it, and after some fine-tuning, it worked. Not all the time. But most of the time. And often very well. 'Trioing' was born. It took about four years ('til 1977) to get it perfected.

Here are the steps that we followed, after 'Trioing' got perfected. (The three people in the Trio are here named A, B, and C.)

1. **Sitting together, but working individually, each of the three write out one of their 'stories.'** Each then jots down in the margin of their paper whatever skills they can see they used, in that story of theirs. This is all done in silence.

If they simply cannot think of any stories, it is useful to first take time (one half day) to fill out "The Memory Net" found in *The What Color Is Your Parachute Workbook.* And then to choose, one story at a time, stories from different time periods in one's life, and from different arenas: work, leisure, learning.
(This typically takes one half hour.)

2. **The first person in the Trio (A) plays 'student,' the other two (B and C) play 'teacher.'** Then the following activities ensue:

a. A and only A reads aloud his or her story, concerning some achievement or "good experience" *(Bernard Haldane)* they had, from any time period of their life. They tell it step by step. It is usually two or three paragraphs in length; no more.

b. B and C listen, jotting down any skills they hear in A's story. If A is reading too fast, B and C interrupt; if A's story is too vague, B and C ask questions designed to get more information from A.

c. A then says what skills he or she heard in their own story, and B and C listen, checking off on their respective lists (from A's story) those same skills if they had identified them.

d. B and C then read off the skills they saw in A's story, that A did not see or mention just now. After each skill, they tell A where in the story, they heard that skill being used. They read the list slowly, to give A time to write it all down.

e. A jots down, in the margin of his or her own story, these additional skill identifications, without argument or protest.

f. When B and C are done, then A asks for further clarification (if needed) as to why B or C said A had this particular skill, or that.

(This process, from a. to f., typically takes 15 to 20 minutes.)

3. The second person in the Trio (B) now plays 'student,' and it is the other two (A and C) who play 'teacher.'
The process in step 2, above, from a. to f., is repeated with this new assignment of roles.

(This process, from a. to f., typically takes 15 to 20 minutes.)

4. The third person in the Trio (C) now plays 'student,' and it is the other two (A and B) who play 'teacher.'
The process in step 2, above, from a. to f., is again repeated with this new assignment of roles.

(This process, from a. to f., typically takes 15 to 20 minutes.)

5. Once all three have had the chance to play 'student,' they study by themselves the list they now have of the skills they used in their own story. They read this list three times, pondering it, then close their notebook, and do not look at the list again.
All of this "Trioing," up to this point has but one purpose: to brainstorm the person's skills, give them new possibilities, and heighten their sensitivity to their real and evident gifts. (Evident to everyone but themselves, at this point.)

(This process typically takes 3 to 5 minutes.)

6. Each member of the Trio now works individually. Each turns to the three lists of Transferable Skills found in 'the

Flower' exercises at the back of *Parachute,* or in the *What Color Is Your Parachute Workbook,* and -- using the boxes labeled #1, color or don't color that box, under each skill, according as to whether they used that skill *in this story* or not. They do not look back at the list from the Trioing. That list was designed merely to heighten their awareness. Trying to 'match' the skills on the Trioing list, with the skills in 'the Flower' is an almost impossible task, since each is in 'a different language.'

(This process typically takes 15 minutes. Total elapsed time for all the foregoing: one hour and 45 minutes. This is considered to be one complete round of trioing. There are to be seven, altogether, before a person's blindness to their own skills is lifted, and they see virtually all their skills without the other two members of their trio any longer having to tell them.)

7. **In subsequent meetings, each person in the trio writes a new story, and the trio goes through all the preceding six steps, all over again.** When turning to the lists in the Flower, it is box #2 under each skill that is used, or not used.

(Total elapsed time: one hour and thirty minutes. The trio gets better at the task.)

8. **In subsequent meetings, step 7 is repeated five more times, until a total of seven stories have been written by each member of the Trio, and analyzed for transferable skills: first, by brainstorming in the Trio, then by using the lists found in the Flower.** Boxes 3–7 get used, each in turn, on the Flower's lists.

(Total elapsed time for each repeat of step 7: one hour and thirty minutes. The temptation is to try to speed up the process, and in these succeeding stories, the Trio tends to get blasé about their skill identification. Tell them to go slower, and savor the joy of discovering who they are.)

All of this has but three purposes: first, to lose your blindness toward your own excellencies. Secondly, to find out what
those excellencies are. Thirdly, to become empowered by discovering these excellencies for oneself, rather than having a
test do the self-assessment for you; in which case you depend
on the test-marker's interpretation of your excellencies, rather
than depending on your own.

Group career counseling enables all of this to happen in
ways far superior to career counseling that is done only with
one individual, by themselves.

CHAPTER 18

Principles of Effective Group Workshops

by Howard Figler

An interactive group workshop for career development can be Real Life 101. Structured properly, the career group can be a microcosm of the world in which the individual is charting a career direction, gathering information, and seeking employment. While career counseling is largely "talking about it," a well-designed career group gives participants many opportunities for "doing it," practicing skills involved in career exploration and job hunting.

Group facilitation is an essential tool for any career counselor. Career groups are not lectures or discussion groups. They are structured interactions among group members that help these participants build and shape their career aspirations and present them to others.

Career groups can be powerful vehicles for behavior change. People who were previously "stuck" in their careers may charge ahead as a result of skills they have learned or insights they have developed about themselves through the group experience. Often friendships are formed as a result of groups and participants provide lasting support and counsel for each other.

As a group facilitator, you can accelerate people's career development by providing numerous exercises that the participants would not have done on their own and giving them access to people who help them in ways that could not have been predicted. A career group can be a shining example of the human community at work, where individuals teach each other, support each other, and urge each other to leap over the hurdles that were previously blocking them.

Purposes of group workshops

A "group" here refers to a workshop of 10 to 40 participants. You can design your career groups to serve one or more of the following purposes:

Self-assessment. Asking participants to examine their functional skills, interests, work-related values, or other career-relevant data about themselves. Reviewing "accomplishments" or other life experiences. May also include drawing pictures of career aspirations, and other right-brained exercises.

Generating career options. Exercises which involve the participants in imagining and creating possible careers, using information they have gathered about themselves.

Skill practice. Engaging the participants in practicing such skills as job interviewing, information interviewing, selling, and others. Participants give and receive feedback about each other's effectiveness.

Information gathering. Obtaining information from other group members, such as ideas, insights, and contacts related to their stated "career problems" or "Yes, Buts." Participants may also share what they know about particular careers.

The time frame of a workshop always depends upon the needs and availability of the participants. A one-time workshop can be as short as two hours or as long as eight. Groups that meet more than once generally meet two to four hours per session.

Many groups meet only once, while others may meet as many as five times. Even longer sequences are helpful, but it's difficult to keep a group together for that long.

Groups can achieve certain results that are not possible on a one-to-one basis. Let's face it. Many individual clients are frustrating. They may respond more constructively to a group, because they don't have the counselor to lean on. Here are some unique benefits of groups:

1. Clients can see the group leader demonstrate skills that are important for career development, such as telephone skills, interview skills, and negotiating skills.

2. Group members can improve their skills by practicing them with each other. Learning through practice in the workshop is a supportive experience. Participants receive feedback without having to suffer the real-world consequences of their mistakes.

3. In every group, clients learn from each other. Each participant sees something different in every other person. A wise group leader designs the workshop so that each member gets input from everyone else in a variety of ways.

4. Groups place more responsibility on clients for their career progress, which is where it belongs. The workshop leader says: "Here is what you need to do to keep your career moving. Now let's use this time to practice." In a group, there's less opportunity for a client to throw the ball back to the counselor and say: "Here, you tell me what to do."

5. An interactive workshop requires individuals to "go public" with their career ambitions. Especially for shy people, this is essential, because many career changers need to deal with their anxiety about "what people will think of me." The feedback they get from others is almost always very supportive.

A career workshop can help the individual to practice conversations she will have that relate to her career. Group members can be asked to role-play job interviewers, bosses, resistant family members, teachers, peers, etc.

Many good things happen as the molecules of group members bounce off each other. Moments of kindness, understanding, or kicks from behind. You recognize your own inertia as you hear the complaints of others. There are smiles and unspoken messages that encourage you to push ahead.

If the leader designs the group according to the guidelines in this chapter, participants will have many serendipitous happenings. For example, an individual who is highly interested in airlines marketing will meet someone who's had experience there. Or a participant who just lost a job in the banking industry will talk with a person who has been through that and can offer much-needed understanding and valuable contacts. Or a person who has been fighting a slow but gradual winning battle with procrastination will offer help and support to another who has the same problem.

Groups can have members with similar backgrounds (all recent college graduates, all laid-off factory workers, etc.), or they can be heterogenous, having a mixture of people with different backgrounds. Participants in a mixed group often are surprisingly helpful to each other, because every member adds to the learning of every other.

A structure for conducting any group workshop

There are many ways to conduct groups badly. One of the more common errors is to ask group members to do exercises without any demonstrations. Sometimes the group facilitator thinks the exercise by itself is enough. This is not so. Participants frequently misunderstand an exercise when they have not seen an example of it. They become frustrated and cannot make progress. Therefore, every group exercise should be presented in the following sequence.

1. **Explanation.** Introduce and explain what the exercise is, why you'll be doing it this way, and why it is important for one's career development. For example:

"I want you to recall every job -- part time or full-time -- you've ever had (or as many as you can remember) and what you liked about that job. This helps you to see aspects of your 'career motivation' even in situations that you did not like overall. You can try to incorporate as many of these motivators as possible in your future career direction."

2. **Demonstration.** The group facilitator demonstrates what he/she wants each participant to do:

"For example, here is my list of past jobs. I had a job as a personnel test administrator. Overall it was boring, but I liked standing in

front of a group and talking to them. I also had a clerk job in the Army. It was deadly dull, but I liked answering the telephone and handling requests for information."

Conduct the demonstration slowly and carefully, to be sure everyone understands what they will do. Repeat the demonstration or do a different one if necessary. Ask the group: "How do you think you'll do when I ask you to do this for yourselves?" If you see or hear any sign of hesitation, do another demonstration.

3. **Doing the exercise.** Participants are asked to practice the skill or do the activity that has just been demonstrated. The group leader circulates to observe what's being done and to answer questions

4. **Group feedback.** After the exercise has been completed, the facilitator asks group members questions similar to these, or other questions designed to check the effect of the exercise:

"What did you learn from that exercise?"
"How did that exercise affect you?"
"In what ways was that exercise helpful to you?"
"What do you wish had been different?"

Key principles in the design and facilitation of group workshops

1. **Assign people for each exercise to subgroups of two, three, or four.** Small subgroups minimize the shyness or threat that many participants feel in talking about themselves or practicing skills. Some exercises can be conducted with subgroups of five or six, but two, three, or four should be the most common arrangement.

2. **Mix up the group members.** As much as possible, arrange the exercises so that each participant interacts with as many different people as possible. The leader should instruct participants as follows:

"On every exercise, I want you to choose the two or three (or four

*or five) others who you know **least** well here in the room. Pick out different people each time. That will insure that you get the greatest variety of input throughout this program."*

It is important that the leader insist on this, because otherwise people will tend to gravitate toward those they already know. Familiarity almost always produces a lower level of involvement, because "friends" think they know what the other person is going to say and why they're saying it. The leader should repeat this instruction ("choose people you know *least* well") for each exercise; otherwise participants will ignore it.

3. **People learn better when they're laughing.** Design exercises so that laughter becomes a natural part of what is happening. As you try different exercise content and formats, you'll learn what is more likely to generate laughing.

4. **Time the exercises tightly.** Announce how much time is allotted to each exercise and stay as close to this as possible. If the participants are not done yet, ask them "How much more time do you need?"

One of the more common frustrations for a group leader is that subgroups will do the exercises at different speeds. Sometimes you may have to interrupt the last subgroup when the other four or five have already finished. In such cases it can be better to get on with the program than have most people sitting twiddling their thumbs, waiting for something to happen.

5. **Introduce as much variety as possible.** Always be aware of the possibility of boredom from repetition. Vary your format from one exercise to the next. For example, if the first activity was a checklist, make the next one a drawing. Or, if the last exercise was a group of five around a table, next have the participants circulate through the room and "interview" each other.

6. **React smoothly to unexpected or disruptive events.** A table collapses . . . there is loud noise in the room next door . . . equipment failures . . . there will always be some "surprise" during the workshop. Learn to roll with it and minimize the distraction to the group.

7. **Respond well to oddball group members.** There is always at least one group member who asks unusual questions, draws attention to himself, or intrudes her personality on the group. The group facilitator must maintain firm leadership so that these individuals are not disruptive or distracting. A group is not a group until you (the leader) have answered the first uncomfortable question. You're expected to handle the loose cannon in your midst.

Physical facilities

The room and facilities arrangements can fit the purposes of your exercises, or they can make your activities very difficult to accomplish. Picture a tightly packed classroom where none of the chairs move, there are no tables, it's difficult for the facilitator to see what people are doing, and it's hard for people to move around. In such conditions, no matter what your interactive exercises are, your workshop will have a low chance of succeeding. Here are some basic principles:

• **Tables.** Give participants tables to sit at, so they can look at each other, interact easily, and have writing space for completion of the exercises. Round tables for six to eight people are ideal, though even square or rectangular tables are much better than no tables at all.

• **Movable chairs and tables.** This allows people to arrange themselves most comfortably to complete the exercises.

• **Space to circulate.** A tightly crowded room makes people feel uncomfortable and it becomes very difficult to have people change subgroups, as was recommended earlier. At least 20% of the room should be open space, where participants can interact, change places, and stretch out when necessary. This space is especially necessary for "mingling" exercises that require moving from one person to another.

• **Microphone.** If you are leading a group of 30 or more, consider using a microphone, because you don't want people straining to hear what you're saying.

• **Avoid breakout rooms.** Conduct the entire workshop in a single large room. Do not send small-group participants to breakout rooms outside of the large room, because you will lose contact with them, they will feel much less involved in the workshop, and they will lower their participation.

Despite the many unique merits of groups, clients are not beating down our doors to have workshops and seminars. We have much to learn about what makes groups attractive and successful. Instead of hoping the demand will increase, we should be improving our group processes and marketing them better. Wider use of group workshops is a breakthrough in our profession that's waiting to happen.

The Present:
Special Problems

CHAPTER 19

The Problem Called "Motivation"

by Dick Bolles

So Near and Yet So Far

I get such letters all the time. A career counselor is having trouble teaching the principles of career planning or job-hunting to some group because -- and I quote -- "they just aren't motivated enough." And always the letters end with the same plaintive cry, "Please give me any ideas you have about how to motivate people."

The problem bothers job-hunters as much as it bothers counselors. I remember well a poignant phone call I once received from Bakersfield, California. "Listen," said the voice on the other end of the phone line, "I just read your book, and I know the exercises there might really help me, but I just can't seem to get motivated enough. I have three minutes right now -- could you motivate me?"

It is easy to understand the root of the problem: it is a Failure to Make A Connection. Over there, we have job-hunters or career-changers who clearly need some fresh ideas, exercises, and tips, that will speed them on their way. Over here, we have a class, a book, a plan, that will give them just what they need. But they can't connect. The job-hunters in question seem unable to rouse themselves from a terminal paralysis or apathy. They are like a drowning person, unable to reach out for the lifesaver that was thrown to them by a nearby rescuer in a boat. So near, and yet so far.

But while the problem permits easy definition, it does not permit easy solution. I am frank to say that after years of wrestling with this issue myself, and listening to learned men and women on the subject, and reading all the books that deal with it, I have no answers. Just some hunches.

Hunch #1

It is not your job to motivate people to do career planning; that is their job.

Some years ago I heard a marriage expert talk about divorce. She threw out a sentence I have never forgotten: "We usually volunteer more information than people really want to hear." I have a parallel sentence to that: "We usually take on more responsibility for the lives of our clients than we really should."

I think it is our responsibility to share what we know about career planning with anyone who will listen. But it is not our responsibility to make them want this information. Our craft is called "career counseling," not "career manipulation." You are called to be midwife, not forceps.

Evangelical fervor on our part is nice: "Hey, but their whole life would be changed if only they would . . ."

But their freedom of will is even nicer. We must not violate that. They are free to say "No" to anything, as are we. That's what makes us human.

Hunch #2

Motivation is not one problem, but a whole family of problems, all lumped together under one umbrella. It helps to separate them out. So, here goes:

a. **Doubt on the job-hunter's part that any job is worth it.** I mean, here you are, a counselor, talking about the fact that you know a process which is going to help your students or clients find a job. However, there's one leetle problem: they have never had a job in their whole life, to date, that was anything but boring, monotonous, oppressive, and just plain drudgery. They listen to your little speech, and what they hear is: "Hey, I've got a great series of ideas that will help you find a boring, monotonous, oppressive piece of drudgery."

You're making your appeal to the wrong life. And it will stay that way until you can give them a brighter vision of what a job could be, at its best.

b. **Lack of experience**. Suppose you were a teacher out in the woods with a bunch of kids. You want to get them to a particular spot. So, you consult your map (or your computer) and plot a somewhat tortuous path that does indeed, eventually, get them out of the woods and to that spot. But it's a very circuitous route, of some ten miles. After showing them the map, and the route, one of the kids raises her hand and says, "Hey, teach, I know a shortcut." And proceeds down a path that within one half hour brings you all to the spot in question.

Well, some of your clients or students listen to you talking about a bunch of hard work -- exercises and strategies, that seem like that ten-mile, circuitous route. But they know (they think) this shortcut: want-ads, agencies, and family connections. Why take the long way around, that you are proposing, when they know this shortcut?

Their viewpoint proceeds, of course, from ignorance and lack of experience; but it is understandable: "Someone out there must know where good jobs are -- just lead me to them, and forget all this stuff about skill identification, informational interviewing, and the like."

c. **Low self-esteem.** So, when you are dealing with people who have low self-esteem, they are perfectly willing to agree that the techniques you are espousing will work for others, but they are quite certain these techniques will not work for them. That is because -- they say -- they have peculiar problems, peculiar challenges, peculiar handicaps, peculiar circumstances, that would prevent these techniques from working -- for them.

Low self-esteem is a double-barreled problem. It is not only that they think too little of themselves; it is also that they make too much of others. It's like a peculiar kind of double vision: seeing yourself as smaller than you are, and seeing others as larger than they are.

Their double false vision makes their low self-esteem a particular kind of hell. They feel all alone. They wrestle with their problems in life under the delusion that they are the only ones who have such problems. They don't talk with other people enough, to learn that many many other people are wrestling with the same problem and have conquered them.

d. **A feeling that they are victim.** There are, indeed, a lot of people whom life has stepped on. But some people come to love this view of themselves, because if they are victim then they are relieved forever of any responsibility for how their life is turning out.

Consequently, they often have a tremendous investment in holding on to this view of themselves. Every new idea, every new technique, every new piece of advice, is examined to see if it might force them to let go of their victim mentality. And if the answer is Yes, the idea, system or subject matter will be resisted, spurned, tuned out, and rejected.

We may think of people who have this victim mentality as people carrying around a very large balloon at the end of a piece of string, floating above their heads. Any belief which threatens this Victim Mentality balloon is viewed as a dart, that threatens to puncture the balloon. And so, the victim will deflect the darts, reject the ideas, find it impossible to 'get going,' so that they can still hold on to that balloon.

Over the years, I have found this particularly prevalent among middle-aged men. As far as I can tell, their thinking seems to run like this: "I have been employed in a number of jobs and been in a number of situations over the years, that weren't terrific. I've excused myself on the grounds that I was always a victim of this or that, and had no power to change the situation. Now you, Mr. or Ms. Career Counselor, come along and tell me that I have a lot of control over what happens to me. And if I accept your premise, about my future, I have to realize it would also have applied to my past. And the thought that I didn't have to put up with all that I have put up with, that I could have changed it all, makes me feel unbearable sadness about all those wasted years. So, of course, I'm going to reject what you are now telling me, and repeat my mantra: I was a victim, I am a victim, I will always be a victim."

In most cases, to be sure, none of this is as conscious as I have just presented it. Ask them why they're ducking the plan you've laid out, and they are likely to just shrug their shoulders and say, "Oh, I don't know. It just doesn't seem right, to me. I guess I'm just not motivated."

e. **The time is not yet.** Remember the job-hunter I mentioned earlier, who phoned me from Bakersfield? The one who said, "I have three minutes, for you to motivate me"? Well, my response was in the form of a question. I asked him, "Are you out of work?" *Yes.* "How long have you been out of work?" *Two weeks.*

And then I said, "You haven't been out of work long enough to be desperate; call me back when you are."

One month later, he called back. "I was never so mad at anyone in my whole life," he reported. "But eventually I came to realize you were right. That's why I'm calling back now. I'm desperate. I'm motivated. What should I do next?"

I referred him to a counselor in his area, and she reported sometime later, that he found a beautiful job.

All too often, as career counselors, we listen to someone who is resisting doing any of the exercises we propose, and then we conclude two things: one, he has no motivation (true), and two, he will never have any (false). Sometimes motivation is like good wine. It just needs some time to ripen.

Okay, there you have it: five problems, hiding under the one umbrella term: "low motivation."

When you are confronted with someone you think isn't

motivated, try to find out which of these five is the actual problem. You can play midwife better, if you know what baby you are trying to deliver.

Hunch #3

We are the problem. When our teaching just isn't getting through to the client or clients that we are working with, it is tempting to say the problem is "lack of motivation" -- thus identifying the client as the problem -- when in fact it is we who are the problem.

How are we the problem? Well, I have observed four different ways in which we *may be.* I see these problems particularly when I observe career counselors teaching some kind of course or group work:

a. The career counselor hasn't run their own life through the process or exercises that they are adjuring their clients to do. They are explaining job-hunting, even though it's been *years* since they themselves last job-hunted. They're teaching skill identification, even though they themselves have never worked through this for their own life. They are sending clients out to do informational interviewing, even though they've never once done it themselves. They're explaining the hiring interview, even though they haven't sat on the job-hunter's side of the desk since dinosaurs roamed the earth. And then -- the ultimate punchline -- they are bewailing the fact that their clients are not motivated, when it is really they themselves who are not motivated.

It is clear that an unmotivated teacher or counselor will always have unmotivated clients, for 'lack of motivation' exists, like beauty, in the eye of the beholder.

b. The career counselor hasn't been sufficiently trained. I get letters every year from career counselors who have set themselves up in practice, after merely reading *What Color Is Your Parachute?* They are stymied by the simplest kinds of problems, stumped over the simplest kinds of questions. There is only one remedy: go get trained. Learn how to teach this stuff. Learn how to deal with common problems. Lack of training (yours) will always *seem* to manifest itself as lack of motivation (theirs).

c. The career counselor is teaching entirely "left-brain" strategies -- words, words, words, I'm so sick of words --instead of complementing these with 'right-brain' strategies -- pictures, context maps, overviews, music, mind-maps, and the like. Many times counselors think clients are turned off by the subject matter, when the fact is that the clients are turned off by the manner of presentation.

This discovery is late in coming, because there are always clients -- particularly in group work -- who *love* words, and will praise the career counselor to the skies; leaving the counselor feeling that the right-brained clients are basically unmotivated. This equation: left-brained = motivated, right-brained = unmotivated, should be avoided at all costs.

d. The career counselor is trying to do all the teaching, instead of enlisting peers of the clients (former clients, former counselees, former job-hunters, former graduates) to come back and testify, explain, and teach that which they know well from experience. Dear counselor: one word from a convinced peer will do more to motivate your students than four hours of speechifying from you!

Hunch #4

Once accurate diagnosis of the problem of 'low motivation' is made, it is within our power to fix parts of it.

Sure, you can't fix *all* of it. But you can fix some of it. Fix it, by changing what you are doing: run your life through any process you are teaching, before you ever try to teach it; get more training; use more right-brain processes with your clients; use peers more often in convincing your clients that what you are proposing is worthwhile.

Of this I am sure: fixing 'lack of motivation' doesn't come

down to figuring out new and better ways to manipulate your clients, but figuring out new and better ways to manipulate ourselves.

Some 'lack of motivation' will still remain, after you've made your best and your brightest attempt to be the best career counselor you know how to be. There is an obstinacy to some problems that will just not go away. Don't beat yourself up about this. Learn to let go.

Commend such clients into the hands of God.

CHAPTER 20

Helping Clients Get 'Unblocked':
The Brain and
the Safekeeping Self

by Dick Bolles

All of us are familiar with clients who get 'blocked' during their job-hunt; they seem to freeze in mid-frame, and cannot carry on their search. Indeed, research reveals that one-third of all job-hunters never find a job because they become blocked and give up.

We need to understand why this happens, and what we can do to help them get 'unblocked.'

In a nutshell, the answer will turn out to be that something is happening in their brain. Therefore, if we are to help them, we must be sure we understand the brain, more than somewhat.

That understanding begins with the two sides of the brain, and it will end in some unexpected places, before this chapter is out. But it is with the two sides of the brain that we begin.

Seeing the Pieces, and
Assembling the Pieces

Now, I realize there is hardly a career counselor alive today who has not heard about this concept of 'the two sides of the brain' -- unless you've been living in a cave.

But since my greatest skill in teaching ideas is 'overkill', let me dare to explain it to you once again, this time with a few genuine twists, as it applies to our clients.

Begin, if you will, by imagining a long freight train going down a railroad track, with two different people watching it go.

The first person is standing right up by the tracks, so close to the train they can almost touch it as it flies by. Suppose they are entranced with the sights immediately in front of them, so that they do not turn their head either to the right or to the left. You will realize they can catch a slight glimpse of that part of the train which has already passed, as well as a slight glimpse of that part of the train which is yet to come by -- but basically all they can see is what is passing right in front of them, sequentially. First the locomotive, then the first car, then the second car, then the third car, and so on and so forth.

Now imagine there is a second person watching that train, but they are not standing on the ground. They are high up in the air, in an airplane or hot air balloon. From that great height they perceive the train in an entirely different way from the person on the ground. Instead of seeing the train one car at a time, they perceive the whole train at once, and every car in it at the same time.

Now, this is a metaphor for the two sides of the brain. One side, normally the left side of the brain, processes information just like the person watching the train on the ground: sequentially, one by one, bit by bit. The other side of the brain, normally the right side, processes information just like the person watching the train from the air: holistically, all at once, intuitionally.

If we want to go into detail, it comes out like this:

LEFT SIDE	RIGHT SIDE
Excels at seeing the pieces.	Excels at assembling the pieces into a coherent picture.
Is good at perceiving details or individual elements (i.e., **text**).	Is good at seeing the broad picture, the overall **context**, at making connections, and integrating elements.
Processes information in a linear manner. Deals with inputs one at a time.	Processes information more diffusely, and simultaneously. Integrates many inputs all at once.

(continued)

LEFT SIDE	RIGHT SIDE
Specializes in logic and analytical reasoning or thinking.	Specializes in intuition and holistic perception or thinking.
Specializes in verbal and mathematical functions.	Specializes in spatial and relational functions.
Specializes in memory and recognition of words and numbers.	Specializes in memory and recognition of objects, persons, faces, music and pitch.
Specializes in anything related to **time**, such as history, planning.	Specializes in things related to **space**, such as body movement.
Is connected to the right side of the body, and the right side of each eye's vision.	Is connected to the left side of the body, and the left side of each eye's vision.

The word that should be emphasized in the list above is "specializes." Which is to say, one side of the brain may *lead the way* in a particular activity, but the other side of the brain often follows, chipping in its complementary contribution too. **The two work in tandem.**

In his most recent book, *The Right Mind: Making Sense of the Hemispheres (1997),* Robert Ornstein emphasizes precisely this truth: "There is almost nothing that is regulated solely by the left or right hemisphere. Very simple chores may be the responsibility of one or the other, but both get involved as soon as any situation becomes slightly more complex . . . We do what we do with all we've got."

That is to say, in our earlier image, both the person standing beside the train and the person flying over the train are in constant communication with each other, contributing their own unique perception and viewpoint.

And we can choose which to listen to, in each situation. We have *one brain with two strategies at its disposal.* Thus, if we try one approach to a problem in career counseling or life, and that doesn't work, our brain offers us an alternative approach -- from the other side of the brain.

We can portray this in a diagram, using the spokes of a wheel. At each end of each spoke, is a pair of alternative approaches to problems, and we can fall back on the one if the other doesn't work -- in a particular situation, with a particular problem:

The Two Sides of the Brain
and What Each Does

The Left Side   **The Right Side**

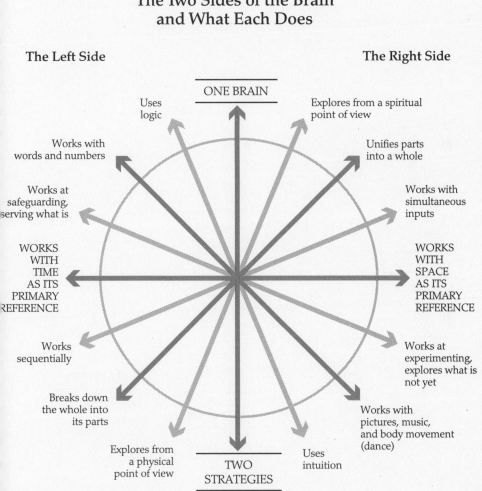

ONE BRAIN

Uses logic

Explores from a spiritual point of view

Works with words and numbers

Unifies parts into a whole

Works at safeguarding, serving what is

Works with simultaneous inputs

WORKS WITH TIME AS ITS PRIMARY REFERENCE

WORKS WITH SPACE AS ITS PRIMARY REFERENCE

Works sequentially

Works at experimenting, explores what is not yet

Breaks down the whole into its parts

Works with pictures, music, and body movement (dance)

Explores from a physical point of view

Uses intuition

TWO STRATEGIES

Seven pairs of strategies, all in all. Many strategies are, of course, missing from the "wheel" diagram on the previous page, because they don't readily divide into pairs.

But if we abandon the idea of pairing, and simply list all the strategies that occur to us -- putting them on the diagram according as they belong *usually, and primarily,* to one side of the brain or the other, there are many more strategies we could add to the diagram -- particularly if we divide the brain into four quadrants, instead of just two -- as we see here:

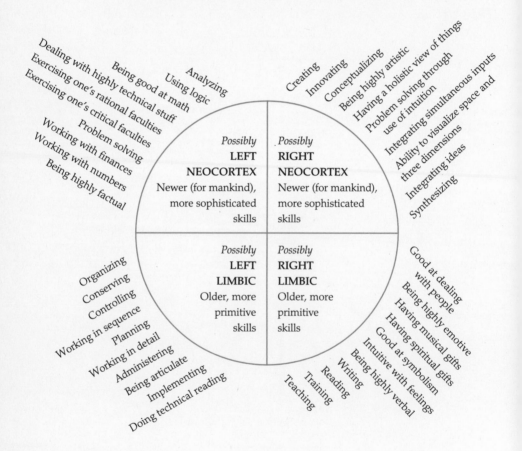

When you study this diagram, you will see that it is really a diagram of 'skills' or 'abilities' or 'talents' or 'gifts,' illustrating where our various skills are *primarily* rooted in the brain.

I am, incidentally, indebted to two people for many of the ideas above: Bob Ornstein, and my friend Ned Herrmann. Ned conceived the four-quadrant model, above, and is the highly popular author of *The Whole Brain Business Book* (McGraw Hill, 1996) and an earlier work, *The Creative Brain* (Brain Books, 2075 Buffalo Creek Rd., Lake Lure, N.C. 28746, 1988). Bob is a pioneer in this whole field of the two sides of the brain. His original work was *The Psychology of Con-sciousness* (The Viking Press, Inc., 1973) which he has updated in sig-nificant ways in his most recent book (at this writing): *The Right Mind: Making Sense of the Hemispheres* (Harcourt Brace & Company, 1997). If you wish to explore this subject further, I recommend the most recent books of both these pioneers. *The Right Mind*, in partic-ular, has a good introductory history of the concept of the two sides (or hemispheres) of the brain.

Specializing in One Side or the Other

When you study the skills listed in the diagram above, if you check off the ones you prefer, you will often see them heavily weighted toward the left or the right side of the brain. Oh, true, we may have a number of skills also on the other side of the brain; but the question is: Where is our primary emphasis, skills-wise?

And it becomes apparent that while each of us is in theory 'whole-brained,' we do tend to gravitate over time toward one side of the brain or the other for our 'primary skill-bank.' We gravitate. We lean toward. We specialize.

And it is in this sense that we may speak of each of us as being *primarily* left-brained or *primarily* right-brained (*except for geniuses, who tend to flip between one side of the brain to the other, with impunity*).

The Bias of Our Educational System

Part of this specialization is due to our innate gifts, of course. Our genes, our inheritance, our family, what have you. But part of it is also due to the educational system in which we grew up. Taken as a whole, that system in the U.S. tends to heavily favor the left side of the brain.

Case in point: our educational system tends to label people who prefer the left side of their brain 'verbal people' or 'logical.' On the other hand, that system calls people who prefer the right side of their brain 'nonverbal.' The latter label has all the air of a defect, as though something were missing from their makeup. A decent educational system, instead of labeling such people in terms of what they do not have ('nonverbal') would label them in terms of what they do have. It might call them, for example, 'picturing people.'

Another case in point: students who are at home in the left side of the brain, people who are verbal, logical, and analytical, tend to find it *relatively* easy to survive our educational system. But the 'picturing people' often get ignored. Picturing people sit in class looking for images: it may be the pictures on the wall of the classroom, or what is going on outside a nearby window. The educational system calls this search for pictures 'daydreaming,' or 'not paying attention' (to the teacher's *words*, that is). Picture-starvation would seem to be a more apt title for the malady.

Outside the classroom, people who favor the right side of their brain will of course continue to be starved for pictures. They turn, inevitably, to the Web, or to TV. Admittedly the quality of the images found there is often lousy, but these picture-starved people are no different than the person starved for food who will consume large amounts of 'junk food' when nothing else is available.

So, our educational system creates much mischief, in skewing the delicate balance intended to exist between the two sides of the brain in each of us, and pushing us toward the left side of the brain.

We will note, swiftly, in passing, that career counseling often contributes to this problem. So many of our tools and instruments (like this book!) heavily favor the person who has chosen to specialize on the left side of their brain: we use words, words, words.

There are precious few career instruments, except those designed to be used in lower schools, that try to use pictures instead of words to aid in the work of career counseling.

Alas! and alack!

The Two Selves within Our Head

Where are we in this pursuit of our subject? Well, we're at the point where we see that we tend to specialize, we tend to lean toward, we tend to gravitate toward one side of the brain or the other. Often it is the left side of the brain, because our educational system pushes us in this direction. That much is clear.

It was George Prince, of the Mind-Free® Group, Inc., who added a new dimension to this whole discussion of specialization. He proposed, a number of years ago, that there is a sense in which these two sides of the brain have very different approaches to life. They function almost like two personalities, two very different Selves. George therefore named them the 'Safekeeping Self' and the 'Experimental Self.'

He suggested that the left side of the brain (in most people) functions as though its mission in life were to safeguard the person by keeping them where they are; while the right side of the brain (in most people) functions as though its mission in life were to lead the person into new and uncharted territory. On the next page is my and Ned Herrmann's summary of how these two selves behave:

The Left Side of the Brain
functioning as

The Safekeeping Self

The Right Side of the Brain
functioning as

The Experimental Self

Guides
Evaluates
Analyzes
Loves Words
Reassures and Supports
Is Realistic
Looks at Consequences
Logical
Is Serious, Cautious and Suspicious
Alert To Danger
Avoids Surprises
Avoids Risks
Avoids Wrongness
Makes Rules, Follows Rules
Fearful
PUNISHES Itself for:
    Mistakes, Wrongness and Any
    Deviations from Perfection

In Touch with Unconscious
Can "Touch" Total Experience
Uses Seeming Irrelevance
Imagines
Intuitive
Speculates
Recognizes Patterns
Makes Connections
Impetuous
Does Not Mind Being Confused
Does Not Mind Being Wrong
Makes Impossible Wishes
Open to Anything
Likes Surprises
Breaks Rules
Takes Risks
Sees the Fun in Things
Feels
Guesses
Curious
Plays

As you can see, the 'Safekeeping Self' is the part of us which likes to maintain our status quo, guarantee us freedom from fear, and give us a feeling of safety because the circumstances are known and familiar -- even if they are grim, as in a bad marriage. On the other hand, the 'Experimental Self' is the part of us which likes to strike out in new directions, and try new things; it is the part of us which craves adventure, and a better life.

In normal circumstances, the Safekeeping Self and the Experimental Self are designed to operate within each of us as a dynamic duo, maintaining balance and equilibrium with each other (just as the two sides of the brain ideally do).

Thus, in a typical situation, the Experimental Self contributes an openness to new things and ideas, curiosity, and imagination; while the Safekeeping Self contributes reassurance, support, analysis, and guidance.

So much for theory. In actual fact, each of us can develop a great preference for one Self or the Other, even as we do with the two sides of the brain in matters of skills, etc.

In some people, for example, the Experimental Self is clearly transcendent most of their lives. They are always rushing off to climb Mt. Everest, or do white water rafting, or ballooning around the world. In other people, the Safekeeping Self is transcendent most of their lives. They live lives of caution, with everything planned as carefully as may be, and risk-taking is held to a minimum.

Mercifully, a great majority of the population switches back and forth, choosing the appropriate Self for the activity at hand: preferring the Experimental Self -- for example -- while on vacation, but preferring the Safekeeping Self at, say, income tax time.

Why Does the Safekeeping Self Go Into Panic?

Inasmuch as job-hunting or career-change is a kind of launching out into the void, it is clear that the appropriate Self for that activity is the Experimental Self.

The problem is, we who are career counselors often see the Safekeeping Self coming to the fore in our clients, just when they need the other Self more.

Why, we ask ourselves, do they choose the inappropriate Self for this activity: career-change or job-hunting? when they clearly need to take some risks? More to the point: why does the Safekeeping Self not only leap to the fore when they are job-hunting, but maintain an iron grip on all their activities?

We who are career counselors may teach them everything we know about new and creative and more effective ways of going about their job-hunt, only to watch in horror as -- when push comes to shove -- our clients fall back on the most archaic and least effective ways of job-hunting, just because they are familiar. Clearly, the Safekeeping Self has them in a death grip. What went wrong?

I will answer in a moment, but first a little bit of background. By and large, all of our lives, we are endlessly finding ourselves living in one of four mental landscapes:

How Am I Doing?

What Am I Trying to Accomplish?

Can I Survive?

What Is Happening?

Mental Landscape #1: By accident or choice, we are thrust into a new and unfamiliar situation: perhaps by the death of a loved one, a divorce, a termination when we least expect it, a move to a different part of the country, an entering into marriage, the children leaving home, a falling into straitened financial circumstances, retirement, or a career-change. Because this new situation, this 'new world' if you like, is so unfamiliar to us, we spend all our energy just trying to find out what this new world is like. Our major fixation: **What is Happening?**

Mental Landscape #2: We are in the new situation, the new world, and we have gotten a handle -- however temporarily -- on what's happening, and now we have moved on in our thinking. We are focused now on how it is we 'make it' in this new world: emotionally, financially, socially, and mentally, even at a minimal level. Our major fixation: **Can I Survive?**

Mental Landscape #3: We have not only gotten a handle on what's happening, but we have figured out that we can indeed survive in this new situation, this new world, and now we have moved on again in our thinking to the question of what we want to accomplish or achieve for our lives, our work, our social relationships, our faith. Our major fixation: **What Am I Trying to Accomplish?**

Mental Landscape #4: We now have a handle (however tenuously) on what's happening, and how to survive, and what we want to accomplish. Now we move on in our thinking -- as time passes -- to the question of whether or not we are accomplishing, with our lives, what we set out to do. Our major fixation: **How Am I Doing?**

We may, then, describe these four mental landscapes as: #1 The Land of Information Gathering, #2 The Land of Action, #3 The Land of Goal Setting, and #4 The Land of Evaluation.

If we observe our clients when they are in Land #3, or Land #4, we generally see them choosing well, between the Experimental Self and the Safekeeping Self, depending on what task is at hand. Normally.

But when life or some internal time clock introduces a jarring note into their lives, as when they are fired, or divorced, or going about the job-hunt, whammo! their Safekeeping Self suddenly comes to full alert, hits the panic button, and starts careening off walls. They often become immobilized, and we as their career counselor wonder what on earth is going on, in them?

Well, the Safekeeping Self is going on in them, panicking in fact, freezing them in their tracks (often) so that they are unable to take the next step in their hoped-for new adventure.

Their Experimental Self 'hangs,' and they don't know why. In this sense, it is just like a computer 'hanging.' If you have such a computer, could you possibly explain why it hung the last three times that it did? Not likely! No more does a job-hunter or career-changer know why they suddenly 'hang.'

But we know why -- that is, if we understand the brain. And therefore our task is to give our clients some strategies that will disarm the overreactive Safekeeping Self in them, and help restore the proper balance between the Safekeeping Self and the Experimental Self.

The Three Rules for Taming the Safekeeping Self

There are three rules that we have found, over the years, work rather well:

First rule: urge your client to put a lot of music in their life. The left brain is the seat of the Safekeeping Self, while the right brain is the seat of the Experimental Self. Music 'feeds' the right brain, activates it, calls it more into active participation throughout each day. Classical music seems to be particularly effective in doing this.

Second rule: help the client to get out of Mental Landscape #1, by having them do lots of information gathering about the new world they are moving into, or contemplating moving into. The more information gathered, the less the new land will seem intimidating and unfamiliar. This means: in a divorce, talk to other people who have been through divorce; upon being fired, talk to other people who have successfully worked through the period afterward; in career-change, talk to people who have successfully moved into the field that is of interest; and so on, and so forth. Information gathering is not an optional exercise for job-hunters. It is crucial, if the Safekeeping Self is to stop panicking.

Third rule: describe for your client, particularly when you see them 'hang,' what the Safekeeping Self does, and how it behaves. Maybe give them a handout with it, along the following lines (it's perfectly OK to reproduce the following, in any way you wish, so long as you include the appropriate credit):

The Sound of the Safekeeping Self during the Job-Hunt

1. *You know your Safekeeping Self is too much in control of your life, when . . .*

You find yourself talking much more than you usually do -- particularly about all the reasons why you shouldn't do this, when you are contemplating making a change in your life. Words, words, words are the way in which the Safekeeping Self manages to keep control and have dominion over the Experimental Self within you.

Remedy: practice silence, and meditation. Put on music. Resolve to gather more information, and then to act.

2. *You know your Safekeeping Self is too much in control of your life, when . . .*

You are using certain words, that are the 'fingerprints' of the Safekeeping Self. These words are:

"I can't"

"I shouldn't"

"I'm not sufficiently (fill in the blank: bright, talented, outgoing, etc., etc.)"

"Yes, but . . ."

"It feels wrong to just do what I want"

"I think I may lose more than I will gain"

"What would people think?"

"This isn't realistic"

"I've never done this before"

"What if I do this wrong?"

"But, I've always done it this way"

"This will never work"

"This is just a waste of time"

"Oh, I've tried this before"

"Convince me"

"This is too hard"

"See, I knew it wouldn't work (after one try)"

"My present job's not so bad, after all"

Remedy: make a list of the opposite of these phrases, and paste that list of affirmations on the mirror in your bathroom, and on your refrigerator. Memorize them. Repeat often, to yourself. Use them as meditations in your silences.

3. You know your Safekeeping Self is too much in control of your life, when . . .

You are feeling very confused about each step along the way toward change, no matter how carefully and well these steps are explained to you. Confusion is of course normal when the road ahead has a fork in it. But confusion normally starts to dissipate after a time. If your confusion not only persists, but -- if anything -- grows stronger, you're almost certainly hearing the sound of the Safekeeping Self. Confusion is one of its favorite weapons, much like the octopus who throws out a cloud of ink when under attack, to obscure and dumbfound and immobilize its enemies.

Remedy: focus on what you do know, rather than on what you don't know; focus on what you are sure of, rather than on what you aren't sure of. It is easier to deal with uncertain ground, when your feet are firmly planted on certain ground. If you are a person of faith, reaffirm for yourself the certainties about "Underneath are the Everlasting Arms," etc., and ask God to lead you through all confusion.

4. You know your Safekeeping Self is too much in control of your life, when . . .

You find yourself being even more obsessive than usual about your little daily rituals and routines. In group workshops this is manifested by: always sitting in the same place, always talking to a few of the same people, etc. This is the sound of the Safekeeping Self: it likes to cling to the familiar routine, as a way of 'planting a flag' which says: I am a creature of habit, not one who goes off on flings into new adventures. In other words, this is the Safekeeping Self saying, "Hell, no, I won't go."

Remedy: practice doing one 'altered behavior' (for you) each day. Practice thus taking one new risk a day, even if it's a little one like speaking to a neighbor you usually never speak to, or whatever.

5. *You know your Safekeeping Self is too much in control of your life, when . . .*

You find yourself engaging in digressions and diversions. This is the old magician's trick of 'keep them busy watching the left hand, so they won't notice what's going on with the right hand.' Digressions are of various kinds. Leaving your job-hunting and career-changing activities until all your other tasks are done, is one digression. Feeling an inordinate need to sleep is another. Devoting more and more time to helping others, rather than giving yourself the time your job-hunting, career-changing exercises need, is another. Physical maladies, such as headaches, tiredness, colds, and the like, are yet another. Essentially, by means of procrastination, the Safekeeping Self is trying to cling to the status quo by getting you to 'put off until tomorrow, the things you could do today.' Except, it is praying tomorrow never comes. Know these tricks for what they are: the Safekeeping Self trying to play Procrastinating Magician, in order to preserve the status quo.

Remedy: Get more physical exercise. That way, you are practicing defining yourself more and more as a person of immediate action, rather than as a person who meets a challenge by taking Flight. No, no, Fight. Leave out the "l".

Biofeedback for the Brain

Well, we set out to see how you could help your clients get 'unblocked.' Once they realize the cause of this 'block' is the Safekeeping Self, overreacting, they're halfway home. The three rules, above, should illuminate the Safekeeping Self in all its questionable splendour, to your clients.

Does the Safekeeping Self alter its behavior once you shine light upon its ways? Yes, it does, often to an incredible degree. Why should this be?

Well, it's like the biofeedback we are all familiar with, vis-à-vis heart rate, blood pressure lowering, and the like. The rule there: give the brain some information about 'attendant signs' that occur when blood pressure is lowered, or heart rate is slowed, and then -- armed with this information -- the brain will be able to reproduce the same results by paying attention to 'the attendant signs.'

So, here too, the brain profits as well from information about itself. Given this information about 'the attendant signs' (above) of the Safekeeping Self, the brain can subsequently regulate the Safekeeping Self when it goes into hyperactivity, and move quickly to restore the equilibrium and balance between the Safekeeping Self and Experimental Self that is its natural state. The job-hunter or career-changer is freed from immobility, and able to get on with the change they desire.

In Conclusion

It's been a long journey, since this chapter began. But, this was an important journey. A rereading of this chapter can pay rich dividends, not only to your immobilized clients, but also to your whole understanding of career counseling. For, after all, the brain is the mother of all skills, the source of all job-hunting strategies, and the fountainhead of all career counseling techniques.

CHAPTER 21

Confronting Clients Whose Actions Don't Match Their Words

by Howard Figler

How often do your clients do what they say they're going to do? By contrast, how often do they say: "I didn't have enough time," "I'll do it next time," or "I know what to do, I just gotta get myself to do it."

Henry said he wanted to be an investigative reporter for a big city newspaper. However, he lived in Kingston, Maine, far from metropolitan areas and seemed to have an uphill climb for this kind of career. Henry and his career counselor agreed that he needed to: (1) Write some articles for his high school paper; (2) contact several city newspapers to find out about their internship programs; (3) ask his neighbors if they can help him to arrange in-person meetings with local reporters; and (4) talk to his teachers about contacts they might have in the world of journalism.

Four weeks after meeting with the counselor, Henry returned and announced that he had done none of these -- absolutely zero. This is not news to warm a counselor's heart. What's a counselor to do? Tell Henry how disappointed she is? Send him out again with the same agenda? Give him a lecture on procrastination?

If your clients follow through on what they say they're going to do even 50% of the time, you're doing really well. But what of the other 50% or more? These situations call for confrontation -- a skill that helps the client to reconcile his actions with his words.

One definition of "to confront" in the dictionary is "to face in hostility or defiance." But that's not what the word means in career counseling. Confrontation is putting the spotlight on the discrepancy between a client's statements and actions, to find out what it means. Henry's counselor might say:

"You said you were going to do these things -- but then you didn't. That leaves me feeling confused about how much you meant what you said. Can you help me understand what's going on?"

Confrontation is a motivation check

When words and action don't agree, something is out of synch. Usually that something is the client's motivation. Henry may not want his career goal enough to work for it. He may want something different. Or, his motivation may be undermined by his beliefs that he will fail and embarrass himself.

Nike's advertising slogan -- "Just do it!" -- caught the public's imagination, because people recognize its simple truth -- no excuses, no whining, no temporizing, you either do it or you don't. In earlier times it was known as "actions speak louder than words" or "talk is cheap."

"Doing it" doesn't mean necessarily succeeding, but it does mean translating your stated motivation into action. Clients who require confrontation usually are confused about their motivation.

Why do people say they want a career goal and then not do anything toward that end? There are probably as many answers to that as there are people who waffle. What matters is what you and the client decide to do about this dissonance. There are two routes:

1. **A motivation test.** Counselor and client agree that the client's motivation needs to be evaluated. The "next steps" are tests of how much the client wants to move toward the goal he has stated.

2. **Change the goal.** The client may recognize that his lack of

action reveals his desire to change direction. Then he sets "next steps" to test his motivation for moving toward a different career goal.

The objective is to have a match between words and actions. In counseling language this is called "congruence." You will know that your client is clicking when she does what she says she will do, and maybe even a little extra. Congruent people are those who say what they want and then bend every energy toward making it happen.

So, confrontation seeks to clarify the client's motivation. It also lets the client know that there's no shame in changing your mind about what your goals are.

It's been said that a lot of people could play professional baseball if they were willing to take about five million swings at a hardball and endure a huge number of misses, being hit by pitches, and bearing massive frustration, until their muscle memories learned how to connect with the ball.

Most of us are not willing to sacrifice what's necessary to swing five million times at a blurry little ball and risk being hit along the way. We don't want it enough. This would also be true of professional writing. If you're willing to write several million words and suffer through endless painful critiques, you'll eventually write something of value. The same could be said of carpentry, public speaking, plumbing, and many other skills. Your clients decide what they're willing to endure en route to the pursuit of their goals.

Of course, others will call out examples of people who seemed to have their skills naturally, "from birth" they say, and apparently didn't have to work hard at them. Well, there may be a few like this, but they're just a few. If you look closely at almost all successful people you will find they have been practicing their activities over and over again, with a lot of stumbling and failures in the early going. The examples are legendary -- Walt Disney was fired from a Kansas City newspaper because he was deemed "not creative enough."

Some will argue that clients are "wasting their time" by seeking goals where the odds seem to be stacked against them. Just think of individuals you know who have achieved goals that most people did not believe they could accomplish. A dogged sense of purpose can be a great equalizer. Furthermore, even if a person fails in pursuit of a goal, she often gains by (a) improving her self-discipline, (b) acquiring new skills, and (c) finding a career related to the original goal.

How to confront

Most clients are slow to recognize the dissonance between their words and actions, so you will have to call their attention to it. I would recommend this sequence:

1. **Outline the discrepancy** you have noticed between her words and actions -- "You said you wanted to move toward this career, but you haven't done much to put it into motion."

2. **Express your confusion** -- "I am puzzled by this difference between your words and actions."

3. **Ask what it means** -- "How do you interpret this discrepancy? Why have you not done anything to move yourself along?"

4. **Ask the client to decide** to reaffirm her original career goal, or decide upon a different goal.

5. **Decide with the client what actions he will take toward the original goal or the newly stated goal.** Tell the client he can anticipate that you'll confront him again if he does not complete his "assignments."

Special issues in confronting

When confronting a client about lack of action, there are certain defenses the client will use that may be difficult to cope with and may make the counselor feel she's putting unfair pressure on the client. Here's what to do about them:

"But I don't have time."

Many clients will use this excuse to justify their failure to complete tasks they said they would do. However, people continually make choices about how to allocate their time. If the client chooses to overlook a career task, it was because she decided to use that time for something she regarded as more important. Unless there is an unusual family emergency, "time" cannot be used as an excuse for ducking career tasks. "Not finding time" can usually be translated to mean "It wasn't important enough to me."

"Something unexpected happened in my life."

This is a variation on the "time" theme. Unexpected things happen in everyone's life on a recurring basis, yet people manage to complete the tasks that are important to them. The old bromide remains true: "we find time for the things that we want to find time for." When assigning "tasks," counselors can state in advance that "excuses" will be seen as exactly that, and the counselor will interpret the client's lack of action as a measure of her lack of motivation.

Overcoming inhibiting beliefs

Lack of action may mean something other than low motivation. It may mean that the client has certain beliefs about herself which inhibit her from taking action. Confronting can also be helpful here. The counselor might ask: *"What beliefs do you have about yourself that may be keeping you from completing these career tasks?"* For example, the client may believe:

"I don't really have the ability to do that, even though I want to. I'd better not try because I'll embarrass myself."

"I'm afraid that I'm not emotionally strong enough to stand the trials and frustrations."

"There are too many people competing for that career. I would just be overwhelmed, because my background is not good enough."

A client may draw exaggerated conclusions from her beliefs:

Belief: "I'm not emotionally strong enough."
Conclusion: "And I'll never get any stronger."

Belief: "The competition is too stiff for me."
Conclusion: "I'll just lose out repeatedly and be humiliated and will never improve enough to become competitive."

The counselor can help clients see these conclusions as premature and unnecessarily self-defeating and assist the client in making new self-statements such as:

"I'm emotionally shaky now, but once I get some experience in this new kind of work I'll calm down and learn the skills I need."

"I'm not competitive yet, but I have developed a strategy for practicing so that I have a good chance of making a place for myself. It's worth working hard to see what I can do."

Recent work by John Krumboltz and his associates at Stanford University is helping career counselors understand how to help clients overcome self-defeating beliefs. They have shown that clients can be helped to overcome beliefs which inhibit their behavior. As they clarify their beliefs, clients may motivate themselves to learn new job skills, take risks, and counter the undue influence of others.

Confronting is a kick and a kindness

Counselors are often hesitant to confront, because it feels as though they are criticizing clients for their failings. However, confronting is a constructive thing to do. It is the proverbial "kick in the rear" from a counselor who identifies with her client's strongest drives and wants to see her succeed.

Confronting is one of the kindest things a counselor can do, because it says: "I'm not just playing around here. I really want to see you get your career plan rolling toward your goals. My reward is seeing you make progress."

When clients do what they say they're going to do, they're on their way to being self-regulating, which is one of the best outcomes a counselor can hope for. When clients are congruent, their words, actions, body, and soul are all moving in the same direction.

Confronting is where a lot of the most pivotal moments occur in career counseling. The client is moving beyond idle speculation and shuffling around. It's time to decide what she really wants, clear out the pretenders and go with the career ideas that have the most promise. Time to decide where her motivation really is and kick the motor into gear. Confronting "forces" the client to decide: "Where am I going to devote my energies? I can change my mind later if necessary, but for now, where does my heart lead me?"

CHAPTER 22

Helping the
'Impossible Client'

by Howard Figler

There are some clients who tie their counselors tails in knots. It's their specialty. They like to see if you can really do career counseling, or if you just take the easy ones and let the problem cases fend for themselves.

The "impossible clients" are one of the main reasons we're in this business. If all we had were the easy ones --those who know what they want and do what they say they're going to -- it would be no fun. Besides, half of us got into this field because we were pretty "impossible" ourselves at one time, so we recognize the symptoms and can testify that the situation is curable.

Give yourself a break, and the client too. When they behave in "impossible" ways, understand that this is part of the grand struggle. Clients benefit from talking about their confusion. Often you are the only one who will listen to their meanderings. Clients need to hear themselves talk.

There is a variety of difficult clients, including many who:

• have a different career plan every day and talk a good game on all of them, but they have no intention of following through with anything

• bluff that they will do something, only to get the counselor's approval

• are continually discouraged, always on the edge of giving up

• blame everyone and everything except themselves for their drooping careers

"Impossible clients" are tests of your courage, your ability to resist your inner demons that tell you to "do something -- quickly!," your ability to be patient with the gradual shaping of the clay.

If you think that she can work this out, then she starts to believe it too.

Client Expectations

Clients often come to counselors as though they are visiting a fortune teller. Oh, Great and Wondrous Career-Nik:

"Tell me what I'm meant to do with my life."
"Make me as happy and successful as that woman over there."
"Tell me the very best careers of the future."
"Reveal to me new industries before they are born."

You're expected not only to know economic changes before they happen, but you must be able to read the client's mind, and divine connections between her and the marketplace.

Clients may be disappointed when you can't do these things. How can you deal with these expectations?

1. Tell the client what you can and cannot do. Be clear with the client about your role:

"I can help you shape and clarify what career options you may want, but I cannot forecast the labor market and I cannot predict where you will be most successful."

2. Help the client process her expectations:

"What did you hope to get from meeting with me, and how does that compare with what I've said that I can do?"

Working with difficult clients

In the face of uncertainty, some people move forward, while others avoid action and give up. The latter make us question our abilities as counselors. It's easy to say they are "difficult," but what do we do about them?

There are several approaches which will help us to work constructively with resistant clients and improve their chances of success:

#1 Believe in your client. We have all met individuals and said to ourselves: "this person will never make it." However, as soon as you believe that, you're both sunk.

Remember that we all once looked as though we might not have great prospects ourselves. Every individual, no matter how forlorn or impoverished, has talents that can be nurtured to success in the labor market, somewhere, somehow.

Take clients who have failed at everything they have tried so far in their lives. These are the people who most need a counselor to believe in them. Often such people have no one in their family who supports their aspirations.

In these cases, the career counselor occupies a special role, and the following approaches will help you work with them.

Above all, believe in the power of every individual to be useful and productive. Furthermore, everyone *wants* to be useful and productive, even if they may say that they don't care.

#2 Define immediately attainable tasks. The best tasks to focus on are the ones that can be done today. Many people cannot see beyond a day or two. If your client is thinking of being a veterinarian (a lot of people fantasize this career and others, but don't discourage them), offer him a book that describes the field, and direct him to a local vet who can show him the nature of her work.

Clients are beset with inertia. Getting them started is good medicine. The more immediate and attainable the task, the better. That leads to the next approach:

#3 Spell out how the short-term steps can lead to longer-term goals. Difficult clients respond well to structure -- a tangible series of steps that, when followed, make progress toward a career.

For example, if you wanted to be an accountant, the steps

might look like this: "Read requirements for accountant in the *Occupational Outlook Handbook* . . . observe a CPA at work . . . decide if you like what you see . . . take accounting and business courses in college . . . get experience at an accountant's office during college . . . complete college degree . . . begin preparation for the CPA exam."

The counselor works with the client to put this structure in place, and then helps the client develop a strategy for completing one step at a time.

#4 Create a support group. Instead of taking sole responsibility for supporting the client's progress, a counselor should encourage the client to have a "support team." This team would consist of four or five people, including friends, family members, or anyone else the client chooses. The client would meet with them for both support and challenge (get out and do it), and would be responsible for reporting to these team members on a regular basis. The "success team" concept is discussed in detail by Barbara Sher in her book *Team Works.*

#5 Recognize and celebrate initial and intermediate successes. People need rituals in their lives to acknowledge their progress. For "impossible clients," small steps of progress are reasons for celebration. Such rituals can include public recognition, names posted at the career center indicating who is doing what, cheers at job search support group meetings, a career center newsletter, and celebratory dinners with support team members.

Sometimes even the smallest token of recognition will spur a person to continue working, and perhaps send them into a higher gear. A counselor once gave a notoriously resistant client named Claudius a button to wear that said "I'm doing it" when he started showing up for classes in high school after years of being delinquent. Until that time, Claudius had never had any recognition for anything in his life.

#6 Acknowledge the client's futility. Sometimes, rather than reaffirming your belief in the client's abilities and pushing her toward action, it can be useful to do what seems counterproductive -- acknowledging the client's give-up-itis and stating it in the extreme:

"So you're saying that no matter what you do, you will inevitably have a bad interview, because most interviewers don't like you and you can't handle all their trick questions and games they play."

"You don't feel you have enough intelligence or ability to stand out and therefore you believe you'll be earning $5/hour all your life."

When a client hears his words played back with an air of finality -- "this is the way it will always be" -- it may jar him into saying: "Well, I didn't mean to say it's quite *that* bad." The counselor encourages him to reexamine his situation.

What if the client agrees with your statement of futility? Tell her you were exaggerating so she could "hear herself talk," and that you believe she can overcome her problems.

What to say when there's nothing left to be said

"I'll never make it. I'm just not cut out to have a place in this world of any importance."

"See, I told you I couldn't do it. Why would you even try helping a person like me?"

Such people have persuaded themselves they are on Team Loser, and they're trying to recruit you to join their team.

How do you end a career conversation in which you feel there has been no progress? Not with a weary sigh or an exhale of utter frustration. Instead, with signs of hope and acknowledgment that the best is yet to come:

"I know you need time to adjust your life to get started with the things that we've talked about. I'm looking forward to when you take those first steps, because I know you have it in you. What's the most immediate thing you can think of doing that would help you?"

For clients who can't think of anything to do to help themselves, counselors can suggest doable first steps and contract with the client to do them.

Some "impossible clients" would like the counselor to confirm their belief about a permanently negative role in the universe. However, the counselor refuses to be suckered in because she knows that most people have been "impossible" at one time or another in their lives.

"Impossible clients" are often waiting to see if you really believe they're worth anything. When you say it, mean it.

How do you know if you're succeeding?

Be careful how you measure your effectiveness as a counselor when relating to "impossible clients." You may have the romantic view that your inspired words will enable such clients to transform themselves and "throw off their shackles and live happily ever after." That's pushing it.

The progress of a counselor is measured modestly, in terms of how much you encourage people toward "movement," rather than closure of their goals. When a client takes a few short-term steps toward a rather distant goal -- that's movement.

Lucinda didn't think she would ever make it to the adult world. Her counselor at Dickinson College listened to her tale of woe on a regular basis: "There's nothing I can do with my History major." The counselor replied: "That's not true. There are many History majors employed in private industry, government, and nonprofit organizations." Lucinda fumed: "I didn't spend four years of college to go wandering around in the labor market!"

The counselor persisted in encouraging Lucinda to do her own exploration. She did nothing except write a letter to the alumni office complaining about the career center -- until after graduation. Then she grudgingly made a few contacts, had a few interviews, and called the counselor to rehash her pessimism. No contact for three months. Then Lucinda phoned to tell the counselor she had a part-time job with the Commerce Department in Washington, DC. She said this would give her access to full-time positions in the month ahead. Lucinda thanked the counselor for his help and said: "It's small, but it's a start. The months of bumping around in confusion were very helpful to me. I learned who I am. Your support and patience made all the difference."

One more case in the life of a career counselor. The rewards are not immediate or thunderous, but when they come, they're gratifying.

Other Factors Related To "Impossible Clients"

1. **Language/cultural barriers**. There are clients who are difficult to talk with because of language difficulties. Others may be culturally so different from you that you have trouble understanding their priorities or appreciating how they view situations. Explore these differences with the client, and express your concern that you may not be communicating effectively. Ask her for feedback.

If you and the client feel that there is a lot of difficulty in your communication, refer her to another counselor who speaks her language and/or has a more compatible cultural background.

2. **Clients who are not introspective**. Career counselors like talking about what goes on inside themselves, and they may unconsciously assume that everyone does. On the contrary, some people think little about their aspirations, goals, values, inner motivators, and such. When you ask them questions such as "What's important to you?" or "What do you feel strongly about?," they give you a blank look. With nonintrospective people: (a) Introduce them gently to self-understanding - - accept minimal responses to questions that call for introspection, and encourage them to do more; and (b) ask such clients to test their career aspirations largely through field experience. Rather than "thinking about" career ideas,

these clients may prefer to have experiences before saying anything about them.

3. **Psychological Issues**. Often there are underlying emotional concerns that make it difficult for a client to focus on career matters. These include unresolved anger, conflict with significant others, and chronic depression. When it's your judgment that such psychological issues are intruding on the client's ability to deal with careers, you should: (a) Introduce your observations into the conversation - - *"I can sense your anger as we talk about these things. Can you tell me more about these feelings?"* - - or (b) recommend that the client seek assistance regarding the emotional issues from someone other than yourself. You would continue to see her as a career client, if you feel she can make progress in this area. If at all possible, it's a good idea to continue career work while the client is getting psychological help.

4. **Personal incompatability with the client**. Let's face it. There are going to be some clients you don't like, or who don't like you. This is not a failure on your part. Some combinations of people just don't work well together. Check with the client to see how he/she thinks the counseling is progressing. If she acknowledges that it's not going well, and you feel the same, ask if she would like to see another counselor. Sometimes the client will say things are OK even when they're not, because they feel they would lose the counselor's approval.

If you sense from the client's nonverbal behavior that no progress is being made although the client says it is, talk to the client about your observations and recommend another counselor if you feel that would serve her interests better. Be careful to NOT communicate that you're "getting rid of" the client. Also, do not refer the client too quickly to someone else. Sometimes a client is getting used to you (starting to trust you) and even though they're frowning and looking glum, they feel something good is happening.

5. **The client was sent by someone else; she really doesn't want to be there.** When the client shows up to satisfy someone else (a parent, a teacher, etc.), you have a barrier that must be dealt with, the earlier the better, because this initial resistance will usually block any of your efforts.

"I understand you're here because ———— sent you. How do you feel about that? How interested are you in talking with me?

After saying "———— sent me," or "I don't know why I'm here," the client may warm up to the process and decide that she has something to gain by talking with you. Ask her: "What do you think a career counselor might do for you?"

If the client persists in resisting, don't push her to talk. Invite her to consider later conversations with you by outlining briefly some of the ways you might be helpful. Tell her that if the referring person calls, you'll inform her/him that the client was there, but *you will not reveal to that person ANYTHING regarding what you talked about.* In other words, you emphasize that she has and will have complete confidentiality with you.

"Impossible clients" are not impossible. Their resistance is a cover for the frustrations they've had with the world of work. They want to prosper as much as the next person, even more so. They're only "impossible" because their career development is all locked up and they don't know the combination. You, of course, help them to find it.

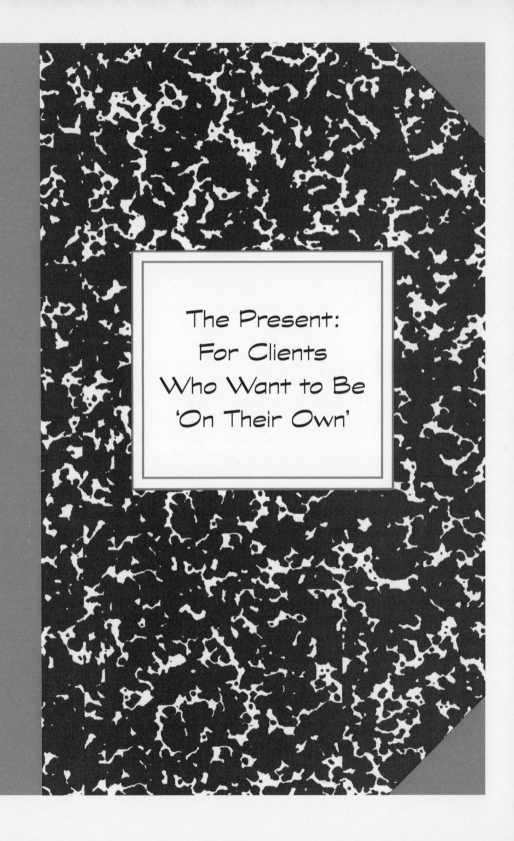

The Present:
For Clients
Who Want to Be
'On Their Own'

CHAPTER 23

A Return to the Real America

by Howard Figler

For most or all of our past memory (1945–1995), "regular employment" has been so much the norm for the working person that American free enterprise was almost lost in the shuffle. That 50-year historical blip is over. In the place of steady jobs, people are learning to regard themselves as self-employed. This is what our country meant all along in calling itself the land of free enterprise. The re-emergence has been brewing for a while.

Dan Lacey predicted the fading of steady employment in *The Paycheck Disruption* (1988) and Cliff Hakim's book, *We Are All Self-Employed* (1994), stated the need to reorient ourselves in the marketplace. Bill Bridges' recent book, *You, Inc.* (1997), confirms the importance of each individual being his/her own enterprise.

In the late 19th century and the early 20th century, being employed was often referred to as "wage slavery." This view made it clear that earning wages was out of synch with the American ideal, which was to be as entrepreneurial as possible.

After a long wait, free enterprise is returning to occupy its rightful place as the economic preference of many citizens. Increasingly, people are giving stronger consideration to business ownership as a possible career, as either a primary or supplementary form of income. American enterprise is reasserting itself for the everyday person. This is the way things were meant to be for our country and economic system.

Free enterprise is an attitude. Even though some of your clients may never own a business, they can participate in this return to entrepreneurial America in several ways. If they ignore these ways, they will be far less prosperous:

1. Be a part of solving the market problems of your employer. Act as though it's your money, your company, and your responsibility for whether the company rises or falls. You'll see your job with a new pair of glasses.

2. Move to the employers who most encourage employees to participate in solving the company's problems.

3. Be prepared to transfer your skills and knowledge to new employers as the market dictates. Don't be afraid to go where the money is or, better yet, where you think it will be in the future.

4. Be prepared to sell your skills to customers and clients on an entrepreneurial basis as necessary. The market will not always have the "regular jobs" you want. Instead, it may offer you opportunities to be an independent contractor or vendor.

Entrepreneuring is woven into the fabric of this country, but we've been oblivious to that because steady employment ruled during every year of our lifetimes, until a few years ago. Listen to what Abraham Lincoln had to say about being enterprising:

> The prudent, penniless beginner in the world labors for wages a while, saves a surplus with which to buy tools or land . . . then labors on his own account for a while, and then at length hires another new beginner to help him. This is the just and generous and prosperous system, which opens the way to all, gives hope to all.

Lincoln's words remind us that self-employment and business ownership are the ways of our country. Employment is only a temporary condition; ownership is the long-term goal. According to Lincoln, it's moral, prudent and makes good sense to have control over your economic life, rather than being employed by someone else.

John Hancock said that ownership is not only good for you, it's good for the nation:

The more people who own little businesses of their own,
the safer our country will be . . . for the people who have
a stake in their country and their community are its best
citizens

Look at it this way -- even if you get a salary check each
week, the company is only renting your skills. And who
knows how long they'll want you? As Bill Bridges has said:
we're all temporary workers, but 80% of us are in denial.

We think of today's labor market as a time of great chaos,
but it's more a time of great opportunity (the Chinese have
the same symbol for both of these concepts -- crisis and opportunity).

Chaos is normal and always will be in a free market economy. If you're in business, you want the market to be dynamic,
so that your business can grow. And you *are* in business.
Everyone is. As Bridges says, your enterprise is you.

We should be happy that the economy is continually
changing. As businesses reach out for new customers and
new markets, they create opportunities for people who have
the skills they need. Initiative, risk taking, resourcefulness, and
sensitivity to the marketplace are all rewarded.

The ground is being tilled for a new entrepreneurial era in
America. Those who see themselves as self-marketers will
prosper. Those who cling to the idea that job performance will
sustain them will become victims of market forces. Job performance is not as important as "adding value" for your
employer.

Let me give you an example. Neil "did his job" as a travel
agent for several years until the agency lost its customer base
and closed its doors. He had seen the service slipping badly.
Tour bookings decreased as the staff lost its enthusiasm. Customer records were lost. Neil watched in dismay but said or
did little about it, fearing that he would "rock the boat." "Not
my job" became a prelude to disaster. Neil has since joined
another agency where he speaks up regularly about what can

best help the business, and is building his capital to buy a stake in the ownership.

The Information Era makes it possible for many people to be self-employed without a large capital investment. You have a set of skills and areas of knowledge. Put these to use where they'll yield the most gain. Your customers (who may include your employers) decide how your skills fit their needs, and money changes hands. Between your skills and their needs is the fine art of selling.

This country thrives by having thousands of owners competing with each other. However, entrepreneuring is puzzling to many people because most of their parents did not have enterprising careers. They had those "steady jobs" which have now disappeared. Thus, our task is to turn their heads around, and it's not an easy one. I suggest that you keep close track of your clients who are most resilient and enterprising in today's economy and tell their stories to your other clientele.

No, not the tale of Bill Gates, but stories such as that lived by Laura, who got on with Texas Instruments through selling her writing skills, then joined the local Chamber of Commerce as VP for Economic Development, then relocated to Baton Rouge where she started a computer software business, folded it, then marketed herself as an economic consultant to industry, then helped her brother open a machine tool shop by providing her business expertise. All this by a woman who had majored in Humanities during college and had never taken a business course.

Is this a great country, or what? Laura changed careers four times in ten years and has many business and job opportunities awaiting her. The more new skills she learns, the more tools she can apply to future career changes.

Many are creating business opportunities related to their personal interests. In the case of Dineh Mohajer, founder of the business Hard Candy, she followed her instincts:

"I didn't start Hard Candy to make a fortune. I started my nail

polish company . . . as a break from the intense amount of research I had been doing (in college) . . . I started the business out of my home with my boyfriend and my sister. Nail polish is pretty easy to whip up . . . During that summer, my boyfriend asked a friend at a Santa Monica boutique to sell our items . . ."

And the rest is history. America was never meant to be a country where people indentured themselves to companies and called this "lifetime employment."

It's no longer possible, and it may not be desirable either for your clients to lock their talents into lifetime jobs with single employers. While a steady paycheck can be nice, it may require the employee to make concessions in exchange for the money. Some employers create significant stress for their employees because of severe work demands, time pressure, and bosses squeezing out "a few more ounces of productivity." In some cases, long-term employment can be like servitude.

In the big picture, lifetime employment for thousands is much closer to socialism than it is to capitalism. People who are used to being employees should develop their entrepreneurial options, so they always have alternative sources of income, if and when working for someone else becomes too unpleasant or even oppressive. When in Rome . . . When in America, be enterprising.

Career counselors must work hard to help people take full advantage of self-employment and free enterprise as concepts, because many are not ready for them. Workers were parented by organizations for a long time. Many will yearn for "the good ol' days," which were not as good as they thought. But of course, assisting people with their difficult career transitions is what we're here for -- to help clients prosper from the reemergence of American enterprise rather than hide from it.

CHAPTER 24

How to Help Our Clients Think about Self-Employment

by Dick Bolles

What Can You Do To Help Them?

You have to be very new to the career counseling field, not to have run into some client who is dreaming about self-employment as their future.

Some clients dream about being self-employed from the day that they were born. They are born entrepreneurs, just waiting for the right moment to take the leap.

Then there are other clients who never seriously considered self-employment until the moment that they find themselves out of work. Then, and only then, faced with the terror of the job-hunt, self-employment begins to look more and more alluring to them. You can see the vision dancing like sugarplums in their wee little eyes: "Maybe I won't have to send out all those resumes, maybe I won't have to place all those telephone calls, ring all those doorbells, go through those dreaded interviews, and wait for those inevitable turndowns. Maybe I can go the self-employment route!"

OK, so how many people are we talking about here, all in all? Well, the Current Population Survey's latest report (at this writing) said that 11.5% of all male workers, and 9.2% of all female workers were self-employed. So, if your client list were representative of the population at large, about every tenth client would want your help with this issue. In your particular practice, of course, the statistics may vary quite a bit from that norm. Up or down.

But the question is: what can you do to help them?

Well, I think our primary function is to make sure they're choosing a card from a full deck. In other words, to make sure they're aware of *all* the kinds of self-employment there are, for them to choose from. And, basically, that comes down to six.

The Six Kinds of Self-Employment

There are six basic types of self-employment, corresponding to the six different *Holland types,* as shown in this diagram:

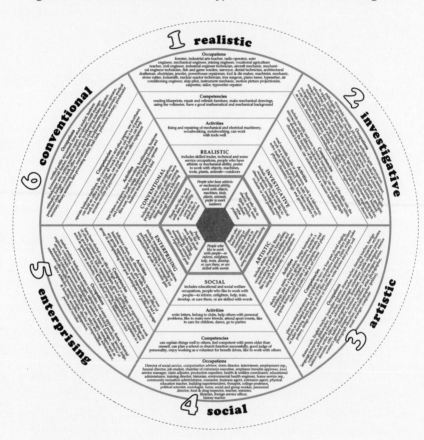

Instructions

You are invited to cut out the next three pages (along the dotted lines) in order to paste or tape them together in the above formation.

Cut out and
paste or tape
together.

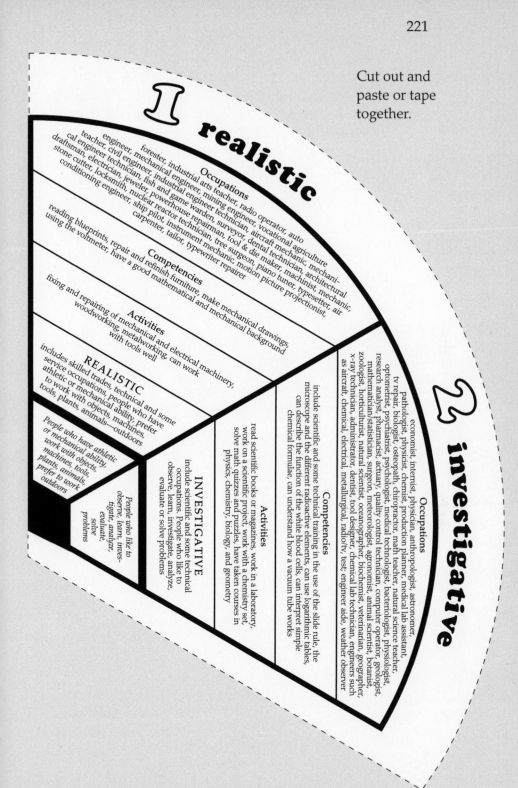

1 realistic

Occupations

engineer, industrial arts teacher, radio operator, auto
forester, mechanical engineer, mining engineer, vocational agriculture
teacher, civil engineer, industrial engineer technician, aircraft mechanic, mechanical engineer technician, fish and game warden, surveyor, aircraft mechanic, architectural
draftsman, electrician, jeweler, powerhouse repairman, tool & die maker, machinist, mechanic,
stone cutter, locksmith, nuclear reactor technician, tree surgeon, piano tuner, typesetter, air
conditioning engineer, ship pilot, instrument mechanic, motion picture projectionist,
carpenter, tailor, typewriter repairer

Competencies

reading blueprints, repair and refinish furniture, make mechanical drawings,
using the voltmeter, have a good mathematical and mechanical background

Activities

fixing and repairing of mechanical and electrical machinery,
woodworking, metalworking, can work
with tools well

REALISTIC

includes skilled trades technical and some
service occupations, people who have
athletic or mechanical ability, prefer
to work with objects, machines,
tools, plants, animals—outdoors

People who have athletic
or mechanical ability,
work with objects, tools,
machines,
plants, animals,
prefer to work
outdoors

People who like to
observe, learn, inves-
tigate, analyze,
evaluate,
solve
problems

INVESTIGATIVE

include scientific and some technical
occupations. People who like to
observe, learn, investigate, analyze,
evaluate or solve problems

Activities

read scientific books or magazines, work in a laboratory,
work on a scientific project, work with a chemistry set,
solve math quizzes and puzzles, have taken courses in
physics, chemistry, biology, and geometry

Competencies

include scientific and some technical training in the use of the slide rule, the
microscope and the different radioactive elements, can use logarithmic tables,
can describe the function of the white blood cells, can interpret simple
chemical formulae, can understand how a vacuum tube works

Occupations

economist, internist, physician, anthropologist, astronomer,
pathologist, physicist, chemist, production planner, medical lab assistant,
tv repair, biologist, osteopath, chiropractor, math teacher, natural science teacher,
optometrist, psychiatrist, psychologist, medical technologist, bacteriologist, physiologist,
research analyst, pharmacist, actuary, quality control technician, computer operator, geologist,
mathematician/statistician, surgeon, meteorologist, agronomist, animal scientist, botanist,
zoologist, horticulturist, natural scientist, oceanographer, biochemist, veterinarian, geographer,
x-ray technician, administrator, dentist, tool designer, chemical lab technician, engineers such
as aircraft, chemical, electrical, metallurgical, radio/tv, test; engineer aide, weather observer

2 investigative

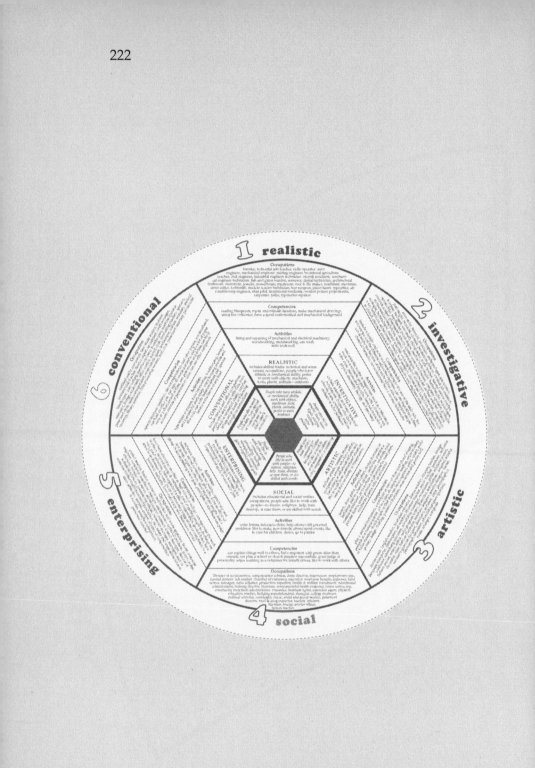

Cut out and
paste or tape
together.

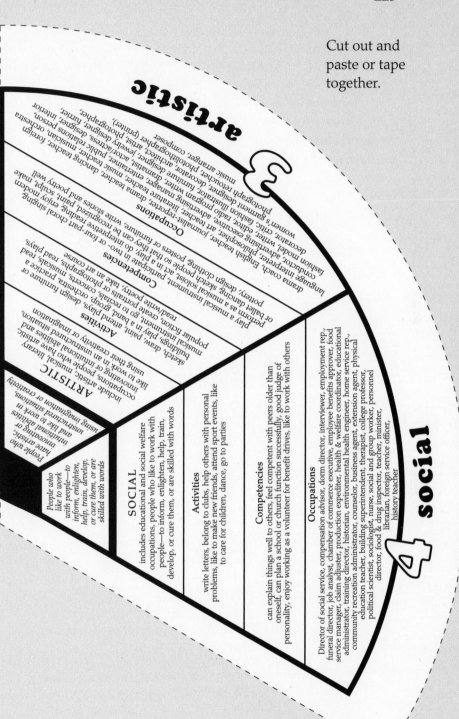

artistic 3

Occupations

foreign teacher, dancing teacher, musician, orchestra conductor, music teacher, entertainer, actor/actress, designer, interior decorator, architect, jewelry designer, artist, photographer, fashion model, fashion illustrator, photolithographer (printer), writer, critic, radio program manager, furniture designer, funnier, advertising executive, public relations person, women's garment designer, music arranger, composer

drama coach, English teacher, journalist–reporter, language interpreter, philosopher, art teacher, literature teacher

Competencies

play a musical instrument, participate in two- or four-part choral singing, enjoy modern or ballet dancing, sketch people so that they can be recognized, paint, sculpt, make pottery, design clothing, posters or furniture, write stories and poetry well

perform as a musical soloist, act in a play, do interpretive reading, read/write poetry, take an art course

Activities

sketch, draw, paint, attend plays, design furniture or buildings, play in a band, group, orchestra, practice a musical instrument, go to recitals, concerts, musicals, read popular fiction, create portraits or photographs, read plays

ARTISTIC

include artistic, literary musical occupations, people who have artistic innovating or intuitional abilities and like to work in an unstructured situation, using their creativity or imagination

People who have artistic, innovating or intuitional abilities and like to work in unstructured situations, using imagination or creativity

People who like to work with people—to inform, enlighten, help, train, develop, or cure them, or are skilled with words

SOCIAL

includes educational and social welfare occupations, people who like to work with people—to inform, enlighten, help, train, develop, or cure them, or are skilled with words

Activities

write letters, belong to clubs, help others with personal problems, like to make new friends, attend sport events, like to care for children, dance, go to parties

Competencies

can explain things well to others, feel competent with peers older than oneself, can plan a school or church function successfully, good judge of personality, enjoy working as a volunteer for benefit drives, like to work with others

Occupations

Director of social service, compensation advisor, dorm director, interviewer, employment rep., funeral director, job analyst, chamber of commerce executive, employee benefits approver, food service manager, claim adjuster, production expediter, health & welfare coordinator, educational administrator, training director, historian, environmental health engineer, home service rep., community recreation administrator, counselor, business agent, extension agent, physical education teacher, building superintendent, therapist, college professor, political scientist, sociologist, nurse, social and group worker, personnel director, food & drug inspector, teacher, minister, librarian, foreign service officer, history teacher

social 4

224

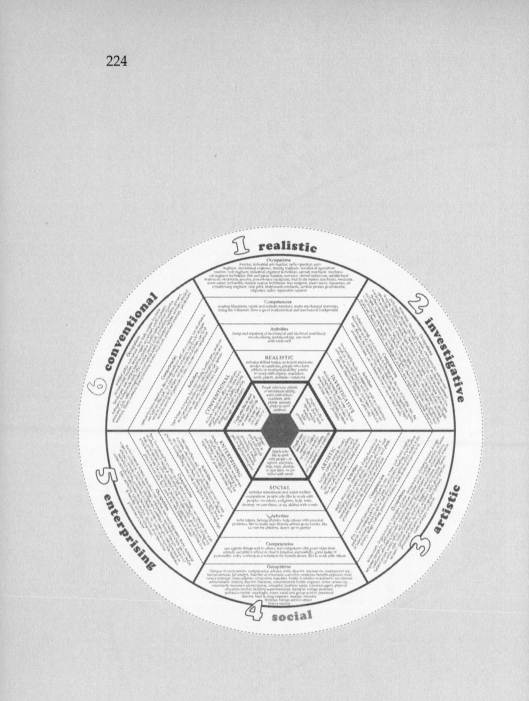

Cut out and
paste or tape
together.

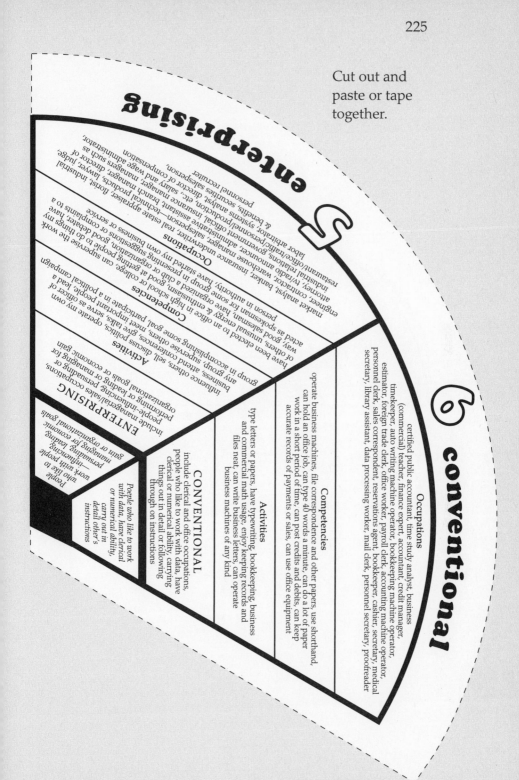

5 enterprising

Occupations
market analyst, banker, insurance underwriter, real estate appraiser, florist, industrial engineer, ttv/radio announcer, government official, salesperson—technical products, lawyer, judge, attorney, contractor, warehouse manager, administrative assistant, insurance manager, director of restaurant/office/traffic/personnel/production, systems analyst, branch manager, director of industrial relations, labor arbitrator, securities analyst, etc., salary and wage administrator, personnel recruiter

Competencies
can supervise the work of others, have unusual energy & enthusiasm, have been elected to an office in high school or college, can organize a club or group in presenting suggestions or complaints to a person in authority, have started my own business or service, good at getting people to do things my way, good salesman, have organized a club or group in accomplishing some goal, participate in a political campaign, acted as spokesman for some group

Activities
influence others, sell things, operate my own business, operate as officer of any group, attend conferences, give talks, serve as officer of business politics, supervise others, meet important people, lead a organizational goals of leading or managing for economic gain

ENTERPRISING
include managerial/sales occupations, people-influencing/persuading or managing for economic gain or organizational goals

People who like to work with people—influencing, persuading, leading, managing for economic gain or organizational goals

6 conventional

Occupations
certified public accountant, time study analyst, business (commercial) teacher, finance expert, accountant, credit manager, timekeeper, auto writing machine operator, bookkeeping machine operator, estimator, foreign trade clerk, office worker, payroll clerk, accounting machine operator, personnel clerk, sales correspondent, reservations agent, bookkeeper, cashier, secretary, medical secretary, library assistant, data processing worker, mail clerk, personnel secretary, proofreader

Competencies
operate business machines, file correspondence and other papers, use shorthand, can hold an office job, can type 40 words a minute, can do a lot of paper work in a short period of time, can post credits and debits, can keep accurate records of payments or sales, can use office equipment

Activities
type letters or papers, have typewriting, bookkeeping business and commercial math usage, enjoy keeping records and files neat, can write business letters, can operate business machines of any kind

CONVENTIONAL
include clerical and office occupations, people who like to work with data, have clerical or numerical ability, carrying things out in detail or following through on instructions

People who like to work with data, have clerical or numerical ability, carry out in detail other's instructions

226

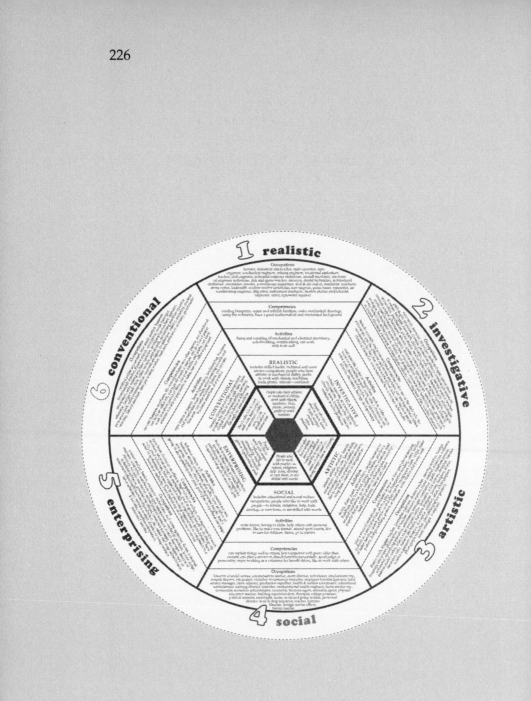

This diagram is taken from pages 426–432 of *The Three Boxes of Life, and How to Get Out of Them: An Introduction to Life-Work Planning,* by Richard N. Bolles (Ten Speed Press, 1978). This diagram was developed and copyrighted by Jerry Hanisko and Lorraine Massaro, 1976, based on John L. Holland's Self-Directed Search, copyright © 1975 by John L. Holland, Ph.D., and reproduced by permission of Consulting Psychologists Press, Inc. The SDS is available online (www.self-directed-search.com), or in paper form from PAR (Psychological Assessment Resources, Inc.), P.O. Box 998, Odessa, FL 33556, 1-800-331-TEST, or www.parinc.com.

Reading from the top of the hexagon diagram, and going clockwise, here are the self-employment types you can use to expand your clients' thinking:

1. **The Self-Employed Realistic Person.** These are the people who love to use their hands, and work with the physical universe. They may think they are not candidates for self-employment, but of course they are. Examples would be auto mechanics, or repairpersons, or piano tuners, or furniture refinishers, or carpenters, or jewelers, etc. -- who are in business for themselves. Sometimes they may have their own shop or store, but equally they may choose to operate out of their home.

2. **The Self-Employed Investigative Person.** These are the people who love to think, and explore, and figure out things. They may think they are not candidates for self-employment, but of course they are. Examples would be researchers, or investigators, or physicians, psychiatrists, dentists, or surgeons, who have their own offices and work for themselves (sometimes by themselves).

3. **The Self-Employed Artistic Person.** These are the people who love to create. They may think they are not candidates for self-employment, but of course they are. Examples would be artists, writers, composers, dramatists, poets, fashion designers, jewelry designers, furniture designers, photographers,

web designers, etc., who create a work and then sell it to an individual or group. This category would also include speakers, entertainers, musicians, etc., who are sufficiently established to have people offer contracts to them. And those sufficiently established in their arts to be able to teach it to others, at home, in community colleges, etc.

4. **The Self-Employed Social Person.** These are people who love to work with others. They may think they are not candidates for self-employment, but of course they are. Examples would be counselors, therapists, teachers, itinerant ministers, career counselors, human resource people, etc., who decide to establish their own practice, or their own offices. It would also include the funeral director with his or her own parlor, the agent who decides to freelance, etc.

5. **The Self-Employed Enterprising Person.** These are the initiative-taking people. Here, at last, we have the kind of self-employment that is most often written and talked about -- often as though it were the only kind of self-employment -- namely, starting or buying and then running your own business or franchise. The skills which most books and government pamphlets single out, as necessary to running a business, are usually Enterprising skills or traits: viz., 'drive,' 'achievement-oriented,' 'willing to take calculated risks,' 'demonstrating leadership skills,' etc. Enterprising self-employed people typically are start-up people, owners of franchises, small business owners, founders of corporations, planners, consultants, salespeople and so forth. They are also those who by the very nature of their business have their own practices: lawyers, physicians, dentists, and the like.

6. **The Self-Employed Conventional Person.** These are the people who love to attend to details. They may think they are not candidates for self-employment, but of course they are. Examples would be accountants or CPAs who are in business for themselves, secretaries who run their own secretarial services, or temp agency, etc.

If you as career counselor talk to any of the six types of workers (above) while they are still working for someone-else, they may get positively misty-eyed over this idea of now working only for themselves. At last, at last, their soul cries out, they will be freed of having to pay attention to the whims and wishes of an employer. No one to tell them what to do, and when to do it! Right? Well, not exactly.

There is a sense in which every self-employed person works for someone else, and therefore has to pay attention to what that 'someone else' wants. Every self-employed person has an invisible, rarely identified employer or employers.

We can therefore classify all self-employed people, regardless of which of the six types listed above they may technically belong to, by who their real employer is.

We can help our clients who are eyeing self-employment, by getting them to think about who their real employer is, with some such words as these:

Who Your Real Employer Is

There are four possibilities:

1. **Many Others.** When you are dependent on many others for your income, then many others are your real employers. These 'many others' are normally called 'customers,' or 'clients,' or 'consumers,' or 'patrons,' or 'students,' or you name it. What you have to offer them is usually a service, or information, or a product. But if they don't want what you have to offer, you will quickly be out of work and starving. That is why it is useful to think of them as your employers. Except they 'fire you' by staying away, in droves. And you need to pay close attention to what they want from you. If, for example, you are setting up a web site, you need to think out who the various audiences are that you want to have come to your web site, then -- finding volunteers from each audience - - ask them what they would want at a web site that satisfied them perfectly; have them go on to your web site, and see if they find

what they want. If not, alter your web site accordingly. Follow this same process regardless of what kind of self-employment you are thinking of. Constantly reinvent yourself and what you are offering the public.

2. **Many Others through One 'Switchboard'.** When your access to many others is through one person/agency/office/agent, then both that 'switchboard' and those many others are your real employers. In the case of an author, the switchboard is the publisher. In the case of an actor, the switchboard is the agent or studio. In the case of a franchise buyer, the switchboard is the franchiser. In the case of a reporter, the switchboard is the newspaper. The point is, you have access to many, but only through this intermediary. Therefore you have to seek to please them plus the many others out there whom you ultimately work for.

3. **One Person.** When one person funds you, that person is your real employer. They control the money, they give you the money. They may give you lots of liberty with that money, or they may keep you on a tight leash. Make no mistake, you have to pay lots of attention to what they want, and what pleases or displeases them. In the case of an artist, it might be a patron or benefactor. In the case of a researcher, it may be a foundation grant. You may think you're home free, but if you forget who your real employer is, you're in trouble.

4. **Nobody.** When you're independently wealthy, either because somebody left you very well off, or you won the lottery, or you've toiled for years and now have enough money to do anything you please, you might think that at last you've come into Valhalla. True self-employment. Working only for your self and your own pleasure. But wait a minute: the Gallup poll has consistently found that 94% of the American people believe in some kind of God. And if you are among them, then of course you still have an employer: your real employer is God. And you will want to take His wishes into account, in how you run your business and how you treat your customers.

Conclusion

When we are dealing with someone contemplating a career-change, our job as career counselors is to show them that self-employment is a viable option for them, regardless of which corner of the Holland hexagon they fall into.

But we must also help them understand that the term 'self-employment' is relative, that there will almost always be someone (or some*ones*) that they have to please, if their business is to succeed.

Therefore, sitting down and thinking out ahead of time who their real employer will be, and then identifying what that employer will want of them, increases greatly their chance of succeeding at whatever type of business they choose.

Our role is to guide them gently through that process, prior to their stepping out into self-employment.

CHAPTER 25

Schooling
and Entrepreneuring

by Howard Figler

___

Why is it that many of our best entrepreneurs have little formal education and many of our most educated people are ineffective at entrepreneuring and selling themselves in the marketplace?

Many entrepreneurs are driven by believing that they had better come up with a product or service the market wants and sell it relentlessly. They learn by experience what a lot of the rest of us could use -- persistence in focusing on your customers, finding out what they want, and giving it to them. The absence of degrees on your resume becomes irrelevant.

Entrepreneurs have that lean and hungry look. They don't sit around thinking of "a little business I might start." They don't sit at all. And they probably act more than they think. They learn by experience rather than by cogitating. The school of hard knocks is a unique educational system. It rewards you when you're right, and when you're not right, well there's always something new to learn.

Of course I am picking on the highly educated because I have seen the problems they encounter in dealing with the emerging entrepeneurial climate in the American economy. Too many years of taking classroom exams and wiggling through the answers seems to dull the senses. Ph.D.'s like me are often the worst.

What is it about schooling that dampens the go-getter instinct? Schooling does a lot of good things, but the years of test taking cultivate passivity. I do what the professor asks of me. Creativity is stifled in the name of keeping some faculty member happy.

How do you go from School -- having professors hanging over your shoulder, challenging every phrase you write or speak -- to Business -- where *you* make the decisions on everything? Not an easy transition.

Master's and Ph.D. graduates are often reluctant dragons when it comes to starting businesses even though they have skills which are greatly marketable. Not only are they not business-oriented, they may especially resist the idea of "selling" anything, including themselves.

There are undoubtedly reasons that well-educated people are often awkward and anxious when selling themselves. Whatever they are, it's unfortunate when many people with undergraduate and advanced degrees avoid this essential fact -- all graduates are salespeople from the moment they walk across that stage.

People with degrees (especially those with more than one academic credential) often tend to belittle "salespeople," thinking of them as crude hucksters and shameless self-promoters. This is exaggerated and inaccurate. Academics may place themselves, in all their pomposity, above the crowd. Down below is where the action is taking place and where people are making money and having fun as well.

Many well-educated people are doing very nicely in the give-and-take of the marketplace, but there are still many more who tremble when they ask themselves: "What do I have to offer if I can't get an academic job?"

Educated people must view Business as an anthropologist would approach a new culture. The norms of business are different from academia, in some ways polar opposites. How to adapt to this foreign culture? The natives (of business) respect action and results. They have their own language -- buzz words. They value and reward teamwork, which is different from academia.

We all need rehabilitation in something, and people with academic degrees need entrepreneurial rehabilitation. Years in school have made them passive when it comes to the marketplace, so let's look at what can be done. This rehabilitation may be necessary for Bachelors graduates, but it will be especially needed for those having more than one degree.

When academically-trained people decide to seek nonacademic employment, or start a business, they must overcome the fear factor -- "I'm willing to work, but do I have anything they want? I don't want to fall on my face and humiliate myself." Acknowledging the fear is a first step and deciding to do something about it is next.

The best way to deal with the fear is through exposure. Volunteer work, part-time work, and any kind of temporary work in the business world will help the naive academic to become familiar with how business people think and interact. The pay will be low and "temporary" work takes time, but this acculturation is absolutely necessary.

Once acclimated, the "educated" will see ways their skills can be used in business and other nonacademic jobs. For openers, research, writing, speaking, and foreign language skills are highly valued. Bachelor's, Master's, and Ph.D. grads have great potential as business leaders because of their superior communication skills and the breadth and depth of their thinking.

Schooling and Entrepreneuring/Selling are not necessarily opposites or contradictory to each other. Once the "educated" overcome their fears and willingly adapt to the business world, a vast pool of talent will be unleashed.

It is also interesting to reflect on why unschooled people are often successful in entrepreneuring and selling. Necessity is often the mother, father, brother, and sister of invention, but that's not the whole story. Since many entrepreneurs succeed without taking any business courses in school, this doesn't say a lot about business theory and what's taught in class. If experience is the best teacher, then entrepreneurs and salespeople are in class all day, every day.

Salespeople have an expression -- "Fake it till you make it." Students, undergraduate and graduate, are not allowed to fake it. In that sense, entrepreneuring may be liberating for them.

Oh, well. Ultimately, the streetwise movers and shakers of business and the "educated" have a lot to learn from each other. Why don't we have a big party and get 'em together?

I admire business people; they are the backbone of our diverse and resilient economy. Degree-holders need to know that credentials are only pieces of paper in a "What-can-you-do-for-me?" marketplace. When the well-educated seize the entrepreneurial spirit, and I am confident they will, it will be an interesting sight to see.

CHAPTER 26

Everyone
Is a Salesperson

by Howard Figler

There is a movement afoot to have all job searchers and career changers think like entrepreneurs and act like salespeople. Entrepreneuring? Urp. Ugh. Selling? Have mercy.

We're not eager to embrace either entrepreneuring or selling. Yet here we are in an era where no job is safe, and most of our clients will wake up one morning having to sell themselves to employers or to prospective customers or clientele. Yesterday I couldn't even spell "entrepreneur" and now I are one.

Entrepreneurs recognize that jobs don't grow in the earth. Jobs exist only when markets are created and promoted. Entrepreneurs find out what people want and sell it to them. Your clients must adopt the entrepreneurial attitude which says: "I cannot count on any demand being there tomorrow. I must continually read what the market wants now and change accordingly. My success will result from my ability (and that of my employer) to adapt to these changing needs." If you work for a company and sales are falling, you must ask yourself: "What can I do about this?"

Selling is directly parallel to the experience of job hunting. Until we invent a better word for it, selling is what we are teaching our job hunters to do. Nothing moves until somebody sells it. Whenever money changes hands in the marketplace, you can be sure that somebody has sold something to someone. If you want someone to pay for your skills, services or products, you'll have to persuade them they'll receive enough value to justify spending their money.

We like teaching job search, but we're slow to warm up to

the idea of teaching "selling." They are similar, and perhaps are even the same thing. Here are key terms and concepts that salespeople use, and how they can be expressed in the language of the job search counselor.

1. **Get in front of people**. The first rule of selling is that face-to-face contact is necessary to maximize your chances of making a sale. In job hunting, it's the same. Information interviews, informal contacts, networking, and job interviews are all ways of getting in front of people. Job searchers learn that the greater the percentage of time they spend in face-to-face contact (60% or more is a must), the more successful they'll be in all phases of job hunting.

2. **Do a needs assessment**. Good salespeople know that if you can't give the customers what they need or want, you're finished. Once they are in front of prospective customers, salespeople ask: "Which of your needs are unsatisfied?" As Dick Bolles has emphasized, the job hunter must do information gathering first, in order to prepare for the job interviews which will come later. This is "needs assessment" by another name.

Effective questions for information interviews can include:

- "What skills are you most willing to pay for?"
- "What are your biggest problems and what do you hope someone will do to solve them?"
- "What can a new employee do for you that will most help the company?"

The more you know about the needs of the employer, the better you can sell yourself.

3. **Outline the benefits**. Once having identified the customer's needs, salespeople explain how their products or services will satisfy these needs. They outline the benefits the buyer will receive. This is similar to how we prepare job hunters for interviews. We teach them to explain: "Here are the skills I have that will give you what you're looking for."

The top-level job hunters are those who can relate their skills to the particular problems the employer is facing. Thus, they are "outlining the benefits" of hiring them, similar to what salespeople do.

4. **Overcome the objections**. Salespeople know that there are always going to be reasons the buyer can find to resist being "closed" for the sale. Their job is to anticipate these objections and counter them effectively. In the same way, job hunters must anticipate their areas of vulnerability and be prepared to show how they're dealing with any "weaknesses"in constructive ways. An employer may have "objections" about the job candidate's insufficient skill or lack of knowledge in a particular area.

Questions about perceived "weaknesses" are what I call Knockout Questions that can occur in job interviews -- you're knocked out if you cannot answer them effectively. All job hunters must anticipate these questions and answer them by telling how they're improving the skills or building the knowledge base that the employer requires.

5. **Ask for the sale**. This is the point in selling and job hunting where people get weak in the knees. It sounds simple and obvious, but salespeople know you have to ask for the business, if you're going to have half a chance of getting it. Let the buyers know you believe you can satisfy their needs and want to do business with them. "Closing" the customer (the employer) is necessary in job hunting too. The individual should say: "I believe I'm the right person for this job, and I want to work for you."

Job hunters have always been salespeople because they ask for money in exchange for their services. Employees have only recently been asked to think and act like salespeople, now that markets are unstable and every company (and all its employees) must "sell" its customers again and again.

In all likelihood, most of your clients will do both kinds of selling in their working lifetimes -- selling themselves for jobs and selling a product or a service in the marketplace. These two kinds of "selling" are interchangeable. You get good at one, you get good at the other.

Used car salespeople have given selling a bad name, but you and your clients do not have to sell that way. Selling is a fundamental human activity and your clients can do it with dignity.

If we get used to the idea of selling, we can help clients to incorporate it and do it well. In a free enterprise economy, if clients are not enterprising, they won't prosper. Selling is not rude, crude, or unsavory. Quite the contrary. We do it all day long. We sell ideas, attempt to persuade others to see our viewpoints, and describe the benefits of actions we want them to take: *"Why don't you get a new jacket like that one? You'll look cool in it."*

You're not going to teach your job hunters to be hucksters. People can sell themselves honestly and adapt selling to their personal styles. Selling can be done low-key, in an "educational" manner, in whatever ways feel comfortable for both seller and "customer" (interviewer, boss, product buyer, etc.). Your clients can sell in their own ways, calmly, confidently, with class and enthusiasm.

First, practice selling in your own career, before teaching clients how to do it. You thought I was going to forget that part. Cozy up to selling. It will hug you back.

CHAPTER 27

Five Business Cards
Instead of One

by Howard Figler

Today's career success may carry five business cards and be serious about them all. We used to laugh at such people, but now they may be showing us the way. Are we turning into a bunch of multiple personality hucksters? No. We're learning that if one source of income is good, then five may be better.

In the dawning era of contract work, layoff as a way of life, and the disappearance of the word "permanent" in the world of employment, we are learning to fend for ourselves. We may not have grown up wanting to be entrepreneurs but, by golly, we'll do it rather than be victims of this change-a-minute economy.

Don't let that "entrepreneur" word scare you or your clients. It used to refer to a special breed that us ordinary folks could not relate to. You know the type -- swashbuckling, rootin'-tootin' gunslinger, cutting down the competition, a fearless innovator of the business world. Does that sound like us ordinary people? No! But just as the Macintosh was designed "for the rest of us," entrepreneuring is now for the 90% who never defined themselves as swashing any buckles.

Now what might those five business cards be that you're carrying?

- two or three different employers who have contracted your services
- a part-time business that supports you when you're between jobs
- a business you've developed to supplement your regular income

- other business ideas that you're cultivating just to see how they feel
- a source of income that you're building for your "retirement days"

That adds up to more than five, but you get the idea. If you don't like my apples, then how about my bananas? Kumquats anyone? This economy is so shifty, it's in your best interests to have many ways to move. You cannot control what the economy wants from you, but you sure can give people several things to choose from.

Life was simple when we all had one job, and the hope that it would last forever. Simple, yes. Idyllic, no. In exchange for the predictability of the job, you got less control over your career. Carrying a few more business cards gives you back some of that control.

A business need not be full time. You can have three customers today and who knows what will happen tomorrow, if the first three are satisfied? It's OK to experiment with a business. Paul Hawken, in his excellent book called *Growing A Business,* recommends that you *not* invest a lot of money in starting a business. Money makes you lazy and reduces your resourcefulness.

I can hear the complaint out there -- "five business cards divides my time, pulls me in all directions at once." Yes, divided attention is a bit of a circus. But, so what? The five cards represent businesses in different stages of development. Five business ideas can coexist. You allocate your time according to what the market wants. I know a woman named Sally who does career counseling on a regular basis, has a greeting card business part-time, teaches on weekends, and tutors math students when time allows. Sally is still working on identifying the fifth card in her "hand."

The five cards can all be clustered in a single field or industry, or they can represent five fields that are worlds apart. That's your choice in this free enterprise carnival known as America.

Donald Super told us a long time ago that we are all multi-potential. It's about time we expressed it. What will life as a five-card person be like? When someone asks, "What do you do?" you may reply: "Do you have half an hour?"

There are numerous advantages to the five-card approach to life -- greater degrees of freedom, more flexibility in the marketplace, probably more income, a variety of spice in one's life, and the ability to replace any of the cards when the time seems right.

Five business cards leave you better positioned to take advantage of the normal chaos of the marketplace, because you're already living in a chaotic state and enjoying it.

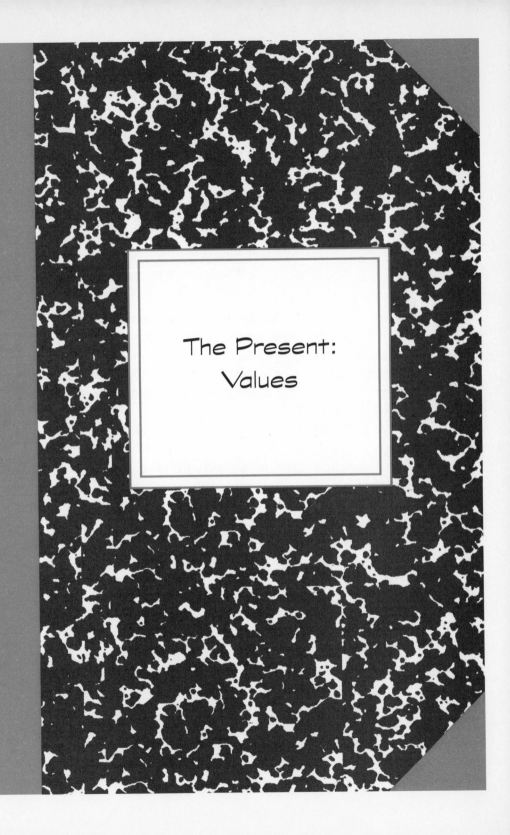

The Present:
Values

CHAPTER 28

Freedom

by Howard Figler

> *This is America. You can do anything here.*
>
> - - Ted Turner

Let's pause for a moment to reflect on how much our beloved field of career development owes to freedom. Every time I hear about a political takeover in another country, or economic controls, or a government dictating its will, I think: "What kind of career development do people in that country have? Not much."

We complain that our markets are chaotic, but that very chaos results from freedom. Customers change their preferences, because they have freedom of choice. Businesses change their products, because they're free to try almost anything they believe might sell. Demographics change, because people are free to move about.

Career-wise, our clients are free to do anything they want to. As you know, that is a blessing which is sometimes perceived by clients to be a curse (so many choices!). But take those choices away, and you would hear screaming of a different order.

I won't pretend that free enterprise as we know it is perfect. Capitalism has led to many abuses and wretched excesses. People are constantly beset by shoddy products and manipulative advertising. But we have recourse. We are free to become wiser and ignore the products that deceive. The alternative to our system is some form of control. Once you see control walk in the door, freedom drops out the window.

When politicians have told people how to work and conduct their lives, the results have almost always been a sorry mess.

"I didn't buy this book to read about political philosophy!" No, you didn't, but you wouldn't have this book to read if free choice of careers were difficult or impossible. So, take a grateful look at all your symbols of free speech (telephone, computer, etc.), salute the flag, and hunker down here for a few more thoughts.

What if you were told that your clients were permitted to do only certain kinds of work? You and they would be pretty resentful. You'd wonder who dropped the U.S. Constitution in the ocean.

Thankfully, your clients' choices are getting more free by the minute. The movement toward self-employment and entrepreneuring is helping many to look at the market as a canvas on which they can paint their own career picture.

Can you imagine a world where you got your job because someone put you there? A significant part of this planet functions that way -- we just don't see it. Americans are insulated from a lot of the indignities that mark people's lives in certain other societies.

In some other countries where you have less freedom, career success is often a matter of luck, what family you were born into, political maneuvering, or other forms of happenstance. In America, your clients have more control over their career futures than anywhere else.

It's no news to you that this is a free country. Why belabor the obvious? Because the obvious can become invisible.

We grow up feeling secure. Some even feel "entitled" to a successful career just because they were born here. Not so fast, Ginsberg. America guarantees the freedom, but not the outcomes.

More degrees of freedom means better career development, but many people resist this. Some would still prefer the "good old days" when lifetime jobs were available in the corporate trenches. They'd rather have more "security" and less

Howard Figler

freedom. Your clients take away some of their own freedom when they look for employers who will "take care of them." Imagine having to encourage Americans to embrace free choice.

Of course, we will always have freedom of choice in America. Oh, yeah? Despite what many clients believe, history did not begin the day they were born. The United States is just a 223-year-old experiment. A mere babe in the woods. It's working well so far, but who knows? No one has invaded our shores. English is the language of commerce. We're fat and sassy.

Don't take freedom for granted. There may be "economic planners" lurking in the wings saying: "Wouldn't it be nice if we had more people doing *this* kind of work?" Economic body snatchers. In any country where planners become dominant, say goodbye to career choice.

Here are things you can do to reaffirm freedom of career choice and stimulate its healthy development in the U.S.:

1. Appreciate freedom and how it encourages clients to make enthusiastic, even passionate career choices;

2. Teach your clients to embrace freedom rather than fear it; this means risk taking, but that is part of the adventure;

3. Help your clients to regard all jobs as temporary, so they will continually develop their skills and look to create new opportunities.

4. Teach your clients to practice freedom by taking opportunities to reshape their careers whenever they see markets open and more Good Work to be done;

5. Expand career freedom by supporting the development of small business wherever you can. Small business is the heartbeat of our economic system, because it allows anyone to enter the marketplace with simply an idea and the willingness to do the learning and work necessary to make it succeed.

The health of the American economy depends greatly upon the individual's willingness to act freely and even boldly in pursuit of their career goals. Career counselors have a key role in encouraging clients to fulfill their ambitions.

Freedom is not automatic, not here, not anywhere. It thrives in the U.S. because we do it every day, and because we continually reaffirm that wide-open career choice is what we want. Freedom is a glorious concept. Support it. Nurture it. Love it. Your clients' careers depend on it.

CHAPTER 29

Helping Clients
Define Success

by Howard Figler

What is career success? We receive images of it every day.
The following quote is taken from an advertisment for
Mercedes Benz that appeared in the June 18, 1998, *Wall Street
Journal:*

Joined the company at 22 . . . made VP at 26 . . . Senior VP at
29 . . . Oversaw 31 annual reports . . . Survived 307 management retreats . . . Stayed awake through 764 presentations
. . . Removed 289 knives from back . . . Raised three kids (two
successfully) . . . Drank 936 bottles of Maalox . . . Payback
time . . . All that struggle up the corporate ladder should not
go unrewarded. Presenting the ultimate compensation pack-
age: the S-Class (Mercedes) . . .

Is this message an updated version of the corporate success
story? Or is it a parody? Let's assume the copywriter is playing
it straight here. Do our clients aspire to this? Do we want
them to? Is it any of our business? Yes.

Do you have to be a Senior VP at 29 to feel you've made it?
What if you're already 42 and you're not anywhere near it?
Will Mercedes take your money or will they send you a letter
of rejection? Maybe you didn't go to the right preschool. Darn.
Gotta tell Mom and Dad about that. Like they really want to
hear it.

What about that Maalox? Do you really want to know what
the inside of that Senior VP's stomach looks like? Would you
want your immune system trashed like his? Do you want to
send your clients out to careers where they gulp tummy reme-

dies in a desperate attempt to fight the stress that permeates their lives? I suppose it's their choices. But am I thus a part of a system that encourages people to want "success" that ultimately may ruin their health? If I go along with success as it is currently defined, am I an accomplice?

What about those knives in the back? If 289 were removed over a 31-year career, that's more than nine knives every year. One knife in the back every six weeks ("Here's your six weeks' report card, Mr. Executive"). Why there's hardly time for the last one to heal before the next one is inserted. Are we to assume that back-stabbing is an inevitable and frequent part of a march to career success? Where does trust fit in in such a working atmosphere? A no-trust environment -- all against all -- would be barbaric.

I suppose the copywriter for this ad wanted to show a sensitivity to the hard knocks of career advancement. And then, of course, The Car will provide ample reward for all the trials that the corporate climber had to endure. A car. That's it. A car will make everything worthwhile.

I've saved the worst for last. "Raised three kids (two successfully)." What is implied here? Two out of three ain't bad? Are we supposed to applaud now? Suppose you're that third kid, the one who got neglected severely while the parent was 31,000 feet in the air, en route to one of many vital corporate meetings? And we know in our hearts the other two kids probably didn't see a lot of that 29-year-old Senior VP either. How much will The Car compensate for ignored children?

What does all this have to do with career counseling? The *Wall Street Journal* and other media have a great influence on how our clients view "success." Do we just sit by and let these images seep into our clients' psyches, and then accept their pursuit of success as it is defined "out there"?

The values revealed in advertisements by Mercedes and others are the values of a consumerist culture. The view is that everyone must buy things to keep the economy rocking along. However, the individual career decision-maker can decide where these values fit among his/her priorities. It takes strength to resist the appeals of the billion-dollar ad industry, and that's where you come in. You can help each client to shape a version of success that reflects his/her most important values.

It gnaws at me to see cultural images of "success" affect our clients unconsciously. I believe that counselors can raise key questions, and still leave the responsibility for choice entirely with the client. You can decide where in the counseling process to introduce questions such as these:

• How is your version of success different from that of others around you?

• How does money fit with the other things that you want from your work and your life?

• How will your career goals mix with your personal and family goals?

• How does your version of success compare to successful people you see pictured in advertisements?

• How do you define career success?

It is essential that clients shape their own definitions of "making it." The career counselor must help in this process by actively raising values questions rather than letting clients passively receive the "success values" promoted in our culture. Career counselors may be reluctant to ask these hard questions about career values, but if we don't do it, perhaps nobody will.

CHAPTER 30

Doing Well
and Doing Good

by Howard Figler

Are Getting and Giving partners, or are they antagonists? How compatible are doing well and doing good? Is there inevitable conflict between profitable business practices and socially conscious motives? Or, can business owners create and maintain Win-Win situations where profits are related to how well people are served? Must social consciousness be limited to being good to your customers?

These kinds of questions are central to career counseling because clients want to know if Doing Well and Doing Good can reinforce each other. If not, the client may have to sacrifice some of one to get more of the other. This would be regrettable. More and more today, people want to have work that affects others in positive ways, at the same time they are being well-compensated.

Doing good is not just for social workers. Social consciousness is everywhere in the world of work, because the main purpose of work is to add value for someone, somewhere, somehow. Hard-core businesspeople, lone-wolf researchers, and even the tax collector can advance the public good as much as any member of United Way. Likewise, social value is added by musicians, lumberjacks, river tour guides, courtroom clerks, and oil rig workers.

The counselor's attitude is crucial here. If she believes that money can only be made by being self-focused, she may direct her clients toward economic gain and minimize their hope for doing social good. However, if she believes that a person's career success is a function of the social value created, she'll encourage clients to seek jobs where giving and getting are intertwined.

Cynics may say that it's a selfish world, but our view is that people help to create the world they believe in. And there is plenty of evidence that businesses can be organizations that provide social value. Just ask the satisfied customers of computer stores, plumbers, graphic designers, music stores, bookstores, restaurants, shoe repair shops, etc. Not all customers are happy, but that just means there are more satisfactory jobs waiting to be done.

If career counselors encourage clients to believe that doing well and doing good are compatible, clients will be more likely to look for, find, and create these opportunities, and less likely to settle for merely "making a living." The counselor's attitude makes a difference, because many clients are oriented toward survival and may believe that social value is out of reach:

Client: *Well, it would be nice to make a difference in my work, but I have to be realistic.*

Counselor: *Here's reality -- a successful enterprise provides social value by enhancing the lives of its customers. Find a product or service you believe in and tell them how you can contribute to their objectives.*

Mom and Dad were Company Men and Company Women, and they did what they had to do to keep the paychecks coming. They didn't think a lot about the social impact of their work. Since then we've seen oil spills and corruption of every kind, in small businesses and large ones, in nonprofits as well as profit-making organizations. And we are the children who watched and wondered how it all happened. We committed ourselves to doing it differently.

Profits versus the Public Good. We used to call this the "capitalism versus socialism" controversy. It is still widely believed today that making money and social good are adversaries.

We will box ourselves into a ruinous debate if we cast these two as opposites. When it comes to career choice, altruism versus profit is a false controversy. People of all persuasions want both -- to do well and do good.

It is severely shortsighted to say that businesses exist only to make money. Profit is their lowest common denominator, but businesses can serve better purposes than that. The narrow profit viewpoint has discouraged many career seekers from aspiring to more socially conscious goals. However, a business can be as socially redeeming and community oriented as its owners and workers want it to be.

One person's work is naturally interrelated with the work of others. More than ever, work is with others and for others. Nearly all work is a matter of doing something for someone else. . . .

From its very beginnings, the modern business economy was designed to become an international system, concerned with raising the 'wealth of nations,' all nations, in a systematic, social way. It was by no means focused solely on the wealth of particular individuals. . .

In a word, businesspeople are constantly, on all sides, involved in building community. . . . capitalism is not solely about the individual. It is about a creative form of community.

Michael Novak, *Business As a Calling,* 1996, p. 125–126

There are two levels of social consciousness that can be practiced by anyone pursuing a job, self-employment, or business ownership:

1. **Serving your customers/clients.** Every good business or nonprofit concern begins with reaching out to people who need what they have to offer. If you run a card and gift shop and treat your customers fairly, honor their requests, and are trustworthy, you have begun your socially conscious relationship with the marketplace.

Doing well and doing good are becoming partners in the most savvy enterprises today. Businesses have learned that customers want to be treated humanely and they'll shop at the stores that give them the most attention.

A business should treat every customer as though she will be a customer for life. Or as though each customer is your grandmother.

You don't want your grandmother to be unhappy, do you? A business owner sees their customers on the street and everyone smiles -- this is the only kind of relationship you want to be a part of.

2. **Your relationship to communities.** Who are these people in the streets blocking your progress as you make deliveries from your flower shop? Whoa! They're your fellow community members. You see many people in your work other than your customers or coworkers. Are your cement trucks dropping loose gravel on the highways which bounces into drivers' windshields? Does your camera store provide photo services for needy organizations during holiday time? Has your computer company developed relationships with the public schools? Does your bike shop alert the public (not just your customers) about riding hazards?

Business has often been a mindless pursuit of profits without much concern for the people being served, sometimes even trying *not* to serve them well, in order to boost profit margins. However, many of today's businesses are paying more attention to building enduring relationships with their customers, their clientele, and their community.

Many enlightened businesses are building ongoing relationships with public education. Better educated graduates help the skills of future employees, and business-education cooperation also raises overall literacy and enhances general citizenship.

The enterprises that try to fool or cheat people in order to make short-run gains will eventually lose their customer bases. It's only a question of time before word-of-mouth reveals how the car really runs, how many glitches the software has, or where that department store dumps its garbage. This is the age of instant communication. People will find out the truth, sooner rather than later.

Doing well and doing good can be highly compatible, if you build ongoing relationships with your employers and co-workers. Even if you change jobs a lot, the "ongoing relation-ship" still holds. People will remember what you did for them, and you'll see them again. If you have a fast-buck mentality, you'll be ignoring doing good in favor of financial gain. Do so at your own risk.

In today's climate of no assurance that a job will last, many say "look out for yourself." Au contraire. Loyalty to one's em-ployer is still a good thing. It shows you care about your work-ing community. Your attitude will be rewarded, not only in Heaven, but also by appreciative customers and bosses.

Many people complain that making money takes all their time, and there's no time left for being socially conscious. This is shortsighted. Every ounce of doing well can be done with an eye toward doing good. Jack's car repair place has a ton of happy customers, including me, because of the good it brings into people's lives. My life breaks down if my car breaks down. Jack does well as a by-product of doing good.

Doing well and doing good at the same time is the best road to success, for both the individual and the organization. If career counselors convey this attitude to their clients, their clients will be encouraged to look for and create situations where economic prosperity results from their ability to give value. Such careers are the most satisfying because all the per-son's energies are moving in the same direction.

CHAPTER 31

Adding Value

by Howard Figler

People wonder how to solve the puzzle of surviving in to-day's economy. What's the right education? How do I escape layoffs? Are my clothes on straight? Should I smile or look tough and commanding? When will employment be stable again?

These questions are off the mark and distracting. Instead, ask: "What do employers pay for?" More than ever, employers are taking a close look at what is worth their money and what they can do without. Business owners ask job candidates bluntly: "Will you help my business move forward? If so, how will you do this?" Whether or not you can do the job is only an intermediate question. The real question that any employer asks any job candidate is: "What will we gain by bringing you on?"

Job seekers must put on the employers' hats and think as they do. "Would I hire me if it were my money at stake?" "Would I be worth the dollars I'm asking for?"

Employers call this "adding value." It's a term that should become part of every job seeker's and worker's vocabulary. How do you add value to a business or other organization? Here are five broad categories of "value" that all enterprises -- profit and nonprofit -- regard as crucial. If your clients can make an impact on any one or more of these, they'll be giving an employer strong reasons to hire them and retain them as employees. Your clients should be taught to ask themselves these questions:

1. **Will I attract new customers or clientele?** A continuing flow of customers is the lifeblood of any company. Whether

you call it selling, marketing, or public relations, any good company does it well. These days almost every employee is tied to customers in some way, or they should be. Am I doing anything to bring in new business? Am I losing some? What can I do that will attract customers?

2. **Will I help to keep present customers?** As every successful business knows, each customer must be "re-sold" every time they have contact with the company. How do you feel about a business after you've received lousy service? Ready to find another store, right? Any employee who cements relationships with clientele is an employee who is earning her paycheck. How would my work affect the company's relationship with its customers/clients in positive ways?

3. **Will I be saving the company money today?** If I'm not saving money, I may be losing it in some way. If I can identify how my work reduces costs, I'll be adding value. Where can money be saved? What tasks or processes might I do more efficiently? Can I talk about when I have saved money in other organizations? I'll think about this company, observe the workplace, and then tell the interviewer where I believe dollars might be trimmed.

Another way of "saving money" is to raise money. Can I propose ways to generate funds (as for a nonprofit organization) and talk about how I would do it?

4. **Will I help the company to be well regarded in the U.S., the region, or the local community?** While they're making money, companies need to maintain their reputations as good citizens of their communities. Involvement in social concerns -- food banks, the schools, reducing crime, etc. -- lets people know the company cares about people, not just profits. As a prospective employee, I may have ideas about how and where the company can expand the reach of its service programs.

Or, I may see more general ways to build the reputation of the organization, through participation in Chambers of

Commerce, speaking to community groups, visibility in the print and electronic media, or ways of educating the general public about the company. Let me think of ways I can get the word out. Open houses? Media? Companies like to be noticed.

5. **Will I enhance the productivity or morale of other workers?** Other workers are not my responsibility? I should guess again. Everyone is everyone's responsibility. I will look for ways the performance of all can be improved. I may create a job for myself. This is not just the old, tired Suggestion Box routine. If I think orders may be lost on the telephone due to poor communication skills, I'll say so, and propose a plan for making things better.

When productivity improves, everybody wins.

I can draw on my past experiences. I can tell the interviewer about methods I've seen that improved productivity at other companies where I've worked. If I introduce a method that enhances efficiency, I will definitely be worth my paycheck.

These five areas of "adding value" are directly related to the success of any organization. They transcend job descriptions, job objectives, and organization charts. Every employee ultimately will be judged on how well he/she contributes to one or more of these five "value" categories. After all, if you cannot pull in customers, hold them, save money, enhance our reputation, or advance worker productivity, why in the world should we pay you?

The "right degree," "job experience," a spiffy resume, or dressing for success become very much beside the point. You can have a wow degree, a pow suit, and zowie references, but if you can't add value to the company's objectives, who needs you? And, why do you even want to be there?

This is the way it must be in the marketplace. Profit and nonprofit organizations alike have no time and energy to waste on employees who take up seats and get in the way. I once worked for an insurance company (back in the dark ages of steady jobs when "value added" was not as important as today) where I compiled and analyzed statistics that were seldom applied to any decisions, did nothing to enhance the company's relationship with its customers, and were lost in the dustbin of corporate research. Why did they pay me anything? Why did I even want the job?

When our clients learn to think and behave like enterprises, they will become comfortable with "adding value" as the overriding criterion for being hired, staying employed, and feeling satisfied with their work. They will evaluate themselves as the CEO would -- by judging whether they are assets that contribute to the company's mission, or liabilities that drag it down.

The "value added" approach will bring us to a more direct and honest relationship between people's work and their satisfaction. In the past, people have been rewarded based upon seniority, office politics, and other mysterious criteria. The relationship between productivity and pay was frequently a muddy one. Today, when you contribute to the company's main objectives, you're rewarded. Every employee is called upon to affect productivity directly, and that is as it should be.

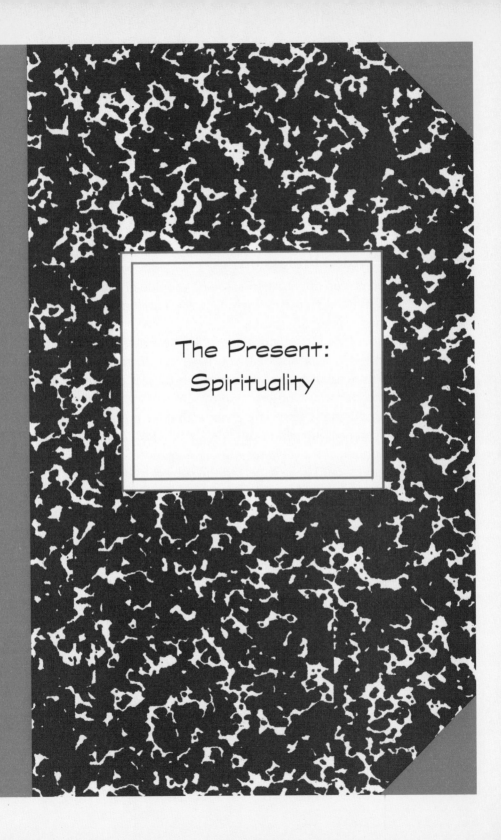

The Present:
Spirituality

CHAPTER 32

The Place of God
In Career Counseling

by Dick Bolles

A Divided Profession

Some career counselors, seeing the title of this chapter, will be offended that it is included in a handbook they had assumed was totally secular.

But other career counselors will be overjoyed to find it here. And there, in a nutshell, you have the dilemma which faces our profession today whenever the subject of God is raised. Some, dismayed; others, overjoyed.

God is not commonly given a chapter in most handbooks for career counselors. But, of course, this is a Figler-Bolles handbook, and anyone who is acquainted with my background would have expected the subject to be covered here (I have been an ordained minister in the Episcopal church for the past 45 years). It is well known that I came to this work of career counseling out of an abiding religious background and concern -- as have many many other career counselors, from the very beginning of our profession's history.

In this, our profession is merely reflective of American society. The Gallup Polls have consistently found that 94% of all Americans believe in God (though what is meant by "God" will vary wildly), and 55% of all Americans consider their belief in God to be "a very important part of their lives" with an additional 30% holding that it is "fairly important."

Our clients are reflective of that same society -- which means that when we are helping people figure out what their mission in life is, and what new career will fit them best, and how they are to find it, the chances are very great that we are talking to someone who also believes in God.

The Conspiracy of Silence

In light of the fact that the overwhelming majority of our profession believe in God and the overwhelming majority of our clients believe in God, it is more than a little bit nuts that our profession by and large thinks it is not permissible to even mention God during career counseling sessions. Why is this?

Well, in part of course it is because some of us labor in settings within American schools or Federal installations, where discussion of religion is greatly frowned upon if not strictly forbidden, under the doctrine of "separation of church and state."

Also, in part this is because some of us who do career counseling today were trained in rigid psychology degree programs, where the subject of God was assumed to be an infantile projection on an adult universe; so we are afraid of being ridiculed if we bring up the subject.

Also, in part our silence about God in the counseling chamber is due to our fear that if we are the ones who initiate any mention of God, we will be misperceived as "proselytizing." So of course it would be nice if at that point our clients brought up the subject. However, when *we* don't bring the subject up, neither do our clients (generally).

Finally, this silence about God is also due to a dismaying trend in our culture toward defining "spirituality" in terms of values, while dropping all its historic and foundational thought forms, most particularly that of "God" (e.g., "Spiritual writing is not about God . . . it is about the human longing for all that God can mean." -- Patricia Hampl, *The Best Spiritual Writing,* 1998). Some career counselors have gotten swept up in this trend.

The end result of all this is clear. We feel constrained not to mention God in career counseling sessions, even if He (or

She) is prominent in the consciousness of both counselor and client. It is all a little bit nuts.

It is as though when the client is ushered into our office, or into our workshop, there were a large pink elephant plainly visible in one part of the room (it had better be a large room), but neither one of us dares to mention that fact -- and must conduct our conversation as though it were not there.

Make that: "truly nuts."

A Saner Career Counseling: God is Discussable

I have, over the years, found it relatively easy to get into a discussion of the pink elephant, in the following manner. During a series of counseling sessions with a particular client (or workshop), I take great care not to mention God during the first or second session -- unless I hear the client mention God first.

Otherwise, I use the first two sessions merely to get into a rhythm whereby both client and counselor talk about what solutions we have found to various problems. Whenever the client mentions a problem, a fear, an anxiety, about their job-hunt, I ask them what they did in the past to solve any similar problem, allay any similar fear, or calm any similar anxiety. I also offer (briefly) my own experiences in dealing with the same thing -- taking care to cite an experience where God or faith *didn't* figure in.

About the third session, however, when this rhythm has become a well-worn path, and it is once again my turn to say what I did in dealing with the problem under discussion, I try to find some experience where my faith in God really came into play.

For example, if we are discussing times when we were scared in the past and how we dealt with it, I might make a comment that runs as follows: "Yes, I remember when I had to be rushed into the operating room, with a gallbladder at-tack. I was scared, but I have a strong belief in God, so I put myself in His hands as I was taken into the operating room, and I felt great calm." (I make sure the story is true, and not one I have made up -- in this case, this actually happened to me in 1994.) Then, after the briefest of pauses (about four seconds), I return to the exercises or whatever it is I am teaching at that session.

I have found that one of two things always happen, by way of response to this casual mention of God on my part. Either the client treats this comment of mine as though it reveals a side to me they hope doesn't ever get mentioned again (pained silence for a moment); *or* they use it as an excuse to bring up some mention of their own faith in God ("Yes, well I had a similar experience myself, when . . .").

So, I have achieved my purpose, which was simply to open a door, that they can walk through or not, as they please.

That, I think, should be our goal with respect to God in career counseling: merely to open a door.

We have no need (we *had better have* no need) to force discussion about God. We want simply to signal the client that it is OK to talk about God in the context of their job-hunt *if they want to.*

Spirituality as Playpen

The purpose of opening this door is that I want to find out if the client has a belief in God that is strengthening or could be strengthening for the client as he or she goes through that difficult passage in life called "The Job-Hunt."

"If . . ." This is always a big question. The fact that a client may believe in "God" does not necessarily mean they draw strength from that belief.

I think it is important to always keep that in mind.

I see spirituality/religion/faith -- whatever you want to call it -- as essentially 'a playpen,' in which each of us acts out the way we see the universe, and others, and ourselves.

The concept of 'playpen' is well known in marriage counseling: sex, and money are the two most common playpens

FREEDOM OF WILL
(the space within
the playpen)

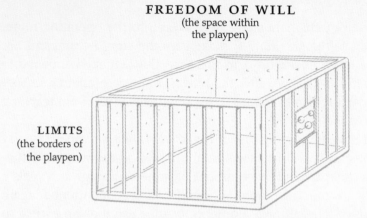

LIMITS
(the borders of
the playpen)

there. If you counsel enough troubled marriages, as I have, you begin to see how you must really pay attention when the couple starts to talk about money or sex in their marriage. It is incredible how people act out all the dynamics of their relationship within these playpens of sex, and money.

Likewise, in career counseling, religion serves as a playpen, in which people trace out and act out all the dynamics of their attitude toward life and work.

Thus the career counselor can learn much about the client by listening to *the form* of that client's religious beliefs. For, in what is emphasized, and what is not, by listening for what to us seems accurate and what to us seems distorted, we can learn much about the client. And we may learn clues which will help us to zero in, on precisely what it is we should emphasize in our teaching.

We are talking here about our approaching the client's faith on two levels. One, is treating it as a practical life skill, which governs how the client is living their life. And the other is treating "religion as symbol" and "religion as metaphor."

All symbols and metaphors divide, it seems to me, into two large 'camps': healthy, and unhealthy, even as there are only two kinds of emotions: appropriate, and inappropriate.

I have prepared a list, over a number of years, of what I consider to be healthy and unhealthy attitudes *within* religious faith. This is only, of course, one man's opinion.

But in case you are puzzled as to how one might distinguish healthy from unhealthy, here is my list, based on my observations over a period of 45 years in ministry:

Healthy Religion	Unhealthy Religion
Is Obsessed with Gratitude.	Is Obsessed with Guilt.
Focuses on the presence of God in the world: sees holiness everywhere.	Focuses on the presence of evil in the world; sees contamination everywhere.
Sees all the world as "us."	Sees all the world as "us vs. them."
Is closely related to mental health with its emphasis on repentance (metanoia) or "Most of my ills stem from what I am doing to myself."	Is distantly related to mental illness (paranoia) or "Most of my ills stem from what others 'out there' are doing to me."
Unconsciously exhibits humility.	Unconsciously exhibits arrogance.
Treasures the differences in others.	Wants everyone to be like them.
Has a high sense of "all the saints" worshipping God together.	Has a high sense of "the individual alone with his or her God."
Believes in learning from others.	Believes in confronting others.
Renounces manipulation of others, and lets them have their own beliefs.	Desires to manipulate others into accepting their every belief.
Wants God's forgiveness toward those who have harmed them or follow other gods; forgives readily.	Wants God's vengeance toward those who have harmed them or follow other gods; often has low long-simmering anger, masked beneath a smile.
Focuses on what one can give, out of faith; anxious to give others benefits.	Focuses on what one gets out of faith; anxious to get for themselves the benefits.
Faith is primarily a matter of actions; words are used only to to interpret one's actions.	Faith is primarily a matter of words used as tests of orthodoxy. Shibboleth and sibboleth.
Is well aware their faith may have some unhealthiness to it.	Doesn't even dream their faith may be unhealthy.

If you discover the client before you is a believer in God, and (as it turns out over several sessions of discussions by the by) their faith is healthy, this can be a great ally to their job-hunt -- particularly in the realm of prayer, as you remind them that they are not alone in their job-hunt, but God is with them every step of the way.

The Counselor's Own Faith

What you must be prepared for, of course, is that the client may have a curiosity about your faith, and want to know about it, and even learn from it. Sometimes this is because your faith is stronger than theirs, and they can sense this, and want more faith in their own life. I do not think that kind of thirst or hunger should ever be dismissed. It is what counseling is, and conversation is, at its best: two human beings learning from each other's life and experiences.

But beware: there are times when the conversation is not what it seems. That is, there are times when the job-hunter's interest in discussing faith is not so much a fascination with faith as it is a fascination with procrastination. You may be dealing with a job-hunter who is just anxious to do anything except get on with their job-hunt, and they will divert you with any conversation down some side road that they can.

If you are not experienced in distinguishing between these two -- the true inquirer, and the false inquirer -- you soon will be.

One of the best ways of staying on track, is to take care that any conversation about faith leads right back to the subject of work. That is, when you 'share your faith' you share what your faith means to you in one particular realm, and that is, the realm of work.

That kind of conversation is often called one's "theology about work." This is not the same thing as "a philosophy of work," though it is easy to confuse one with the other. But look at the etymology: "A *philosophy* of work," a Greek word springing from *wisdom* (-sophia) and *love* (philos), is essentially some wise thoughts about the nature and meaning of work.

"A *theology* of work," on the other hand, springs from *a word* (-logos) about *God* (theos), and is essentially an attempt at some higher thoughts about the nature and meaning of work, based on the nature of God.

In other words, philosophy deduces itself from our own nature. Theology deduces itself from the nature of God.

Each of us who does career counseling, and has a faith of our own -- whether Christian, Jewish, Muslim, Hindi, Buddhist, or any other persuasion -- needs to think out what our theology is about work; and it is this which we seek to share, if the client wants to walk through the door we slightly open as I described above.

I find that career counselors generally want some guidance about what such a theology of work might look like, before they fashion or trace out their own; and I am somewhat limited in giving help here, because my own orientation is so thoroughly rooted in Christianity, from my youth up.

But if you can translate, as it were, out of Christian thought-forms into your own thought-forms, then I can give you an example of what a theology of work might look like. Here 'tis:

A Sample Theology of Work

My reading -- my Christian reading -- of God's nature, is that there are six characteristics of God which have broad implications for our calling and our work. They are as follows.

1. **God is, above all else, omniscient, all-wise and all-knowing.** As we are created in His own image, it is essential for us from the beginning to prize this side of ourselves: knowledge, wisdom, and preparedness. If we want to help people with their Work, we must first of all know *more* about the job-market, and how it works, than the average person, by far. We must know more about job-hunting, than the average person, by far. We must know more about career-changing, than the average person, by far. Our faith requires of the career counselor more study, more reading, more meditation, than the average person. We must go into battle prepared.

2. **God is eternal.** The implication of this for our understanding of Work is that we must view what is happening in the world of Work in a longer *time view* than most people do. For example, we must understand that changes in welfare, etc., etc., are not a cause for panic. When people in our culture see these kinds of changes, they tend to get riveted in the moment, and -- lacking any historical perspective -- run around yelling "The sky is falling, the sky is falling" -- the job-market is just doing what it's always done. *Theology's unique contribution must always be to give perspective: we must teach people to take a long-range view of the job-market.* To insist that, not only with the Lord, but also with the job-market: *a thousand years is as a day.*

One way to gain some perspective is to recall what it was like in the settling of the Old West, circa 1870. You rode into town, you decided what skills you had to offer -- you were a cowhand, or a waitress, or a farmhand -- you figured out who might need your services, by 'asking around,' and then you went to see them, asking if they needed help, and what wages they paid. No employment agencies, ads, resumes, no social/government 'apparatus,' no 'safety net' -- it was up to you to get a job. This was little over a hundred years ago, not a thousand. Well, we're back to that day and time, more and more, with the reformation of 'the social contract' currently going on in the workplace. Theology insists on the long-range view of time, and says, "This is nothing new. We solved it before, we can solve it again."

3. **God is Creator.** *Our contribution, particularly to welfare recipients and others newly losing 'the safety net' they've been accustomed to, is to offer a theology of work that is first of all a theology of creation.* We need to say to every person out of work, "We are all partners with God in creation, and you are a lifetime partner with God in creating your life here on earth. Think of yourself as a sculptor: you are given rough materials out of which you must carve a life. You may wish you had a better

childhood, a better marriage, a better work history, etc., but your history merely dictates the materials out of which you still must sculpt your life. Work with the materials you've got. You may wish it were marble, that you have to work in, but you have been given wood instead. Don't waste time lamenting the material you have to work with, get on with sculpting out of that material a life that is pleasing in God's sight, and a fulfillment of your destiny -- the reason you were put here on earth.

4. **For the Christian at least, God is 'Three in One.'** To speak of God as a Trinity, is to speak of 'Him' as three different natures, bound together in One: God above us, the Father; God beside us, the Son; and God within us, The Holy Spirit; yet all one God, whose Name is 'Love.'

One in three -- that is the key.

God's gifts to each of us are likewise one in three: the gifts He has given each of us are *but one gift:* namely, the ability *to love (God, neighbor, and self)*,

But, there is a threeness within this Unity, in the gifts that He gave us, for He gave us three abilities: the ability *to achieve*, the ability *to learn,* and the ability *to play.* These are His gifts to our will, to our mind, and to our heart. Any decent theology of work, therefore, must see Work as a city within the large kingdoms of: achievement, learning, and play.

To look briefly, at each of those kingdoms in turn:

Achieve. Work is but *one part* of our larger vocation, and God's larger call to us, *to achieve.* We are called to achieve many things (besides Work) and God gives each of us the requisite talents to achieve each of the following:

to achieve the acting out of *love,*

to achieve *character,*

to achieve *growth toward God's image,* and

to achieve *those tasks and projects God wants us to, both inside or outside of 'a job', either with people, or with information, or with things.*

God's emphasis is on *achievement*, broadly conceived as in Jesus' famous words: "Not everyone that says unto me, Lord, Lord, shall enter the kingdom of heaven; but *he that does* the will of my Father, who is in heaven." "Does," is the operative word, here. Achievement is the goal. Work is but one part of *that*.

Learn and **Play.** Our ability to achieve, in turn, cannot be looked at except as *one part* of God's other gifts to us: the ability to learn, and the ability to play. We tend to divide these arenas into different linear 'time frames,' -- 'now I am at work, then I am at school, and then I am at play.' In reality, as people of faith, we must seek a synthesis of work, learning, and play, in our lives.

This leads us to the next truth about God, that determines our theology of Work:

5. **God is He who transfigures -- first, Christ, and then, all creation.** Any decent Christian theology of work insists that work can and *should* be transfigured, for this has always been God's work in the world.

To speak from an overall view, Work can only be transfigured (in the eyes of faith) if it is infused with a constant awareness of God's presence there, with us, in our work: it is He and we together, seeing every vision, doing every task, accepting every compliment.

But, to be more specific, the way in which our work is transfigured by God's presence is when *in each and every moment we feel we are not only 'at work,' but also 'at school' and 'at play.'*

That is to say, transfigured work is by definition work that has been (by our attitude and consecrated intent) turned into *a learning experience,* wherein we are constantly asking 'What am I learning, here, today; and how could I make tomorrow teach me even more?'

And, transfigured work is by definition work that has been (by our attitude and consecrated intent) turned into *a playful experience,* wherein we are constantly asking, 'What fun and joy did I have today, in the very doing of the task; and how could I make tomorrow even more fun, in the very doing of the task?'

6. **God is Love.** A theology of work teaches that, for the person of faith, the commandment: "Thou shalt work" is a sub-heading under the larger and more imperative urgency: "Thou shalt love." "Thou shalt love the Lord thy God, and . . . thy neighbor as thyself." A theology of Work insists that work is one of the ways (along with learning and play) that we act out our *love* (for God, our neighbor, our self).

When we speak of work *as love*, we come into a common confusion: the confusion between 'priority of importance' and 'priority of learning.'

In terms of *importance*, our order of priority for the three loves must be: first God, then neighbor, then self.

However, in terms of *learning*, inasmuch as the Scriptures say, quite realistically (I paraphrase), "How can you love God, whom you have not seen, if you do not first love your neighbor, whom you have seen?" to which I would add some words of our Lord which sound like an exhortation, but I believe to be a law of nature (again, paraphrased): "You will, inevitably, only be able to love your neighbor as you love yourself," we are left -- in sum -- with an inverse order, from that of *importance*. (I exaggerate this, to make a point. It is obvious, of course, that all three loves are being learned at once, and forever.) But if we *were* to think linearly, just in terms of learning, our order of priority for the three loves would be: first self, then neighbor, then God.

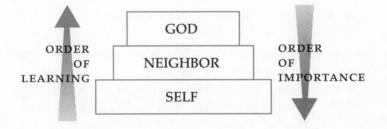

By the imperative of *love*, therefore, *the first work we all are given* is to learn to love the self, of which a large part (in my experience) is learning to inventory, know, and love the gifts which God has uniquely given to each of us. This is the first imperative of love, and it is also the first imperative of true stewardship. As our love for self (the appreciation of God's gifts to the self) grows, so in turn will our love for neighbor, and our love for God.

In Conclusion

If we who do career counseling have a faith in God, we must each think out in something like the manner I have just illustrated, what are the implications of God for the realm in which we live and move and have our being: the kingdom of Work. And then be ready to share a little of this thinking, or a lot, as the client may need or want it. But only as the client may need or want it.

There will be many counseling encounters with clients where none of this ever gets mentioned, from start to finish with their job-hunt, because the client has no interest at all in the subject.

But we must be ready when they do have an interest. We must be ready to ensure that there are no pink elephants in our counseling office which everyone notices but nobody mentions.

Let's sum this chapter all up, in a nutshell: we are called to be as helpful to each client as we possibly can be, consistent with honoring their free will, and our determination to empower them, not simply do the work for them.

In that determination to be helpful, faith is one of our strategies; God is one of our allies.

And always, and ever, we keep in mind: "More things are wrought by prayer, than this world dreams of."

The Future

CHAPTER 33

Five Rules
for Dealing with Change
in the New Millennium

by Dick Bolles

The Millennium is the symbol of a new era, a New Age, where all changes are possible. It is a career counselor's milieu, for we are fond of saying, "We are agents of change. We help people effect the changes in their work and their life, that they are hungering for."

People will want help in dealing with this New Age, and some will turn to us (as change agents) for that help. "Tell me how to deal with change," they will ask, in one way or another, spoken or unspoken.

What shall we tell them? There are, of course, so many things we could tell them. But let's see if we can reduce it to just "Five Rules for dealing with change, in the new millennium."

1. In the midst of all the changes you are going through, always look for the things that remain constant.

In the Old Testament, the story is told of God's voice commanding the prophet Elijah, "Go forth, and stand upon the mount before the LORD." And then a series of changes passed by Elijah: a tornado, an earthquake, a fire, etc. The story goes: "behold, the LORD passed by, and a great and strong wind rent the mountains, and broke in pieces the rocks before the LORD, but the LORD was not in the wind; and after the wind an earthquake, but the LORD was not in the earthquake; and after the earthquake a fire, but the LORD was not in the fire; and after the fire a still small voice." (1 Kgs. 19)

This is, of course, a story about, "Where is God to be found?" but what is most interesting to me about this story is that the first thing the Lord told Elijah to do in this story was to find a firm piece of ground to stand on, from which he could then deal with all the changes that were going to come at him.

Likewise, it seems to me that whenever our clients are dealing with a series of changes in their life, they need this sense of a firm ground under their feet. They need a sense of the things that remain constant in their lives, on which they can firmly plant their psychological feet, before turning to deal with the maelstrom of changes that the new millennium will bring to their lives; or the changes that they will initiate in their own lives.

The more changes they must deal with (divorce, career, geography, illness, grief) the more they need to know what remains constant in their lives. It is this thread of constancy, running through all the changes, that will help keep our clients sane.

Our job, therefore, is not merely to be "change agents." It is to be, equally, "identifiers of constancy." You must figure out ways to help any clients overwhelmed by changes, to sit down and make a list of all that remains constant in their lives.

As an example, my own list of constants in my life would include: the loving God I have known all my life; who I am and the values I have held all my life: honesty, love, compassion; my loved ones who have given me constant love over many many years; the things I learned to appreciate as a child and still do: the beauty of this earth, the warmth of the sun, the exhilaration of exercise and movement, the beauty of light, the glory of color, the sound of beautiful music, etc.

A meditative time, daily, when each of us sits and fixes our attention on the things that have remained constant in our life will always be restorative, and strengthening beyond belief. It gives us the mount on which to firmly stand, as change whirls around us, and in us.

2. In the midst of all the changes you are going through, search for the largest context you can find, for viewing those changes.

When someone falls ill, the graver their illness the more you can see their mental horizons shrink and shrink. You can see this clearly if you are visiting them regularly in the hospital. If *all* they can think of is food, sleep, and their bodily functions, then you know they are gravely ill. Their mental horizons have shrunk to the boundaries of their body.

But if, after time, they start to recover, you can equally measure how fast their recovery proceeds, by how fast their mental horizons start to expand. First they ask about you, then they ask about the family; over time, they ask to see a newspaper, then they ask about the city, then the world. You know they are on the road to health. Their mental horizons have expanded out again to embrace the world.

So, the equation becomes clear: Shrinking horizons = illness. Expanding horizons = health.

Change often affects people just as physical illness does. And often we can measure how badly those changes, such as unemployment, are affecting our clients, by how much their mental horizons start to shrink.

Our advice to them, in such a case, should always be to keep their horizons as broad as possible. Do whatever they can to achieve that: reading the daily papers, listening to beautiful music, getting plenty of sleep, going out for walks in the wide world beyond their dwelling place. The larger they can keep the context within which they live and move and think and have their being, the healthier and stronger they will be, in dealing with life's changes.

For those of our clients who are people of faith, it goes without saying that their belief in God offers them precisely the kind of context we are talking about. If they have faith in God, then we should encourage them to work on giving priority to that faith as they are wrestling with life's changes --

even as *the point* in the story of Elijah, mentioned above, was to look at all of the experiences which passed before him, and try to see where God was, in those changes.

3. In the midst of all the changes you are going through, learn to break things down into their component parts.

Changes in our clients' lives can seem intimidating and overwhelming to them until they learn to break them down into smaller bite-size concepts. Here are some examples we can commend to our clients:

Don't think just of 'your *life*.' Break it down into 'various *phases*.'

Don't think just of 'your *career*.' Break it down into 'various *roles*.'

Don't think just of 'your *job*.' Break it down into 'various *tasks*.'

Don't think just of 'your *projects*.' Break them down into 'various *skills*.'

Don't think just of *'employers*.' Break them down into 'those who *will*' and 'those who *won't*.'

Change is always a challenge to be overcome. The key to overcoming, is always to break an overwhelming thing down into its component parts.

Our clients can master change when they can transfer what they had in the past, to something new in the future. This 'transferability' is difficult for them to see, when they are dealing with large concepts. But when broken down, their 'transferability' to another realm is easier to see.

'Careers' are hard to transfer. 'Roles' are not.

'Jobs' are hard to transfer; 'tasks' are not.

'Projects' are hard to transfer; 'skills' are not.

Our clients will increase their mobility, their ability to move around on a changing millennial landscape, if they travel on a mental moped (think small), rather than on a mental tractor-trailer (too big).

4. In the midst of all the changes you are going through, work constantly on developing alternatives.

In today's world of rapid change, having one plan is not enough. Things totally beyond our control may occur, to upset that plan. One must always have alternatives: alternative careers in mind, alternative places of work in mind, alternative styles of work in mind, alternative ways of getting income, alternative clients and customers in mind, alternative services or products to offer.

Debra Angel and Elisabeth Harney, authors of *No One is Unemployable*, 1997 (Worknet Training Services, P.O. Box 5582, Hacienda Heights CA 91745, phone 888-9-WORKNET) have evolved a very interesting approach, based on this principle of "always have alternatives." They ask their clients always to develop three options, or possibilities, for any situation or decision facing them. Then they help the client list the pros and cons of each of the three options. After which, the client (not the career counselor) chooses the option that seems best to them, and the career counselor unfailingly supports them in exploring that option -- even if the counselor feels the option chosen was not the best of the three. Debra's and Elisabeth's reasoning is that the worst that can happen is the client will get a good learning out of a mistaken choice, and then return to look at the other two options they earlier rejected.

The late John Crystal used to heavily emphasize the importance of always having an alternative in place. He applied this particularly to one's present job. He was fond of saying, "The time to begin your next job-hunt is the day you begin your present job." Clearly he was right; the best way to help our clients who are frightened at their present place of work, scared they may lose their job at any moment, is to help them evolve a plan and have it fully in place for what they are going to do *next*. Then they will lose their fear of what is happening, or what might happen, in their present job.

5. In the midst of all the changes you are going through, act, then reflect; act, then reflect; act, then reflect.

Every age seems to have two kinds of people in it: 'action people,' who are good at leaping into action and doing what is necessary; and 'reflection people' who like to think out all the ramifications and consequences of an action before it is taken.

We find 'action people' everywhere, keeping busy, busy, busy, all day long, and then falling exhausted upon their bed at night.

'Reflection people' tend to be found in monasteries, in private or government 'think tanks,' in academia, or in the philosopher's study.

But when our clients are faced with a time of great change, such as the new millennium, or great change is occurring in their lives, we need to encourage our clients to become 'action/reflection people.'

My friend Jack Schwarz, founder of *Alethia* in Mendocino, California, is such a man. Definitely a man of action, he developed the self-discipline of sitting down each night, in front of a blank wall in his living room, and imagining that he is watching on that wall a video replay of his entire day. He asks himself what he learned, what he felt good about, what he would do differently in the future.

A similar discipline may be just what some of our clients need, in dealing with profound changes in their lives, during this new millennium. If we suggest this to them, we should also suggest some questions they might ask themselves as they 'watch' this video replay of each day:

"What did I have the most enthusiasm for, today?"

"Was there any time today when I lost all track of time, and if so, what was I doing, what skills was I using?"

"What were the things or issues or people I was most sensitive to, today?"

"What questions was I trying to find answers to, today?"

"At my work, what is the real business I am in?"

"Who was I, today?"

Always, always, the best way to deal with change in one's life is to act, then reflect; act, then reflect; act, then reflect, in a continuous yin-yang cycle.

Well, there are the five rules about helping our clients deal with change in the new millennium. Do I really need to add that these five rules apply to us also? And that we had first better practice them in our own lives before we ever dare to offer them to our clients?

CHAPTER 34

How
to Stay Up-to-Date

by Howard Figler

It's easy to develop your own professional ruts that feel comfortable and acceptable, because you've been running in those grooves for a long time. You're making a living. So, what could be bad?

The purpose of updating is to jar yourself, to introduce new and dissonant information into your system, to force you to reexamine what you're doing and what you believe you know. Once you think you've got it down cold, that's when you don't.

The two (most common) ways to keep up:

1. **Attend professional meetings.** Such meetings are the life-blood of your professional relationships. The conversations you have there are critical to keeping yourself current about what others are doing and thinking. It's been said the best learning at a conference takes place in the hallways. This heady brew of perspectives among hundreds of people cannot be duplicated electronically. Conversations across computer lines are not the same as the give-and-take of eyeball-to-eyeball meetings. Computers allow both speaker and receiver to hide their feelings and their faces; it's an incomplete dialogue at best. Do as much conference attending as you can afford, and even a little more.

The Career Planning and Adult Development Network Newsletter (800-888-4945) gives a monthy preview of many professional meetings for career counselors across the nation.

2. **Read as much as possible.** Read the whole range of publications, from professional journals and newsletters to the

more commercial items such as the *Wall Street Journal* (there's a career column every week by Hal Lancaster), the *National Business Employment Weekly, Fast Company,* and others. Read a wide array of books that discuss people and their work, workplace trends, spirituality and work, job search methods, and work as it relates to the rest of our lives.

Meeting and reading are fine and necessary, but it's not what you know as much as what you do with what you know. Therefore, the following guidelines are recommended:

What You Must Do

1. **Take a risk.** At least once each year, take a flyer, try something new that you developed from your own creative hotbed, an innovative approach in your practice that tests an exciting idea you have about what might work better for your clients. Be bold. Whip yourself into a froth about a new way of doing things. See what happens.

2. **Meet with three professional soulmates.** Find three other professionals and meet with them once every month, without fail. Reveal what you've been doing lately in your practice. Tell all. Ask for feedback. Talk about ideas you have for the future and about work related problems. Everyone gets air time. These three soulmates give you a real-world sounding board that you can count on each month, so that you don't get trapped in the "washing machine of your mind."

3. **Write at least one article.** Write an article for any publication (journal, newspaper, newsletter, etc.) about a topic that moves you. Writing forces you to be a much closer observer of a practice than if you are just talking about it. Writing helps you keep up-to-date because it requires you to think carefully about a subject and take a stand, and it elicits responses from others. Even if you don't like writing, do it because you need to hear yourself think.

4. **Give public presentations.** Give speeches, talks, seminars, or other presentations to professional colleagues about prac-

tices or problems that interest you. Once again, giving talks will force you to study subjects more closely and will heighten your desire to dialogue about these subjects with your colleagues.

Both writing and speaking will encourage you to be more up-dated on specific topics than if you simply talked about them informally. The more writing and speaking you do, the better. Passion is the key. If you have energy on a given topic, don't keep it to yourself. Pass it around.

5. **Allow others to observe you at work.** By receiving feedback from colleagues, you can have your blind spots observed and critiqued. Part of keeping on top of your game is knowing where you're stepping in holes and not realizing it. Firsthand observation is one of the best ways to help you stay clear of poor or ineffective practices. Ask for feedback from both professionals and untrained individuals. The nonprofessionals can sometimes identify more easily with the client.

Before you get too carried away with all these things you're going to do to stay updated, ask yourself: "Why am I doing all this?

To be hip? To dazzle my friends and cohorts with all the latest methods? To bolster my resume? To impress my mother?"

Those are interesting reasons and I'm open to them. It's always important to keep your mother happy. In addition, you're updating yourself in order to improve the service you provide for your clients. We still know very little about what works consistently for individual counseling and group workshops.

The Changing Knowledge Base

So far we've been talking about updating counseling processes and skills. There is also knowledge to be concerned about, in two categories: (1) The changing sociology of the marketplace; (2) The emergence of new occupations and the disappearance of old ones.

The changing sociology is important for you to understand because it refers to broad sweeping changes in the labor market which affect everyone, but which clients might be slow to recognize. Examples include:

- The gradual but significant movement toward self-employment
- The flattening of hierarchies in many businesses
- The dramatic increase of contract work in private industry
- The increasing presence of "project teams" in businesses

To keep apprised of these kinds of changes, read as much as you can in major business publications which examine broad movements in the world of work, such as the *Wall Street Journal*, the *Harvard Business Review, Fortune, Forbes,* the *Business Journal* in your local metropolitan area, and others.

Changes of occupations are hard to track and difficult to remember even once you have identified them. Make good use of the Internet and other sources such as *Career Opportunities News.* Contact the federal government's Bureau of Labor Statistics office nearest to you and ask for their most recent publications. However, occupational changes are so numerous, detailed, and fast changing that you'll want to encourage and teach clients to do their own firsthand investigations, customized to their needs.

I do not recommend that you try to be a walking encyclopedia of jobs and careers. As Bridges notes in *Job Shift,* occupational titles are less common. People are often moved from project to project, depending on their skills and the organization's needs.

A good way to sample changes in the marketplace is to do follow-up on your clients' career paths. Real people make jobs come alive. You'll certainly learn about some emerging occupations and how the fluid nature of the world of work (see Bridges' *Job Shift* and Charles Handy's books, *The Age Of Unreason* and others) is unfolding in real life.

Check out other counseling philosophies and practices

Choose one or more professional colleagues whom you respect, who have approaches to counseling or group work that are very different from your own. See what you can learn by talking with them about their methods and by observing their work, if possible. For example, you might know of a counselor who does a lot of role-playing, and you do none at all. Ask about her perspective and how her clients respond to this practice.

Keeping updated is an acknowledgment that our profession is growing, changing, and continually reinventing itself. What worked yesterday may not work tomorrow. Staying up-to-date is necessary because people and their work are dynamic. By reacting to an ever-changing landscape, you can change and expand your repertoire as often and as much as necessary.

CHAPTER 35

Where
Is Career Counseling Heading?

by Howard Figler

The widespread need for career help presents an opportunity for this profession to become well established in the American economy. People of all ages, educations and backgrounds expect to have many career transitions in their lifetimes. Some will turn to career counselors for help and others will wish they had.

If you think of the huge numbers of people who could benefit potentially from career help, there would seem to be a promising future for the career counseling profession. Nonetheless, there are many uncertainties about how well the public understands the nature of career services. To the typical consumer, "career counseling" is a service that is not especially familiar. I will outline some of the possible changes in our profession that lie on the horizon. These can clarify career services in the minds of potential users and may lead to continued growth in the profession.

Positive movements, but it's unclear if they will occur

There are certain changes in career counseling which offer promise, but there is no clear indication that they will occur across the profession. Each of these would be greatly beneficial to all practitioners:

1. **Feedback regarding one's career counseling skills.** One significant roadblock to the advancement of career counseling quality today is that career counselors seldom see each other practicing their skills.

A career counselor might practice for years without observing another counselor at work. This is not a formula for improving one's competence. It is a prescription for an advanced case of rust and rigidity.

Counselors are beginning to talk more about in-service sessions where they would give each other feedback, but the movement in this direction is slower than a turtle with a hangover. Perhaps it's asking a lot for a professional to expose his/her skills to others and suffer the self-doubts that may occur. However, that could also be seen as an excuse for being defensive and self-protective. Most importantly, watching each other do career counseling is a prime opportunity for personal growth.

Physicians observe each other performing surgery and they somehow get used to it. Surely career counselors are capable of making this leap to self-improvement without collapsing in a puddle of anxiety. We do not have programs or procedures in place to enable counselors to observe each other. Since they don't yet exist, we will have to invent them.

2. **Greater use of career groups.** Groups provide benefits that cannot be duplicated by individual counseling, just as one-to-one counseling has unique advantages of its own. Career counselors must become proficient in both one-to-one practice and group workshops, for the sake of their clients.

The benefits of groups are numerous -- participants learn from one another, clients can practice their self-assessment and job search skills, and participants often provide tremendous emotional support for each other. Career group workshops are often both fun and beneficial at the same time.

Many career counselors acquire their group skills through trial and error. In-service training programs should be developed to focus on group skills, because there are many ways to design and conduct groups that facilitate learning.

It is not clear yet whether counselors will increase their practice of group workshops. Groups represent a golden opportunity to expand our services to greater numbers of career changers. Many potential clients will prefer group programs to individual work. Practitioners need to respond to this latent demand.

3. **Less reliance on standardized tests.** Approximately 30 years ago, counselors relied heavily on test results to suggest career possibilities for their clients. Today testing is still widely used by many counselors, but test results are only one option in a wide array of methods that clients can use to generate career alternatives. Self-assessment tools are more widespread, group exercises such as analysis of "accomplishments" are better understood, and information interviews are used frequently to explore career ideas. Furthermore, the dynamics of career counseling allow clients to generate career alternatives as part of the counseling sessions.

Overall, the client has much less need to ask the counselor to "give me some tests that will tell me what to do." Furthermore, today's counselors recognize that using tests in that way allows clients to sink into a state of dependence upon the counselor and the tests. By contrast, everything else the counselor does acts to discourage dependence and enables clients to take responsibility for their own decisions.

It is our hope that the trend continues to be away from testing. In the past, clients have tended to believe their test results too readily, sometimes inferring that "the test is telling me what I ought to do." Such dependence on external authority makes the counseling process more difficult. We recommend that tests be eliminated entirely, because they go against the flow toward self-empowerment and self-reliance that characterizes all other career counseling services.

Movements that are likely to continue

There are several trends that are gathering steam and are likely to become even more prominent. Each of these will broaden the presence of career counseling and make it a more effective service.

1. Less emphasis on career prediction and more on career development. Some years ago career counseling focused on a prediction model, suggesting that if you knew certain things (abilities, interests, etc.) about individuals, you could forecast the careers where they would be successful and satisfied. This was a mechanical model, emphasizing that each person is a fixed set of attributes, not likely to change over time.

The mechanical, prediction model is essentially pessimistic -- it says that people cannot grow or develop very much. The prediction model is discouraging and often destructive because it tells the client: "You're not in control of your career. Here is what you can and cannot do." Tests are often used as the centerpiece of the prediction model.

In contrast, a career development model encourages clients to identify the skills they would like to improve or develop in order to gain entry to certain jobs or careers. It renders the prediction model useless. The career development message is: "You can jump on the learning curve of almost any skill and make significant improvement if you're motivated enough." This model says that each person is in a continuous state of growth and development and that the individual accumulates skills and knowledge through the experiences he/she chooses. This philosophy has been explained most effectively by John Krumboltz's social learning theory.

The career development approach is optimistic. It offers clients the hope that they can learn and grow into many career fields by exercising the timeless virtues of hard work, focus, and dedication to learning. This approach affirms that the individual is in charge of the progress she makes toward the career choices she has defined for herself.

2. **Building the knowledge base.** The career counseling profession has been steadily accumulating knowledge and disseminating it to practitioners. Theorists such as Krumboltz and John Holland have made great strides in enabling practitioners to apply key principles of career development.

Holland's theory of personality applied to career choice has enabled counselors to observe how their clients' experiences and preferences cluster in one or more of the R-I-A-S-E-C categories.

Recent work by Krumboltz and his associates has helped us to understand the powerful role that beliefs and cognitions play in people's career development.

The Career Is Dead: Long Live the Career, by Douglas T. Hall and Associates (1996) makes a compelling case for the emergence of relationships in careers. Hall, et al., write about relationships of all kinds -- between employers and workers, between career-seekers and their families, among people of diverse backgrounds, and others. They assert that the depth of our relationships will be a key to career success and personal happiness.

Much more knowledge building is needed. When the day comes that counselors routinely observe each other's individual counseling skills and each other's group workshops, it is likely that a great many more books, articles, and theoretical propositions will result.

3. **More emphasis on "career self-reliance."** This is a useful and contemporary term that was coined by the Career Action Center in Cupertino, California. It refers to the necessity for all individuals to take full responsibility for adapting to the ever-changing world of work.

One factor that has made career self-reliance a more urgent proposition today is the expansion of self-employment, entrepreneuring, contract work and other independent forms of income earning. Two things are happening at the same time --the market is forcing people to adopt an attitude of being more self-employed, and more people are finding they like the autonomy and strength that comes with self-reliance.

It's vital that people adopt a self-employed attitude when they are workers, because: a) The employees who best understand the needs and goals of the organization will be most productive; and b) a team approach is necessary to solve problems. Everyone is on the same ship; they hold steady or run aground together.

As Betsy Collard and the Career Action Center have emphasized, career development does not apply only to the career transitions in one's life; a career encompasses all one's working days. According to Collard, people must be proactive to get what they want in their careers, not simply wait for transitions to occur.

4. **College and university career centers.** Career counselors have become established on the campus, because they speak directly to the career needs of students -- "How will my major affect my job prospects? What skills should I be developing? How important are overseas experiences? How can I get an internship? What kinds of summer jobs are available?" As long as higher education continues to prosper in the U.S., thousands of people will have one of their earliest exposures to career counselors while they are students. These counselors have highly active professional associations governed by the National Association of Colleges and Employers, based in Bethlehem, PA.

5. **Companies and organizations providing career counseling for employees.** Career counselors are increasingly common in corporations, government agencies, and nonprofit organizations. As layoffs have continued, organizations have felt a greater responsibility to help both those who depart and those who remain. They counsel their employees to take charge of their careers and prepare themselves for many changes.

Given the turbulent nature of employment today, organizations are likely to maintain their commitments to career counseling and perhaps even expand them. This is a welcome development, since it gives many people the opportunity to build their career development skills on a continuing basis.

An alligator in the water

One change that this profession needs to make is to rid itself of retail practitioners who, often calling themselves "career counselors," charge very large up-front fees ($1000–$5000) and deliver no more than what a person could get for much less money. Potential clients for career counselors have heard about those high fees and may well be scared off as a result.

These high-fee "counselors" prey on people who have lost their jobs and are grasping for help, by selling them hard. Such "counselors" convey the image that they will provide "top-notch contacts" and other ways of accessing good job opportunities. In fact, their contacts are far more meager than referrals that people can generate on their own. It is unclear how the career counseling profession will handle these practitioners in their midst, or whether they can even handle them at all. Thirty-five years ago this problem existed and nothing much seems to have changed.

The reader may wonder how clients can unwittingly pay $1000-$5000 while similar services exist for reasonable rates all around them. Desperate people take desperate measures and often they misapply the philosophy that "you get what you pay for," believing that the higher fee is an index of value.

Since high-fee "counselors" seldom do anything illegal, other practitioners will have to work hard to distance themselves from those who undermine their credibility. This alligator continues to be a threat to broad public acceptance of the many career counselors who provide value in exchange for their more reasonable fees.

Possible Future Developments

1. **Nonprofit career centers.** There are a small number of nonprofit centers today which offer multidimensional services. Prominent among them are the excellent centers noted earlier -- the Career Action Center (Cupertino, CA), the RLS Career Center (Syracuse, NY), and the Career Resource Center (Rochester, NY).

While these centers have been notably successful, they have not spawned a generation of such organizations in other towns and cities. Why not? It takes a lot of coordination and leadership to make such a center work, and there has to be a sufficient financial base in the area to support it.

Communities which are looking for a way to support their citizens might do well to create nonprofit career centers. Now that the knowledge of career development is solidifying and there are many more able practitioners around to offer their skills, this is a mission that would touch the lives of numerous people.

The nonprofit career center may be a movement that is waiting to happen, an idea whose time has come.

2. **Crossfertilization between career counseling and psychological counseling.** This one has great potential, but it's a long stretch to say that it will occur. To date, psychological counselors have shown little inclination to get involved with career counselors. Many feel that career work is "beneath them," or they have the misguided view that it does not have enough psychological content. Other therapists say they don't know enough about careers, thinking (mistakenly) that career counseling is information-centered.

The emotional dimensions of career counseling are quite apparent to any practitioner. Psychological and career counselors would have much to learn from each other. Psychological clients have career concerns, and career clients have emotional problems. There is a natural collaboration that could exist between the two professional groups; each has strengths that the other needs.

As Astrid Berg notes, "There are many career issues that have psychological content, such as the dysfunctional workplace, workaholism, and others. Many of my clients are dealing with these issues; therefore career counselors need to be versed in psychological problems."

Perhaps the psychological counselor will continue to be too busy emulating the psychiatrist to give much attention to career counseling. That would be regrettable. If career counselors and therapists were to become collaborators, all of their clients would benefit greatly.

Recently there have been signs of change. When their client loads have diminished due to competition in the health care field, some marriage and family counselors have sought to develop their career counseling skills.

3. **Retail career centers for reasonable fees.** Given the thousands of people today who are changing jobs or careers, you might expect that low- to moderate-fee retail career counseling centers would already be commonplace. However, they are not.

Thousands of people who need career help are not receiving any, or what they do get from public agencies may not be enough. A combination of services would be attractive -- individual counseling, group workshops, print and computer resources, videotape skill practice, job search support groups, resume critiques, etc.

Examples of such centers recently have begun to appear. Two organizations in Seattle --the Center for Life Decisions and Centerpoint -- are developing creative and diverse approaches to attracting clientele. They offer multiple services, including weekend retreats, other group programs, and referral systems.

4. **Career counselors and financial counselors working together.** This is a potential collaboration that is a stretch; nonetheless, it is interesting to contemplate. Each deals with money, but in different ways. When you lose a job or gain a job, financial matters are affected. Conversely, financial decisions often affect career decisions. The more successful you are with investment decisions or other financial choices, the more degrees of freedom you have in career selection.

Career counselors and financial counselors could have professional partnerships or less formal working relationships. Such arrangements could expand the market for both professions.

This chapter has outlined several emerging themes in career counseling, and some others which represent tantalizing possibilities. The broad background for all these possible changes is the large proportion of the population which needs more career help than they are getting. Unmet needs are waiting for our profession to respond to. There is no assurance that the career counseling profession will get itself together enough to satisfy this enormous potential demand with diverse programs of high quality that can be understood and trusted. The opportunity awaits.

CHAPTER 36

When to Hang It Up
As a Career Counselor
and Seek a New Career

by Howard Figler

- Are you thrilled when you get phone messages saying that certain clients have cancelled their appointments with you?
- Are you trying to find surgical remedies for the problems expressed by your clients?
- Does goat ranching look infinitely more personal to you than career counseling?
- Are you focusing on the clients' heads nodding and not on what they're saying?
- Are you having nightmares where clients ask you: "Do you have two minutes? I'd like to know what I should do for the rest of my life."
- If you hear "I want to work with people" one more time, you'll start screaming?
- Do you cringe when you hear a client say: "I don't know why you're asking me that question. That's why I came to see **you**."
- Do you feel as though every day you listen to three movements of the Whiners Concerto?

"Is this what's troublin' ya, cousin?"

Eddie Lawrence, "The Old Philosopher" who was immortalized on records during the 1950s, used to ask this question and then answer: "Well, lift your head up high, walk into the sunlight, and never give up (da-da-da) the ship!!"

Nonetheless, Eddie didn't have to hear the same career stories endlessly, watch parades of clients say one thing and then do another, and listen to hand-wringing ambivalence day after day. Career counseling has its frustrations. If they're driving you to distraction, maybe it *is* time for you to do something else.

Nobody said you had to do this forever

This was not necessarily meant to be a lifetime contract. If you change to a different line of endeavor now, you'll be guaranteed a place of honor in the Book Of Good Work. You're far ahead of most people in terms of contribution to the betterment of others. You're way up the list on nobility points. You're a model citizen for all the patience and fortitude you have shown in shepherding people through the trials of career change.

Don't stay in there just because you feel guilty that you ought to help a few more. You should consider hanging up those counseling shoes if any of the following are true for you:

1. **They all sound the same.** After a while, the clients all melt together, you can't remember who said what, and you may feel as though you haven't accomplished anything. When that frustration hangs heavily over your counseling head, it may mean you've racked up enough points in the Good Book Of Career Counseling, and you should find a different form of life excitement.

2. **A more concrete job is beginning to look more appealing to you.** There are jobs which have visible outcomes, where you can get from A to B more easily. Jobs dealing with things. Or working with people who are coping with easier problems. If you find yourself daydreaming about a job that doesn't have quite so many uncertainties, go for it. That job will have its own problems, but they may be the ones you want right now.

3. **You don't want to admit what you do when you're asked at social occasions.** Someone at a party asks you: "Oh, what do *you* do?," and you feel like saying: "Consultant, adminis-

trator, self-employed, mnmnmnmnnmnm, razzafrazz," or something equally vague. You don't want people to start asking you career stuff or sending you their relatives, or whomping you with their own career problems. In other words, you don't want to hear it anymore. Enough is enough. Back up the moving vans. Time to look for a new door to enter.

4. **Your empathy tank is low.** "What was that you said? I was just nodding off a little here." Maybe you'd rather listen to something else for a few years besides: *"There are sooooo many things I could do for a career. Oh, my. I just can't decide."*

Career counseling is not like bricklaying, where you can grouch about things out loud and still get the job done. You have to want to do it. You must have a combination of enthusiasm and tolerance that will allow you to work with difficult clients. If you've done it for many years, blessings on you.

The memories of your career counseling will be warm ones. There were soaring moments. You were part of many people discovering themselves. Now you're finding a new role for yourself. You'll waffle and wriggle like every client you've ever had. Finally, you're the counselee, with new energy, new missions, and a unique array of skills that have been developed by your life as a career counselor. Go forth and do good deeds.

Index